Praise for *Witness to Belief*

"Russ Levenson's collection of heartfelt conversations is a book that you will just want to savor, sitting in your favorite chair with a fresh cup of coffee, getting to know this diverse group of famous people on a far deeper level, as they share heartfelt stories about faith and life and abiding hope. By the time you get to the end, you will be ready to start reading it all over again!"
—Bishop Michael Curry, world-renowned preacher and author of *Love is the Way*, *The Power of Love*, and *Songs My Grandma Sang*

"The secret to the ministry of Jesus was that God was at the center of it. The profiles in this fine book, *Witness to Belief*, invite us all to follow and stay anchored to our 'center.'"
—Gregory J. Boyle, SJ, founder, Homeboy Industries

"Russ Levenson's book is not only interesting, it is inspiring. What an engaging way to 'witness to belief'! Each interview witnesses to a unique aspect of a vibrant faith for today's world. Indeed, each person's story is an authentic and clear statement of the power of faith."
—Jeanie Miley, author, spiritual director, and retreat leader

Praise for *Witness to Dignity*

"Reverend Levenson was a dear friend and spiritual mentor to both my beloved grandparents. His stories of friendship will fill you with hope and inspire grace."
—Jenna Bush Hager, host, *Jenna and Friends*, and bestselling author

"They were not perfect, but as Russell Levenson's personal and pastoral memoir tells us, they strove to be faithful people of God."
—Jon Meacham, canon historian for Washington National Cathedral, Pulitzer Prize–winning author and historian

"Congratulations to my friend Russ Levenson. He has captured a compelling story of faith, family, love, and leadership."

—Max Lucado, bestselling author and minister,
Oak Hills Church, San Antonio

"Russ's book truly reveals the inside story of this remarkable couple and the extent to which their lives were informed by their faith."

—Jean-Pierre Isbouts, historian and *National Geographic* author

WITNESS
to
BELIEF

....

CONVERSATIONS ON
FAITH AND MEANING

BY RUSSELL J. LEVENSON, JR.

Copyright © 2025 Russell J. Levenson, Jr.

All rights reserved. No part of this book may be reproduced, stored in a retrieval system, or transmitted in any form or by any means, electronic or mechanical, including photocopying, recording, or otherwise, without the written permission of the publisher.

Unless otherwise noted, the Scripture quotations are from New Revised Standard Version Bible, copyright © 1989 National Council of the Churches of Christ in the United States of America. Used by permission. All rights reserved worldwide.

"The Great Creator of the Worlds" by F. Bland Tucker from The Hymnal 1982 © 1985 is reprinted by permission of Church Pension Fund.

All images used with permission.

Morehouse Publishing
19 East 34th Street
New York, NY 10016
www.churchpublishing.org

Morehouse Publishing is an imprint of Church Publishing Incorporated

Cover design by David Baldeosingh Rotstein
Typeset by Andrew Berry

ISBN 978-1-64065-857-8 (hardcover)
ISBN 978-1-64065-858-5 (eBook)

Library of Congress Control Number: 2025934359

This work is dedicated with gratitude of heart and soul to my wife, Laura, who is the constant companion along the way, and to

The twelve pilgrims you will meet in the pages that follow, whom I have come to know and admire and to whom I offer my profound gratitude for serving as witnesses to belief.

TABLE OF CONTENTS

Preface ix

Dr. Francis Collins 1
The Honorable Dr. Condoleezza Rice 21
Gary Sinise 35
Ambassador Nikki Haley 55
Denzel Washington 73
Admiral William H. McRaven 89
Amy Grant 109
The Honorable James A. Baker III 127
Jim Nantz 143
Sam Waterston 157
Brit Hume 175
Dr. Jane Goodall 193
Closing Thoughts 215

Acknowledgments 230
Author's Note 232
Notes 234
Suggested Further Readings and Viewings 249

PREFACE

"Jesus said to them, 'Follow me . . .'"

—Mark 1:17

Dear Reader, what you hold in your hands is an invitation, and I thank you for receiving it.

One of the things that strikes me deeply about the work of Jesus of Nazareth is that after having submitted to baptism by his cousin John, emerging from temptation and declaring his mission, he begins widening his circle of disciples with two simple words, "Follow me . . ."[1]

Jesus does not cajole; he does not demand; he does not force—he invites. Some followed, some did not, and, I suspect, some pondered before making any decision at all.

And so, it is this invitation I am offering you. What follows is a collection of twelve conversations with people you are likely to know from a broad cross-section of vocations—actors, producers, a sports commentator, a singer-songwriter, a journalist, an admiral, a scientist, a naturalist, an ambassador, and two former secretaries of state. This is how you know them—you know their names, their faces, their voices; you have read their works or read about them. Each, in their own way, has what many in today's world hold as the summum bonum—things like fame, influence, power, wealth. And they have each, also in their own way, chosen to respond to Jesus's ancient invitation—to follow.

Why write such a book?

Now let me ask you to stick with me for a bit. You may be tempted to flip over to one or more of the conversations yet to come, but I would like to set them within a particular context first, so sit tight; read this first.

Having stepped well into the twenty-first century now, there is a great deal of confusion about what it means to be a Christian. I was baptized as an infant, confirmed as a teen, had an experience of coming to faith in my later teen years—all of which played a role in my call to ordained ministry.

I entered the vocation of priesthood in the Episcopal Church at the age of thirty and now am well past the age of sixty. In more than three decades of ministry as a priest and pastor, I have had more conversations with people about what it means to be a Christian than I could ever number. But I confess to you, my reader, all of those conversations have made me no expert, only a fellow pilgrim along the way who also has chosen to follow. I still stumble and fall. I still doubt and still sin.

There are many things about a life in Christ about which I am still learning. In many ways I remain very much an amateur. In most every way, I am still growing in my faith. I also find, with each passing day, how much I need what I have found in a life of following Jesus, and how I need him not less, but more.

That said, I have come to learn and understand a lot about what Christianity is *not*.

Christianity is not a political movement. I dare say the lines that have been deeply blurred in recent decades between religion and politics have likely done more damage to the truth of what Jesus invites us to receive than many forces of evil. This aberration is not new and is in part what inspired Jesus's words, "Give to the emperor the things that are the emperor's, and to God the things that are God's."[2] Regardless of your political affiliation, too many people have mistaken allegiance to a political party as on the same par as allegiance to God. Few things could be further from the truth.

Christianity is not inextricably bound to a particular denomination. Of the 2.6 billion Christians on Earth today, recent studies show that by the end of 2025, there will be as many as 49,000 different Christian denominations.[3]

Followers of Jesus were not called "Christians" until several years after his death and resurrection, around the year 40 AD in the south-central city of Antioch, Turkey.[4] Unfortunately, division within what the Apostle Paul called "The Body of Christ" has also plagued the faith since its earliest days, and a call to a unified faith was a frequent subject in Paul's New Testament writings.[5] By and large, the Roman Tradition took center stage for the first 1500 years of Christianity, and in the last five centuries, one split after another has been a bruising interference to that simple two word call of Jesus.

Christianity is not the sole property of any particular ethnic, geographic, racial, or political identity. Since Jesus's call, people from every walk of life, every station of life, every color, every gender, and every continent on the earth have chosen to follow him. One of the most quoted passages of Scripture is Jesus's call, "Come to me, all you that are weary and are carrying heavy burdens, and I will give you rest."[6] His prophetic word about his own crucifixion was equally inclusive, "And I, when I am lifted up from the earth, will draw all people to myself."[7] Jesus's words were not *some*, nor *just a bit*, nor even *a whole lot*, but *all*. His invitation to follow was, and still is, an open invitation to anyone willing to receive it and then make their own choice about if, or how, to follow.

And while some may argue to the contrary, Christianity is not simply a philosophy. Of course, certain aspects of Christianity include philosophy—a way of looking at the world, a particular way of living, a particular set of beliefs. But Christianity is not primarily about any of these things.

So, if Christianity is not, at its core, a matter of politics or denomination, identity, or philosophy—what is Christianity?

Toward that end, I have to borrow from the words of my dear friend and mentor, the late Anglican Priest and theologian, the Reverend Dr. John R. W. Stott. His words, and those he borrows from others, put a point on the question of what Christianity is:

> "Jesus Christ is the centre of Christianity, and that therefore both the Christian faith and the Christian life, if they are to be authentic, must be focused on Christ. . . . The late Bishop Stephen Neill wrote: 'The old saying, "Christianity is Christ," is almost exactly true. This historical figure of Jesus of Nazareth is the criterion by which every Christian affirmation has to be judged, and in the life of which it stands or falls.' Professor John

Mbiti of Kenya has expressed the same conviction even more succinctly in the words: 'The uniqueness of Christianity is Jesus Christ.'"[8]

John's point, of course, is that Christianity is not about many things—but one, not just another religion. In fact, it could be argued that Christianity is not a religion at all. Christianity is a call to relationship with God—full stop. When trying to convince a very divided Christian community known as Corinth, the Apostle Paul would write to them to recall that when he lived and taught among them, trying to bring about the birth of the early faith among them, that "I decided to know nothing among you except Jesus Christ. . . ."[9]

Maybe some words Denzel Washington, shared with me in one of our conversations, brings the message a bit more clarity. . . . "You don't get to heaven by what you know, but by Who you know." I could not have said it much better than that.

Why am I starting here, at this point, trying to shed some light on what Christianity is, and what it is not? Because I think many are missing out on the joy, the hope, the promise, and the peace one can find in Christ, because there are so many alluring promises from the material world that surround us.

One of the core beliefs that springs to life in the very first chapter of the Hebrew Scriptures, Genesis, is that God created everything, including humankind, as an expression of His love. God chose not to keep Himself to Himself and, in a very real sense, could not contain Himself, so creation was birthed as His gift of incredible generosity.

Christians hold to the belief that we exist because God wanted us to exist, and we were created out of His love to live in that love. All the gifts of the world around us are merely gifts—gifts to be enjoyed, shared, and used with care and caution to bless us, but they are not, in the end, God.

Some people have mistaken the gifts for the Giver and, in doing so, take on more and more of what this world has to offer in lieu of authentic nourishment for the soul. And thus, weighed down by the material aspects of creation, they find themselves spiritually sinking, and never rising to sail into the bliss of life for which they were created.

Why write this book? Borrowing from the words of the Apostle Paul to his protégé Timothy, this book is an invitation to "take hold of the life that really is life."[10]

Making a Case to Accept the Invitation

Those who agreed to sit for a conversation with me about their faith will make their own case as to why they have made their decision to follow Jesus.

But it is fair to say they, like you and me, have some pretty stiff competition. In a world that literally thrives on the accolades social media pours upon the material world, it is hard to see beyond the shiny objects placed before us, but one set on those objects alone often experiences the futility of their impotence once they have been attained. This is nothing new, of course. Let me offer just a few examples.

The Roman Emperor Septimius Severus wrote, "I have been everything, and it is worth nothing."[11] Napoleon wrote to his brother Joseph, "I am tired of glory at twenty-nine; it has lost its charm; and there is nothing left for me but complete egotism."[12]

Fast forward a bit, and we find that Jay Gould, the nineteenth century American financier (who died unlamented) worth some $100 million, is said to have exclaimed with his dying breath, "I'm the most miserable devil in the world."[13]

But it cannot be denied that many people do, in fact, find a lot of satisfaction in the material world. When I asked some of those who agreed to sit for an interview, "What would you say to those who believe that you have so much and would like to have what you have?" more than a few said, "I cannot say that I am not happy that I can put food on the table and have a roof over my head." Then more than one at least turned the question back to me, "Do you think the material world and spiritual world are necessarily at odds?" And to that, I would have to say no.

People often misquote the Bible in saying that the Apostle Paul said that "money is the root of all evil." Paul instead wrote a clarifier, "The love of money is a root of all *kinds* of evil."[14]

If reader, you object to the idea that fame, power, wealth, or success are in and of themselves intrinsically bad for the soul, your objection is sustained; and yet that is not the point I am trying to make.

Here, former President Barack Obama, in speaking about his own journey into the Christian faith in his book *The Audacity of Hope*, makes the point:

Each day, it seems, thousands of Americans are going about their daily rounds—dropping off the kids at school, driving to the office, flying to a business meeting, shopping at the mall, trying to stay on their diets—and coming to the realization that something is missing. They are deciding that their work, their possessions, their diversions, their sheer busyness are not enough. They want a sense of purpose, a narrative arc to their lives, something that will relieve a chronic loneliness or lift them above the exhausting, relentless toll of daily life.[15]

What the president is suggesting is not that the things of day-to-day life do not matter, but that they do not meet the deepest need of the human soul, . . . food for the body cannot, at the same time, be food for the soul.

Jesus talked about this a lot, . . . perhaps *warned* is a better word, when he asked some of his followers,

"What does it profit them if they gain the whole world, but lose or forfeit themselves?"[16]

So, Listen to the Need

In my years in parish ministry, as I have lost count of the number of times I have had discussions with people about the meaning of Christianity, I confess I have also lost count of the number of people with whom I prayed at the moment of their deaths. Early in my ministry, I thought I would keep count of things like that—baptisms, marriages, funerals, and such, but it became clear to me that was simply another way of tallying up the things of this world. That may seem a bit silly to a person who is not in ordained ministry, but I can assure you that the allure of one-upmanship is as alive and well in the church as it is in the secular world!

But this I do know—when the end draws nigh, the things of this world are given their proper perspective. Job, of the Hebrew Scriptures, put it well: "Naked I came from my mother's womb, and naked I will depart."[17]

I have been with many people when they take their last breath, and no one cries out for more money, more success, more fame or power, . . . none of those things. No, those who, as we say in my vocation, "die in peace" have found the truest meanings of life—and I think they did so because they listened to the deepest hungers of the soul.

The Quaker pastor and author Richard Foster wrote, "Superficiality is the curse of our age. The doctrine of instant satisfaction is a primary spiritual problem. The desperate need today is not for a greater number of intelligent people, or gifted people, but deep people."[18]

Where do we find those deep people?

Honestly, they are all around us. In 2007, I was called to be the rector/senior pastor of St. Martin's Episcopal Church in Houston, Texas. Among the members there were the former President of the United States George H. W. Bush and his wife, Former First Lady Barbara Bush.

Over time, I came to know them not just as members, but as active churchgoers. By God's grace and in His time, my wife, Laura, and I got to know them better and better as our years increased and they became dear friends.

What I experienced in that growing friendship was a deep and profound faith. I was with both in the final weeks and days of their lives, was with them at the times of their deaths, and officiated and preached at their funerals and burials. I have written extensively about all of this in my book *Witness to Dignity: The Life and Faith of George H. W. and Barbara Bush*.[19]

On the heels of writing that book, I began to receive letters from—literally—around the world, from peoples of all walks of life. They would write to tell me how inspired they were to know people who had attained so much of what this world had to offer yet were still faithful believers—said their prayers, went to church, served others. To know that a former president and first lady were truly humble, kind, and loving to everyone—not just a few, but everyone and anyone they encountered—seemed to be a moving testimony to the power of the Almighty in their lives.

I received many letters along the lines of "If they can do it, I can do it too," and "I have never really taken the Christian faith seriously, but I am willing to give it a try." One gentleman wrote me and said, "I have thought about going into ministry for years, and after reading this, I am pleased to let you know that I have been approved to enter the Lutheran seminary this fall."

What was going on? Just this. Reader, when I walk into the grocery, donned in a clerical collar, people expect me to talk about Jesus or invite them to church. Maybe they expect me to inspect their grocery basket and pass a little judgement (as long as they do not inspect mine!).

But the response to *Witness to Dignity* confirmed a truth I had long believed—the faithful witness of those who are not clergy people packs a far more potent punch than what may be preached from the pulpit or offered at the altar. In this case, I was able to give testimony of two people who were among the most powerful who have walked the earth, and yet, they believed, prayed, worshipped, and practiced the tenets of their faith and, evidently, many were deeply moved by their story.

I had no intention of writing what I guess could be called a "sequel" of sorts to *Witness to Dignity*, but after a long season of reflection, I thought, "If others can be inspired by the faith of those who have also attained much this world has to offer, then, perhaps, should I tell more stories like this?" The fruit of that question is the book you hold in your hands.

My intent here, is to introduce you to twelve people whom you may know from their public lives but not their personal lives, . . . their spiritual lives, . . . people who found that they needed God, and found beyond needing God, what God had to offer.

A New Invitation

Obviously, given the title of this book, my intent is to be a "witness" to the belief of the twelve people you are about to encounter. But in a very real sense, I am merely being a witness to the witnesses, for it is the personal journeys of these pilgrims that also serve as a witness—to their own experience of encountering the reality of God.

Listening to witnesses is important, whether in a courtroom, a conference room, a church hall, or a kitchen table. When people share what they believe, those of us who are seeking to plumb the depths of life's meaning should engage critically with the testimonies of others—whether we take them at face value, or not.

Before leaving planet Earth, Jesus gathered his followers around him and said, "You will be my witnesses . . . to the ends of the earth."[20] Over thirty percent of the world's population today declare themselves to be Christian.[21] Thus the mere fact that the largest body of religious adherents are followers of Jesus is testimony to history's long line of witnesses to belief. That, alone, should speak volumes to us.

What the story of the followers of Jesus puts before us is something of ultimate importance. To borrow the words of the Anglican apologist C. S. Lewis, "One must keep on pointing out that Christianity is a statement which, if false, is of no importance, and, if true, of infinite importance. The one thing it cannot be is moderately important. . . ."[22]

What you have here is the testimony of twelve witnesses to meaning and purpose they have found in the important truth of God. They have been given much the world has to offer. As you will read here, what they have been given is a gift from God, and a gift they choose to use to bless the lives of others and the world in which we live.

They listened and listen (past and present, I should note) to their need of God. They opened their lives to the truth God is, and they each, in their own way, experienced and experience (past and present again) a new lens through which to take in the whole of life. As Dr. Lewis wrote, "I believe in Christianity, as I believe that the sun has risen, not only because I see it but because by it, I see everything else."[23]

Jesus's invitation to follow speaks directly to our deepest need and invites us to know and experience satisfaction to that need.

A few caveats . . . and then away we go . . .

You may wonder about the order of these conversations. With two exceptions, the conversations in the chapters that follow have no particular order. The first exception is that I did decide to begin with my conversation with Dr. Francis Collins, because his journey to faith came in large part because of his own reflections on the origins of life—the beginning, the "genesis," if you will. The last interview is with naturalist Dr. Jane Goodall, and it will be apparent why her words of wisdom are the last shared by these special guests.

I almost resist offering the following caveat, because—well, an author wants to sell books, . . . right? Yes, but I hope you can see in this preface that my mission is far more about inspiration than compensation. I have spent my entire adult life doing what I can to invite others to the marvelous life of grace and peace one finds in Christ.

As I have already shared, I am a pilgrim. I am still growing. Yes, I am a Christian and, yes, I am a disciple of Jesus Christ. But what I have learned and am learning, in large part due to the conversations you will read here, is that "how" God goes about doing that, in Christ, is beyond my capacity to comprehend.

You, reader, need to know that I have learned from the people in the pages that follow. . . . I have been inspired by them. Some of my questions are the same to more than one person, others are more tailored. Often, we found our conversation would lead in ways neither the one I interviewed, nor the interviewer, expected, and I think that is to your benefit.

You will not find perfect people here, nor will you find people who have lived without the bruises, wounds, and scars of life, and all of them have drawn on their faith to get through the darkest moments of life. And while all of them have, in fact, accomplished and attained much, they have not failed to recognize the One from Whom all blessings flow—even, at times, the blessing of suffering.

You are about to meet twelve people whom I greatly admire—some of whom have become close friends. I laughed with each one of them. I have listened to each one of them. I have learned from each one of them. I wept with some of them, . . . and I have prayed with each of them.

As you read, you will see I alternate in my description of these twelve, calling them "followers," "disciples," "pilgrims," "children of God"—for I believe each to be all of those things in their own way. So, toward that end, you will find here, twelve disciples of Jesus, from different vocations—men and women, Black and white and brown, from a variety of denominations—who seek to understand Jesus, and pray to Jesus, and worship Jesus, and follow Jesus in different ways.

I invite you to read on and see if God might very well show up for you in new ways, or deeper ways, or maybe even for the first time! For indeed, as Shakespeare's Hamlet observed, God did not give you such a huge power of thought and divine capacity for reason in order for you not to use them![24]

So, patient reader, if you have decided to accept this invitation, then may I invite you to invite the One Who invites us all . . . with his words, "Follow me."

And wait, with an expectant heart and soul, as the One Who invites you, when invited in return, always comes. This I promise.

Russell Levenson, Jr., 2025,
a fellow pilgrim, along the Way

Photo credit: © Diane Baker

"I can't turn back now. The only thing I can do is go forward."

—Dr. Francis Collins

Dr. Francis Collins

As I was preparing this book, a good friend of mine, who also happened to be my cardiologist for several years, and his wife took a shine to the project, but they both said to me with no small measure of enthusiasm, "If you are looking for laypeople to talk about the meaning and purpose of faith, you need to ask Dr. Francis Collins!" My friends had heard Dr. Collins speak at the Chautauqua Institution in Chautauqua, NY, and they said his words were not only spellbinding, but life changing.

Everyone who knows even a little bit about the world of medicine and science would know Dr. Collins' name. He was the second director of the famed Human Genome Project, serving under first President Bill Clinton and then President George W. Bush. He went on to become the director of the National Institutes of Health (NIH) under President Barack Obama, and served under both President Donald Trump and President Joe Biden, until his retirement from the directorship in December of 2021. He currently leads a research group at NIH that is focused on diabetes and aging. His list of accomplishments and awards could fill a small volume.

But I had absolutely no idea that he was a believer who had personally made the journey from atheism to Christianity.

Upon setting up the interview, I set out to read as much of Dr. Collins' work and watch as many of his recorded lectures as I could. And like my friends, I was both moved and mesmerized. Here was a scientist who spoke of his faith and his personal journey into that faith, in much the same way C. S. Lewis did nearly one hundred years ago in 1929.[1]

I was welcomed, virtually, into Dr. Collins' office on the Feast Day of the Epiphany, January 6, 2025. As we began, I suggested to him that it was a bit providential that we were meeting to discuss the faith on the day when Christians celebrate the manifestation of the news of the Christ-child to the greater world.

I was just coming off a bout with the flu and joked with Dr. Collins that whatever formula the NIH had developed for this year's strains did not keep me from getting the flu because I got my shot! He reminded me, through a smile and laughter, that if I had not gotten the shot, I could have very well ended up in the hospital with pneumonia, and I agreed.

As I wrote in the preface above, I am beginning this collection of reflections with Dr. Collins, for reasons I have already shared. However you come to find yourself reading this book, whether as a skeptic, or a believer, or somewhere in between, I would invite you to approach the pages that follow with the same measure of openness that led Dr. Collins to his own embrace of the faith.

With that, let's begin.

In a talk some years ago, you began with a PowerPoint presentation showing a photo of the Rose Window at Westminster Cathedral and an image of the long axis of DNA, showing the radial pattern.[2] You said this was a unique way of representing two different worldviews, ... faith and science, ... and you asked, do these two world views have to necessarily oppose one another—in other words, "Do you have to choose?" So, my first question is, indeed, "Do you have to choose?"[3]

Absolutely not! Yet a message that has been widely distributed, particularly in the United States, is that the science and the faith perspectives are somehow irreconcilably opposed to one another. I have not found that to be the case since I became a Christian at age twenty-seven. In fact, it has brought great joy to have these two ways of finding truth in my own life. I do love that image of the stained glass and the DNA double helix, because they are both beautiful!

One of our great aching needs as human beings is the desire to discover things that are beautiful. My faith does that for me, but science does that for me too. It gives meaning, . . . the sense that there is something more than just the material world that is calling to us. For me that kind of beauty is a signpost to God.

But God has given us curiosity, and we can use science to discover beautiful things in God's creation, if we are just willing to put the time in to find them.

Can you say a bit more about that experience of joy? As you know, that is one of the experiences that C. S. Lewis unexpectedly found when he came to faith and about which he writes in his book, Surprised by Joy, *a book you say helped you in your own faith journey.*[4]

When I was trying to understand what evidence there might be for the Creator God, the concept of joy—coming from C. S. Lewis originally, but then realizing it in my own life—became powerful and important. Those experiences of joy lift me out of the daily experiences of whatever else is happening.

You know, just waking up this morning in Washington, DC, and looking out the window and seeing an incredibly beautiful snowscape (which we don't see all that often here), I was struck with joy, and said to myself, "Ah! God has given us such a beautiful creation—and here it is!" That kind of an experience of joy gives you a sense of the numinous, a sense of gratitude that such moments are possible.

Certainly music—which is a big part of my life—is one of the ways in which that experience of joy finds its way into my daily experience. Music can lift me into a place, sometimes quite unexpectedly, that is hard to put into words.[5] Maybe that's why Lewis chose the simple word *joy*, although it has so many other meanings.

The beauty of music creates this sense that we are made for something more than just this material world. It can bring about a sense of ecstasy and longing, perhaps even an insight into who we are called to become, if not in this world, then maybe in the next one.

Can you share a bit about life in your home growing up—you have been open about a wonderful, loving home and parents, but religion and spiritual practice was not part of the matrix there.

Yes, my parents were wonderfully creative people who made the decision to homeschool their four sons, because they felt they could do a better job than the local schools. And I think they were right about that. But it was not a homeschooling that was based on religious training. There was none of that. My parents were highly educated, but we lived very simply. We lived on a farm with no indoor plumbing. It was a fairly austere way to grow up, although growing up that way you didn't know it was austere until you met other people.

You talk about having a kind of innate curiosity about the world around you. Did you parents inspire that?

Yes, I loved the experience of learning new things. That was a gift I was given by my parents' skills as teachers, one that I carry with me to this day. The homeschooling ultimately gave way to public school by the sixth grade. I was the youngest of four boys, and understandably, my parents' energy for educating all of us began to wane by then. But it was in public school where I fell in love with science.

Tell me a bit about how you, let's say, "landed" in a place of atheism early in life.

Again, I had a wonderfully loving and creative home life, but no particular religious background. When I got to college and listened to those conversations in the dorm about religion, I thought the atheists had the better hand of it. So I sided up with them. I liked the idea of not having to be responsible to anybody outside of myself. By the time I enrolled in graduate school to study physical chemistry, I was pretty much an atheist.

But then things began to shift for you?

Yes. First, I had a major change in my idea of how I wanted to spend my professional life. I realized that my attraction to physics and chemistry had caused me to ignore biology. As I belatedly explored that domain, I found a strong pull to change direction and study the science of life. I made a rather dramatic shift from quantum mechanics to medicine. I arrived at medical school as an atheist. But a couple years later, I found my atheism was rather thin when I sat at the bedside of people who were dying. I watched those who had faith strangely comforted by their own sense of peace, and realized I would not be at peace if I was in their circumstances.

And you have this wonderful encounter with one of your patients that really cracked open the door a bit for you. Can you share about that?

Yes, there was a moment of encounter with one of my patients. She was a grandmotherly person with advanced heart disease, and I was a bit attached to her. She was very open with me about her faith. One day after sharing her own love for Jesus, she looked at me and asked, "Doctor, what do you believe?"

It was a question that just burned into my brain. Even to this day, I can see the room. I can see her. I can feel the color rising in my face when I realized [that] I've been asked the most important question that I've ever been asked.

And I had absolutely no answer. The ice was cracking under my atheist's feet. I realized I had no defensible response to the sincere question from this wonderful, loving, honorable woman. That's when I figured that I'd better do something about this. I needed a better way to defend my atheism.

That began a two-year personal journey, trying to understand how reasonable people could actually believe in God. The first and rather shocking step was to recognize that atheism is probably the least rational of all the choices.

Atheism requires that you have a version of faith—to assert that there is no God. This is the assertion of a universal negative, which scientists are not supposed to do.

Think about it this way. Suppose you were asked to draw a circle that represents all the true knowledge that has ever existed or ever will exist. You would draw a massive circle in the air. Okay, now suppose you are asked to draw on that same scale a circle that represents what you currently know. Even the most arrogant person will draw a circle much smaller than the larger circle of universal knowledge.

But suppose the knowledge of God's existence is outside your circle. How then could you possibly say, "I know there is no God"?

So the next step for me was agnosticism.

Which I have heard you describe was kind of a "safe place" for you, . . . at least for a while!

Yes, agnosticism was a good landing place after what I realized was an indefensible, hard-edged, atheist position.

Agnosticism leaves all the options open. But after a while, it ended up being kind of a cop-out for me. It was a way station to avoid doing the next set of hard work to figure out what really might be the knowable truth. If we are asking the honest questions, if we believe there is more to know, then we don't stop.

That's what kept my inquiry going. I rested there for a few months, but then I realized agnosticism didn't answer my patient's question, "*Doctor, what do you believe?*"

Where then to look for evidence? I gradually began to see that science itself had pointers to a Creator that I had ignored, despite my love for science.

I had to come to terms with the fact that there's something instead of nothing. As a scientist, I knew that there was the "Big Bang"—that out of nowhere, out of nothingness, came the universe, about 13.5 billion years ago. How could that happen without a creator outside of nature, space, and time? "Uh-oh," I thought, that started to sound like God!

I also began to realize that those beautiful and elegant equations about matter and energy that I had studied in physical chemistry inspired a question: "Where did those come from?" Why should mathematics describe the universe, unless there's a mind behind it? Even more riveting, I learned about fine-tuning—the fact that those equations have constants in them—like the gravitational constant, the strong and weak nuclear forces, and the speed of light. Astoundingly, those constants have to have exactly the value they do, or nothing interesting can happen. The universe, if it existed at all, would just be a lot of boring particles.

All of this was leading me to recognize there's a really strong case for an intelligence behind the universe. I learned that even Einstein recognized that.

That led to the next big question: "Does this Intelligence care about me?" That's an even harder question to answer. Here's where C. S. Lewis came in and really helped me think that one through—specifically with the first chapter of *Mere Christianity*, which was titled, "Right and Wrong as a Clue to the Meaning of the Universe."[6]

Lewis asserted that unless there is a source of morality, then the very concepts of good and evil really don't have any meaning. He was right. Good and evil. They exist. We humans, down through history, all seem to know that. But wait a minute, if that is true, . . . where do these concepts come from?

Well here it was. I was looking for a God who was not just a Creator of the universe, but who cared about me and other humans. And here I found this signpost in my heart, pointing me towards what is good and holy, calling me to be like that, even though I often fail.

There was also that other signpost that I couldn't really explain from a purely materialistic perspective—beauty. Both of these clues were pulling me towards a conclusion that there's something more to humanity than just atoms and molecules.

But then, I realized I had a problem. If this God does exist, and cares about me, and as a holy God wants me also to be holy—well, I'm failing. Failing a lot. So just as I was beginning to realize that God might be real, God was emerging in my mind as a Judge who must look upon me as a moral failure. How could I deal with that?

How did you deal with it?

Well, I guess you could say, God dealt with it. Because just as I hit that brick wall, I met Jesus.

I had thought of Jesus as a myth. I didn't realize the historical evidence of his life and death was so incredibly compelling. Even more astounding, hundreds of witnesses testified that he was raised from the dead, some of them going to their deaths insisting on the truth of the Resurrection. What was the point? I had heard Christians talk about Jesus dying on the cross for them, but I didn't understand that. I believed people just said that, because that's what they were supposed to say. They could not actually mean that, I would think to myself.

But then, I came to understand. I realized what they meant. This was the solution to my estrangement from God. In the words of a hymn I later learned to love, "For God hath regarded my helpless estate, and has shed his own blood for my soul." Jesus did die for me. . . . And then he was resurrected from the dead to give me the hope of new life. And now I can have relationship with God, despite all the things that I know are not right with me—because Jesus provides that bridge.

I realized the search had come to the place that made total sense. I couldn't prove it, but it had every attribute that I've been searching for.

And then you made a decision . . . ?

Yes, I still had to decide. I realized that faith is not acquired passively; it requires a commitment. That ultimately came to pass on a beautiful day, hiking in the Cascade Mountains.[7] There was a riveting moment where I was overwhelmed by the beauty of nature. It was in late October. I turned a corner and saw in front of me a frozen waterfall, spread like a veil, cascading down from the top of a high cliff. I could no longer resist. I realized, "I can't turn back now. The only thing I can do is go forward."

C. S. Lewis describes his own experience of coming to faith as "the most reluctant convert in all of England." I might have not been quite that uncertain, but I was certainly not a convert shouting, . . . "Hooray. I'm saved!" It was more like, "I don't know what I'm doing, but I'm going to take this leap."

I love that you quote a sonnet by Sheldon Vanauken, "Our only hope: to leap into the Word / That opens up the shuttered universe," in relation to your conversion moment. How did your leap begin to open up that "shuttered universe"?[8]

Beauty, . . . joy, . . . a call to be holy, . . . immortality, . . . knowing where everything true and good is coming from suddenly made those experiences a whole lot more important—and provided a way of connecting outside of myself to the Source.

You give the doubter a wide door as you have written, "Doubt is an unavoidable part of belief," with a nod to Paul Tillich who wrote, "Doubt isn't the opposite of faith; it is an element of faith."[9]

Absolutely. Probably most believers have doubts but aren't comfortable saying so because it feels dangerous. They have concerns like, "What will other

Christians think of me if I am having doubts? Does that mean my faith is actually much more fragile than I thought it was . . . ?"

I actually worried about that when I had a faith crisis about a year or two into my Christian experience. I felt like I had somehow lost the thread completely, and went through several weeks of deep distress, feeling all alone. A chance encounter with another scientist-believer was what rescued me. He helped me walk back through how I came to believe in Jesus, and I realized again that those were really compelling arguments. It wasn't that I had somehow been trapped by some emotional experience and abandoned rationality. The evidence was still there. I just had lost the connection for a bit.

I haven't had anything as disruptive as that since then, but I've certainly had plenty of moments where I've encountered a doubt and had to work through what I felt God was trying to teach me through the scriptures, or what God might be trying to say to me in a given situation. Doubt turned out to be a reliable signal of an area where I needed to do some work. I learned not to be afraid of it.

Can you talk a little bit about your prayer life?

I mostly focus on that early in the morning, partly because my own professional experience during the day has tended to be quite intense and unremitting. But at five o'clock in the morning, it is less likely that I will be interrupted.

I'm usually up at 4:30 or 5 a.m., trying to start the day with some kind of reflection. Sometimes that's reading scripture, other times reading the words of other people that I have learned a lot from, like Dallas Willard with his wonderful exhortations about spiritual discipline; or Philip Yancey, who is so good at identifying areas where I need to do some work. I'm also in a book club with an amazing group of other men who are serious believers and who have become my spiritual mentors.

I pray during the day when something gives me a nudge; I pray with my wife at every meal, and not just in a superficial way, but in a real way that tries to reflect on what's on our hearts.

And when there's a real crisis happening—and there are plenty of those, whether it's a family crisis or a professional crisis or a health crisis—prayer is the place I go to.

You have worshipped in several denominations, but do you have a denominational home now?

I confess I am puzzled about denominations. I'm still bouncing around now after forty-eight years. I came to Christ in a Methodist Church. I have worshipped in an Episcopal Church and a Presbyterian Church. Yesterday, I went to a Baptist Church because a friend of mine was preaching there.

Honestly, when I am walking into a Christian church I don't pay much attention to the name on the door. I figure we're all there to worship God, to learn from the Bible, and to try and follow Christ. It is surprising to me that some people seem to attach such significance to denominations.

I know you are a student of a lot of theologians, but do you have one to whom you draw a lot from?

Yes, it's Tom Wright, who I've had the good fortune to get to know and spend time with. He is a prayerful man and a deep thinker. When I read his books, essays, or Bible commentaries, I have to read them more than once to get my head around what he is saying.[10]

My other spiritual mentor was Tim Keller. I got very close to him in his last two years, while he was being treated for pancreatic cancer at NIH.[11] I would spend a lot of time with him in the afternoons just learning from him. He didn't want to talk about cancer, he wanted to talk about Jesus!

Watching him, I learned how to live, and I learned how to die.

In your writings and talks, you have spoken with a great deal of insight and wisdom about the various reasons people choose not to believe in God. One of those reasons that you say they point to is the corruption of the Church. Can you expand on that a little bit, just for folks who are reading?

Yes, God has created us in His image. But He pours the clear truth and grace of His Holy Spirit into rusty containers—human beings like me.

Jesus gives us clear teachings of the kind of Christians we are called to be—just read the Sermon on the Mount all the way through.[12] Ask yourself if we are living up to those exhortations—as individuals or within our churches.

Especially in these current times where there is so much divisiveness and animosity, there is a wide gap between how most of us live our lives and what Jesus calls us to do.

The problem is, "we" get in the way. Our own desire to be important and our pride invariably pops up. Our sense of being threatened or angry takes over. We see that happening prominently right now in the United States, and it's affected many church communities.

People who aren't believers look at Christian churches right now and see strife and hypocrisy. They might hear Christians talk about love, but all too often what they see is animosity, anger, fear, and political messages that are the opposite of the "love your neighbor" foundations of the faith.

To be fair, the vast majority of Christians have not fallen victim to the strife, and they are grieving about the loss of love and grace. But they don't get much attention. The loudest voices are often the most egregiously set apart from the principles that Jesus calls us to. That makes it easy for people to say Christians are all hypocrites.

Yet God is still in charge. God is still sovereign. Our shortcomings seem to have no limit, but God's love has no limit. And despite all of this, I think that God's love and grace will sustain us and will still draw people to the truth.

You have also pointed out that "suffering" is another reason people turn away from a belief in God. If we have a loving God, why is there suffering? What is your response to that?

That is the hardest question for a believer. I wish I had an answer that was totally satisfying.

But I do think in my own life experience, suffering has often been the moment where I have learned the most. When things are going smoothly, and everything's fine, it's easy to just coast along and figure, "Well, I'm all right. I don't really need God today." But then you get hit by a crisis—and I've had my own set of family tragedies. Then you realize that, as much as you are grieving, and as much as you are hurt and distraught, this is also a chance to understand what really matters in life and, particularly, what matters with your relationship with God.

As a Christian, I have a source of comfort in those moments of suffering. I know that I worship God to whom I don't have to explain suffering. Jesus suffered for me on the cross in an agony that I can't possibly imagine. And for me to say, "God, why are you letting me suffer?" I need to remember that God has already done the suffering for me.

I also see that suffering has to be interpreted in a wider context: what matters most might be more than what you see right here in this moment. We are here for an eyeblink of time in the context of eternity. Suffering that seems so unbearable for our little eyeblink may somehow make perfect sense in the context of eternity.

This seems the right point to ask you about your daughter, and the suffering she, and you all as a family, experienced because of her own horrific tragedy. To me, this might be where the rubber really hits the road. When you have been through the sexual assault of your daughter, plenty of people would say you have every right to say, "Okay, that's it, I'm done." But you and your beloved Diane, and your daughter, did not do that. How did your faith help you through that?

My daughter was an undergraduate. She was working in a university lab in the summertime in between her sophomore and junior year. And this evil man broke into her apartment with a knife and raped her. He was never caught.

I could hardly believe such a thing could have happened. And how could God have allowed it?

For a while, I was consumed with anger and grief. I didn't know how to think this through. I still don't know that I completely do, but I can look back now and see that God must have grieved too. God gives free will to all of us. That doesn't prevent some humans using their free will to do terrible things to each other.

It's impractical to think that God should jump in supernaturally and intervene multiple times a minute to stop these kinds of evil events. If God did, the whole nature of order in the universe falls apart.

So, should God not have given us free will? If so, that would be a very different world, and we wouldn't be given a chance to find Him for ourselves.

But suffering can also lead to spiritual insights and personal growth. I watched the way in which my daughter worked through this awful experience.

She was motivated by this to reach out to other women who have also suffered sexual assaults. My daughter, now as a physician, is able to counsel them, reassure them, comfort them. That simply would not be possible if she didn't know personally what their experience has been.

This says so much about her—she did not run away from the opportunity to work through similar crises with others. She ran towards it. That is a blessing that came out of a terrible crime.

Thank you for sharing that. That's powerfully humbling and inspirational at the same time.

Let me shift just a bit. While a lot of people know you from your work with the Human Genome Project, and the NIH, I suspect a lot of people, unless they read you directly, might not know you spent a little time as a missionary doctor in Nigeria. How did that impact you?

Oh wow, in a big way. It was a turning point part of my own life and faith experience. Since I had become a Christian during my medical training, I wondered if there might be something medical I was called to do in other countries.

An opportunity presented itself and so my daughter and I went together to Africa—twice, first when she was an undergraduate and then again when she was a medical student.

The experience really forced me to put myself in God's hands. We were stationed in an incredibly challenging environment, a small hospital in the middle of the jungle in Delta State, Nigeria. All of the technologies and laboratory capabilities that I, as a Western-trained physician, was used to were simply not available.

The diseases that I was seeing were often ones I'd never seen before, only read about in a book, and yet I was supposed to provide the right care.

I knew my own competence was wildly short of what was needed, and I realized I would just have to depend on God for the rest.

I didn't like that at first. I liked being a physician who was in control of everything. But it was an important moment to let go and let God be the source of wisdom. I don't give that control up so easily. This was a giant opportunity to do just that.

Having this shared experience with my daughter was particularly meaningful, and we really bonded together during those weeks. I learned a great deal about life, faith, and courage from those amazing, good, honorable, hardworking Nigerians who were my coworkers—and my patients.

The hospital was so full of patients that many of them slept on the floor, because there were not enough beds. In the clinic every afternoon I might see sixty or more patients in three or four hours. That's about six times what you would see in an American setting.

One afternoon, I saw a young farmer with massive swelling of his legs and very low blood pressure. With some uncertainty because there was no imaging available, I concluded that he probably had tuberculosis and had developed a life-threatening accumulation of fluid around his heart. Without intervention to remove the fluid, he would surely die in a few days. I had never done this procedure, called "pericardiocentesis," before. I could easily have killed him if it had gone wrong.

And yet it did work. A quart of fluid was taken off, and he had a rather miraculous improvement in the space of twenty-four hours. I was briefly exhilarated. But then I felt discouraged again. I knew in this environment, he might not be able to get the drugs he would need for the next two years to cure his condition, or some other illness might get take his life.

I went to see him the morning after the cardiac procedure. He was reading his Bible and looked dramatically better. After greetings, he looked at me and said, "I get the feeling you're new here."

"Darn it," I thought—it wasn't supposed to be so obvious.

And then he said, "I get the feeling you're wondering why you came here."

I really didn't expect that. I was sure the Nigerian medical residents with me on rounds were all thinking, "Oh boy, this patient has really nailed this green American doctor."

And then the farmer said, "I have an answer. You came here for one reason. You came here for me."

I confess to you, my reader, at the telling of this "punch line" I was overcome with emotion and began to tear up. We both paused for a moment.... And then Dr. Collins added:

It's great to have grand schemes and plans, but when it comes right down to it, you and I are mostly just called to touch the life of another person. In this case, in the story I just told you, I was given the gift of touching this farmer's life, and he then he touched mine. And in the process, Jesus touched my heart and soul in a way I will never forget.

Well, thank you. Thank you for that. I'm glad I asked that question. Let me try to wrap it up.

As a Christian, and as a pastor, I think it is really important that people have a chance to hear a belief of yours that I share—and you make a wonderful case for it—there's absolutely no reason to not believe in Genesis 1 and 2 and not believe in the Big Bang or whatever scientific theory one wants to pick for creation. Some, sadly, have chosen their position as their own personal line in the sand, and have used it as yet another reason to divide from one another. See if you can help that person who gets too hung up about those kinds of things.

I do feel bad for people who have been taught, many of them from their earliest Sunday school lesson, that Genesis 1 and 2 must be interpreted as textbooks of science, with literal days of creation that are twenty-four hours long.

John Walton, the Old Testament scholar at Wheaton College, has helped a lot of believers to understand what the original readers of Genesis must have thought of those words. In Walton's books, including *The Lost World of Genesis One*, he makes it clear that those first readers would never have thought this text was describing twenty-four-hour days.

The insistence on a literal interpretation is a relatively recent development, particularly in conservative Christian churches in the United States, dating back to the mid-nineteenth century, in part as a response to Darwin. After the 1925 Scopes Trial,[13] belief in a literal interpretation of scripture became almost a litmus test for serious faith.

That strict literal interpretation, often referred to as "young earth creationism," required its adherents to believe that the theory of evolution is wrong, and potentially even evil. Also seen as a threat was the growing evidence from multiple scientific perspectives that Earth is about 4.5 billion years old, not 6,000 years old. To defend their position, young earth creationists came up with their own alternative explanations to explain fossils, geologic strata, and relatedness of species. These were mostly well-intentioned but ultimately doomed because of their failure to fit the evidence.

This perceived conflict between the biblical story of creation and what science has unequivocally revealed about origins still persists in many conservative churches. The greatest tragedy is what this has done to generations of young people who have grown up in dedicated, well-meaning, loving Christian churches, but are told they must believe in creation that occurred in six days of twenty-four hours.

But then that young person attends a university and begins to seriously study science. The data in support of an old earth is overwhelming. Evolution, as a means of explaining the relatedness between living things, including humans, is now about as well established as gravity.

When faced with that evidence, those who hold to the young earth position are faced with terrible questions: "Am I going to reject this evidence? Is science not trustworthy? Is it maybe even evil?" If the answer is yes, that person may walk away from being the next great scientist, maybe even the next Nobel Prize winner. If the answer is no, this person may reject their faith in order to embrace what appears to be objective truth about origins.

But this is all unnecessary! The literal reading of Genesis was never required, even before recent science came along.

I would love for more people to go back and read Augustine.[14] He was somewhat obsessed with Genesis and wrote several volumes about it. He ultimately concluded that no human can really understand what was being described and warned believers not to attach themselves too tightly to a single interpretation, lest new insights about creation might make their interpretations no longer viable. That was written 1600 years ago!

Furthermore, there are plenty of clues in the text that Genesis isn't intended to be taken as a scientific textbook. As you know, there are actually two creation stories in the opening chapters!

Yes, and the details of those two versions are quite different from one another!

But this can all be resolved. There is no need for those days of creation to be twenty-four hours. And if God chose to use evolution as the means of creation, ultimately resulting in big-brained creatures in His image who would seek Him, who are we to say we wouldn't have done it that way? The Bible teaches us "why?" Science can teach us "how?" The perceived conflict between the Bible and science can thus be resolved in this way. Those interested in deep discussions about this synthesis of rigorous science and Christian faith can find good company in a foundation that I started sixteen years ago—BioLogos (www.biologos.org).

Let me ask you one more question. Your new book The Road to Wisdom *has just been released, during this season in time when our nation, if not the world, is seeing these deeper, deeper divides, along issues of politics and religion.*[15]

And I think you kind of hope in this book to turn the focus away from that division in the public square through that ancient virtue of wisdom. And, as I understand it, you give your reader four plumblines to the kind of wisdom that have the potential to heal our cultural divides—truth, science, faith, and trust.

How would you counsel us as we look at where we are? How can we better turn to wisdom? How can we pull on those four strands as individuals in a way that helps us heal these great divides?

We are living in a difficult time. I don't know anybody who would say that our cultural divides are not a serious problem. In many aspects of our daily experience, everything seems to be about grievance, animosity, and polarization, often along political lines. These tensions are getting in the way of our ability to flourish the way that God wants us to.

People of faith ought to be in a strong position to help turn this around. Look at all the exhortations in the Sermon on the Mount. You must not just love your neighbors, but you must also love your enemies. There's not a lot of that going on right now.

The premise of my book is that we need to recapture that path towards wisdom. For people of faith, if you want to learn about wisdom, read the book of Proverbs!

Wisdom is referred to in many places in the Bible. I love the verse from James 1:5, "If any of you lacks wisdom, you should ask God, who gives generously to all without finding fault, and it will be given you."[16]

Ask God. Are we people of faith, frustrated with all of the divisiveness around us, asking God and seeking out the road to wisdom? That journey might provide insight to help guide us in our own interactions with our families, our friends, and our nation.

In the book I argue first that wisdom can't be achieved unless we reclaim the position that there is such a thing as objective truth. Facts are facts, even if you don't like them.

Science is, of course, a wonderfully reliable way to discover truth. But transcendent truths about the meaning of life and our relationship to God are not approachable by the scientific method—here's where faith comes in.

And then there's trust, which is in short supply these days. It is vitally important to be thoughtful about how we assign trust. Are we withholding trust from reliable sources because they're not part of our own tribal grouping? On the other hand, are we granting trust to people who are feeding us nonsense, but our guard has been let down because they are part of our own social bubble?

The current societal crisis, which has deeply affected the church, requires some deep self-reflection. We won't find our way out of this polarized situation from politicians or from the media, and certainly not from social media. We will have to find it as individuals.

In the final chapter of the book, I call on all of us to do two things: First, we need to do some self-examination about how we decide what is true, and whether our own storehouse of truth has been contaminated by misinformation. Second, we need to counter polarization by making a commitment to build real bridges with people we don't agree with, to become the kind of people who are able to listen, and not just shout.

People of faith and houses of worship could lead this healing process. We have the principles, values, and tools to do so. Perhaps then we can find our way out of what is unquestionably a dark time.

God is still sovereign. God can work through us if we're willing to be those channels—where we are not about hate anymore, we are about love.

I think that is a beautiful way to end our conversation, but may I ask you to close us in prayer?

Yes.

Dear Lord, thank you for the chance to speak together through this virtual connection. I guess, mostly, it's been about me telling my story. But I know you've touched Russ's life in many ways. I'm thankful for his dedication in trying to distribute these stories for individuals who are still searching. May we both seize those opportunities to share your good news, even at times where it doesn't seem very convenient or we're not sure if it is appropriate or timely. Help us to be willing at all times to let your light shine through our lives. Even though our own lights are often inadequate, yours is never inadequate. So thank you for this time. May these words touch lives down the road through the skills of Russ and the rest of his team that are putting this all together. I ask all of this in Jesus's name. Amen.

DR. FRANCIS COLLINS

Dr. Francis Collins is a physician-scientist. Under his direction, the Human Genome Project produced the first finished sequence of the human DNA instruction book. His contributions to science, medicine, and society have been recognized by the Presidential Medal of Freedom, the National Medal of Science, and the Templeton Prize. A former atheist, Collins became a Christian during his medical training, and wrote about that in a best-selling book, *The Language of God*. Subsequently he founded the BioLogos Foundation, to provide a meeting place for individuals interested in serious and civil discourse on the potential harmony between science and Christian faith. From 2009 to 2021, Collins served under three presidents as the Director of the US National Institutes of Health, the largest supporter of biomedical research in the world. Following a year in the White House as the President's Acting Science Advisor, he oversaw a research laboratory as a Distinguished Investigator in the intramural program of the National Human Genome Research Institute. He also led a bold administration initiative to eliminate hepatitis C in the United States. His most recent book is *The Road to Wisdom: On Truth, Science, Faith, and Trust* (Little, Brown and Company, 2024).

Photo credit: © Courtesy of The Hoover Institution

"Guide my feet in ways that will glorify your kingdom."

—The Honorable
Dr. Condoleezza Rice

The Honorable Dr. Condoleezza Rice

Say the name Condoleezza Rice, and a myriad of adjectives come to mind—brilliant, tenacious, wise—and in addition there are her many positions of esteemed leadership—security advisor, provost, secretary of state. The Honorable Condoleezza Rice is arguably one of the most gifted and notable public figures of the last and present generation—so much so that she has repeatedly declined invitations to consider running for the highest office in our land.

For now, she has settled into to her latest role as the director of the Hoover Institution at Stanford University, a post she has held since September 1, 2020. An academic, author, speaker, as well as an accomplished ice skater, golfer, and concert pianist—Condi Rice has been, and is, many things, but perhaps the one word that captures them all is *daughter*: the daughter of two loving parents and the daughter of her heavenly Father.

She unapologetically pays homage to both in her writings and when speaking publicly: "Every night I begin my prayers saying, 'Lord, I can never thank you enough for the parents you gave me.'"[1]

Before the interview you are about to read, I had only met Secretary Rice once, at the twentieth anniversary celebration of the Baker Institute, where I was offering the invocation. That evening, as always, I found her remarks spellbinding. We shared two other moments, where she attended the

Memorial Service for Barbara Bush in Houston, Texas, and the State Funeral for President George H. W. Bush, during which I presided and offered the homily at both services.

But through my reading and mutual connections with other people, what intrigues me most about Secretary Rice is her deep commitment to her Christian faith. In a moment in history when religion is more likely to be used by those seeking power and privilege to further their individual purposes, Secretary Rice stands out as one who is, instead, used—perhaps *employed* is a better word—by her faith to better the world around her and around all of us.

Toward that end, with transparent admiration, I offer to you in the following excerpts from an interview I recently conducted with Secretary Rice; a portrait that I hope will encourage you, as it has me.

One of the things you've said in a couple of places but certainly in the memoir as well, is that you're somebody that always believed in God, and I think that was the fruit of your parents' devotion and the way in which you grew up, but that also of your community of Titusville, [Alabama.] I liked when you said there were no atheists or agnostics in your middle-class community. But indeed, kind of paralleling that with the years of Jim Crow, segregation, Bull Connor Birmingham and all that, were there times when your faith was challenged?

I don't think that my faith was challenged, . . . remember I was pretty young too, . . . [2] and I think certainly everybody feels at some point, particularly probably my parents' generation, "Where is God if this is all going on in our community?" But the funny thing about it is that the tendency instead was just to strengthen one's faith and to go to God even more fervently as things got difficult. I have often reflected that maybe it comes from the history of slavery where during the darkest periods of time slaves wrote *"Nobody Knows the Trouble I've Seen"* and *"Glory, Glory, Hallelujah,"* which I've always found is an interesting and awed response to the circumstances.[3] And so, I do not remember my faith being challenged during those times, but I was pretty young. I also don't remember any indication that my parents' faith was being challenged during that time.

You are clearly a person of prayer, and it sounds like you're somebody who prays upon rising and prays before you go to bed at night. And I love that you begin your prayers with giving thanks to God for your parents—but can you tell me a little bit more about the shape of your prayers? What does that look like? How do you pray? Are there times, more times than others, outside of regular devotional time you might pray? And then, lastly, what does your prayer life bring to you?

That is an interesting question. I just had breakfast last weekend with my former pastor, John Ortberg, at my church, but I still consider him my pastor in many ways.[4] John and I were talking about this very thing, about prayer. My days are very busy and begin early, so I shared with John that my morning prayers are often brief and simple. I will pray something like, "*Guide my feet in ways that will glorify your kingdom,*" which serves as a reminder to me in the morning of who I am called to be and what I am called to do.

And, throughout the day, I will often use what I would call tiny prayers, automatically, "*Lord, help me get through this,*" or "*Give me wisdom*" or "*Help me to be someone who helps in this circumstance, and doesn't detract from Your guidance.*"

But my prayers in the evening are very different. Before I go to bed, I offer my prayers in a pretty structured way, maybe that is just the Presbyterian in me—you know, we Presbyterians like structure! So, as you pointed out, I begin my prayers thanking God for my parents. I have a prayer for gratitude of everything I have been given. I pray for my family. If there are particular family or friends that I know are in distress of some kind, I offer my prayers for them.

I pray for special circumstances like the people of Ukraine.[5] So I then spend time in prayer for others, particularly those in distress, but also people that I pray for, like my aunt, my stepmother, etcetera, so there is a "prayers for the people" section. I pray for good health. And then end my prayers by asking that God would specifically use me to serve Him with these words, "*Help me to be an instrument of Your peace, a better disciple and to be a blessing to others as You have been a blessing to me.*" After that, I offer the Lord's Prayer.

So, I confess, my prayers are pretty structured, and as I was saying to John [Ortberg], . . . I have to keep refreshing my prayers and the way I pray, because while I believe it is certainly fine to be structured, I do not want my prayers to become rote.

And funny enough, Pastor, when I was working in the government, I would come home sometimes so tired, and if I waited to the end of the day I would find myself falling asleep while I was praying, so I started right when I walked in the door, I would get down on my knees and do my prayers while I was still conscious enough to talk to God and was not falling asleep in the middle of our conversation!

But I have come to believe that the way I practice prayer gives me a sense that I have been attentive to all of the things in my life that are good, all of the things in my life that are challenging, and that is really what prayer does for me. Prayer opens up a conversation with the Lord. As a Protestant Christian, I believe that our personal relationship with the Lord is so important—and because it is personal, I do not need intermediation and so that's how I think about it.

That said, I remember a moment when my Protestant faith was on display for Pope John Paul II. It was during my years of service in the Bush administration and, honestly, I walked up to the Pope, and I said, "*God bless you, Holy Father.*" And then I thought to myself, "*What a Protestant thing to do! I bless you, you bless me, we all kind of bless each other!*" But then I questioned my words, and thought for a moment, "*No that was the other way around, the Holy Father blesses you, you don't bless him.*" But I am a Protestant, so I really do believe that when I pray, I have no need for an earthly mediator and can go directly to our Lord in prayer.

May I ask, what is your posture during prayer? Do you sit? Or kneel?

I kneel.

And what role does faith play in your prayers?

I often wish that I had that sense of absolute faith that I saw in my maternal grandmother, who, whenever I think of someone who was totally and completely faithful, I think of her. She died when I was about twenty-two, but I could just feel it and see it—it was almost as if there was a forcefield around her. I think that is something I want, I think we all would like that.

That's wonderful, and I would agree. Dr. Rice, you have certainly had seasons of deep pain in your life, not only some of the many stories that you share in your memoirs about your movement through the Civil Rights season and the ongoing challenges we all faced there, but also the death of your parents. How did your faith carry you through those times?

Well, I think the only thing that carries one through those times is faith. Because you cannot do it on your own—it is not as if your brain will carry you through it. I think particularly of my mother who was so young when she died, at the age of sixty-one.

When that happened, of course, I wondered why? Now I will say, my father had something that really helped me in that period, which is that he reminded me that my mother first had breast cancer when I was fifteen. He told me that during that time, he prayed, "*I don't know how to raise a fifteen-year-old girl.*" After that prayer, my mother went into remission, and she lived 'til I was thirty, until the breast cancer returned. But she got to see me become a professor at Stanford. She got to read my first book, and so forth. So, I am very grateful she did not die when I was so young.

But I am an only child, and my parents were the center of my life in so many ways, so I naturally thought, "*How am I going to be without my mother?*" So, yes, my mother's death was very painful, and yet my faith carried me through that, and continues to do so. What my faith offers me in times like that is "the peace that passes understanding." To me, that is what faith is all about, you cannot understand it with your mind. I am a believer in the Lord expects you to use your brain. I was never encouraged to be one of those people who never question, who never think through the ways of God, life's challenges, and so on. But in those particular times, thinking, your intellect, just fails you. You have to rely on your faith.

For instance, it helps if you are a believer in resurrection, which I am. If you are a believer in that hope, then I believe in one day being reunited with my loved ones who have gone to death before me. Though, I would not be telling you the truth if I said that I do not know quite how I think life looks after death. I was talking to a friend several months ago who has also worked with me. We talk about faith from time to time. And he said, "*Do you really believe Christ really rose from the dead?*" and I said "*I do. I believe in the Resurrection.*" I said, "*I have to tell you I'm not really sure what it means to me—is it immediate, do I have to wait awhile? I'm not really sure on the details.*" But if you believe that death is not a final chapter, I also believe that helps when you lose loved ones as well, and for that, I have to rely on my faith.

I have read about a particular moment in your faith journey when an important epiphany occurred. You were listening to a sermon on the prodigal son, and you identified with the elder son and how that shifted something for you, and I felt like that was a journey we all need to make, but tell me a little bit more about that if you would?[6]

Well, when people tell the prodigal son story, it seems to always be about this kind of wild kid who ran away from home, and everybody focuses on prodigal, and it can elicit sympathy for the elder son who stayed home and did all the right things. But it was a sermon delivered by one of the pastors at Menlo Park Church, named Walt Gerber, and he gave a sermon from the perspective of the elder son, in the sense that it was all about self-righteousness. He pointed out how one can kind of "fall back" on just doing the right things. But what he pointed out, and what struck me, is that when your Christian faith is focused on what you do, rather than what Jesus does for us, such thinking is at odds with the concept of grace.

And as I listened to that sermon, I realized I was becoming like that elder son. I was doing all the right things. But I had to ask if my faith was such that I would have been able to do what the younger son did, which was to leave everything, and basically fall prostrate in front of the Holy Father and say I am a sinner too.

I think what I began to realize is that I was following the path of the self-righteousness of the elder son. And with that, I also realized how important it was to constantly search to revise and revisit my faith and refresh it and not take it for granted. That was a real turning point for me, and I still go back to that sermon and its wisdom from time to time.

How do you ... understand grace? Because you have become a person of extraordinary achievements, and it seems like every time you've used up all of your talent to ice skate or to play the piano, you take up golf or something else! One could say you're a highly achieving workaholic, which could get in the way of one's faith, but how do you understand grace then?

I understand grace, as a gift of God, as not deserved, as freely given. And again, there are these mysteries of our faith. How does it work for people who are not good people that could still receive grace? That is a constant question. For instance, think on Hitler. Did Hitler receive grace? When I head down those kinds of roads, I have just decided that I will leave those ultimate kinds of questions up to God.

But I receive grace as completely undeserved. One of the most challenging parts of the Bible really for me is that grace does not come through good works. Does that mean that I just sit here, and I do not do good work? I think the answer to that is no. As a Christian, I am still supposed to do good works. In fact, the early Christians became mostly known, not for their preaching and teaching, but for their good works. These first followers of Christ were the ones who began institutions like orphanages and hospitals—which offered things that many people did not believe important to be given to the ones Jesus called the "least of these."[7]

And yet Jesus taught that caring and serving in this way was what He was all about. So, yes, our faith is in part about works—so it is important to struggle with everything Jesus taught, not just one part or the other, which is a constant reminder that we do not have all the answers! But again, I believe that grace really is not deserved, not earned, it is given, it's freely given to all of God's children.

So let me ask what you would say to someone who might say, "I am young, and I have my life in front of me. I want to have all kinds of things that Secretary Rice has. She has achieved so much, and yet she is a person of faith. Why is that so important to her?"

I give my father a lot of credit for the way in which my faith developed. As a theologian, my Father was always asking me to ask questions. One time, he gave a sermon in this little church which some who heard it believed to be kind of controversial. But he invited his listeners to consider the story of Judas from Judas' perspective. My father was kind of always pushing the limits. So, I think because he let me use my mind, my faith was not separate from the rest of me. So, I am the kind of person who never really questions the existence of God. In every season of my life, it never occurred to me to abandon my faith, it just occurred to me to try to access it more.

For instance, after the terror attacks of 9/11, it was to try to access it to just stand—keep upright and to have wisdom and to try to put aside the hurt and the pain and the regret and just do what had to be done.[8] I never doubted God's existence and in fact found myself asking Him every night, "Can You just help me get through this?"

And, of course, in other seasons of life, as I mentioned earlier, when we face the death of loved ones, we have to rely on our faith. I do.

But just before I accepted the position as the Director of the Hoover Institution, I was really feeling like I had kind of ground to a halt.[9] I was doing a lot of fun things. I had left government, and I was teaching, and I was speaking. I was also able to do some consulting. All of this was really great, but I felt unfulfilled. I did not feel like I was contributing in the way that I thought the Lord wanted me to contribute.

My Church was offering a "Summer at the Movies" series, where they show films and encourage those attending to think about various religious themes. One of the films was Disney's *The Lion King*.[10] The elder lion, Mufasa, says to his son, Simba, "*You are more than you have become.*" And all of a sudden, I thought, "Yeah that's the problem, I'm more than I have become, and what really is this next chapter—is there a next chapter? Lord, are you really okay with me doing this the way that I'm doing this or is there something more that you want?"

And I prayed about that, for an entire year, and talked with my pastor about it. And then, of all things, I was at the Good Friday performance that the St. Lawrence String Quartet does at Stanford of *The Seven Last Words of Christ*.[11] And the director of the Hoover Institution had just stepped down, and the provost, Dr. Persis Drell, came up to me and said, "I want to talk to you about the Hoover job, and who should we have?"[12] A few days later, I went to meet with her, and she asked, "Would you take the position?" And I said, "Persis, I have negative zero interest in this. You're a physicist and you're going to be really offended because negative zero is not an integer, but that's how much I don't want to do this job."

And then I'm walking along this campus where I started my career as a young person from Denver, who probably never should have ended up on the Stanford faculty, and I started to think, "Maybe there's something that I owe this place, maybe this is a chance to mobilize others to work on big problems that we have as a country, maybe I can do something to make America a better place." And I called her [Dr. Drell] back and I said, "Well maybe it's not negative zero—we can talk about it."

But here is my point, which I think speaks to why my faith is so essential to my daily life. All of this came about, after a year-long prayerful search for what the next chapter was going to be. And it was rooted for me completely and totally in asking God if He had another chapter in mind for me and what did that look like. And no answer.... No answer.... No answer—until that Good Friday. To me, you could not write a better movie scene. On Good Friday in the church, it comes to me, and so I do not believe these things happen by accident. And so, with each phase of my life, faith has been there in different ways.

Such a powerful story. I love the closing line of your memoir, how you wish your mom and dad had seen you in the office, but at the same time you could hear your dad's voice, saying that you are God's beloved child. That's a lovely word.

So somebody is reading this interview—because they are curious about somebody like you, and says, you have all those things, it's easy to say you need God, but what would you say to someone who says, "You may want all those things, but you still need God on top of that?"

You are right, because ultimately those things will not matter in the long run. One day, you will be, as you approach your last chapter, your death, and what you achieved and what you accomplished will, of course matter to the world, but it does not matter ultimately to your soul. That soul can only be saved and preserved, when it either arrives in heaven immediately or at the moment Christ comes again. That is preserved through faith in God. And so it goes back to those works. I fully believe you try to do good works, but in the final analysis that is not what's going to matter—it is God's grace, which we receive by our faith, which produces good works; not the other way around.[13]

That's beautiful, beautiful. Well, one final question. When do you most experience God?

I think I most experience God when I think back on my own life and think there is no way to explain how I came from Birmingham, Alabama, to where I am. My life is totally and completely improbable. And I think, okay, there was a plan there. I was not even executing on it very well sometimes. I mean I thought the plan was I was going to be a great concert musician and obviously that was not the plan. I was supposed to do something else—I bumped around trying to figure out what that was quite a long time—changing majors, you know, doing odd jobs until I could not "figure it out," but until it was finally revealed to me.

My life has been so improbable that I think it has been a revelation step by step. And I suppose there is a part of me that has not even figured it all out. It can be hard to do that—I often see that with my students, because they want to figure it all out. The ones who want to express their faith I say, just spend enough time with God and it will be revealed over time. For those who do not have an active faith, I suggest that they keep searching for what it is and what is going to make this make sense to them individually. But I start by saying, "*Look, when I was your age, I was a piano performance major, okay, so don't worry too much about the future!*" And I think that "don't worry too much about the future" comes from deep faith. So faith is something I just keep returning to again and again, and I have to work on it.[14]

And then let me share one final story. So, I was part of the government entourage that attended Pope John Paul II's funeral. And Pastor, it was a gray cold day, and it was, of course, a very long service. You know when the Catholics offer Mass, it takes a while! My job was to get everybody—President Clinton, President George H. W. Bush, and President George W. and Laura Bush to the front so we could get out first, because our motorcade was so long the Vatican wanted us to leave first. So, my job was—and it's not easy with Bill Clinton or, as you know, with George H. W. Bush, they love people—and love to stop and talk, so I had to kind of keep pushing everyone toward the front.

So, we all get to the front and the pallbearers come and they turn the coffin toward the crowd and, on that cold, dark, gray day—the sun breaks out. And I thought, "Oh boy, did I feel that." And what was odd was, that moment was not reported by any of the journalists or anyone. But as we left the service, I asked Laura [Bush], "Did you see that?" She said, "Yes." And then on the plane back to the United States, a number of us spoke about noticing that.

A few weeks later, I was in Argentina and the foreign minister, who is a very faithful man, brought it up and he also asked, "Did you see that?" All of this prompted me to ask myself, "*Did only people of faith see it? Is that what happened?*" "*Could you only notice that moment in a service that proclaimed resurrection unless you had the eyes of faith to see it?*"

And so, there have been times that I have felt the presence of God very, very strongly. And I have come to believe that each of these moments throughout my life, . . . really that all my life has simply been preparing me for that moment when what I have believed in faith, I will see, and experience, the fullness of resurrection.

May I close using some of your own beautiful words? You wrote in your memoir that despite the deaths of your parents that "often, it has been their presence, not their absence that I've experienced. I could almost see John and Angelena Rice at the door of my West Wing office and hear their words, 'You are well prepared for whatever is ahead of you. . . . Now don't forget that you are God's child, and He will keep you in His care. . . .'"[15] *It seems to be, living in that knowledge not only of being the daughter of your wonderful parents, but also the daughter of our Heavenly Father, has been a source of strength and peace your whole life through. Would that be a fair assessment on my part?*

Yes, without question—my parents provided me with a strong foundation built on love, faith, and high expectations. When faced with the difficult challenges of life, my faith has guided me, lifted me up and sustained me—it has allowed me to be an optimistic person. All in all, I have been blessed beyond measure.

The Honorable DR. CONDOLEEZZA RICE

The Honorable Dr. Condoleezza Rice is the Tad and Dianne Taube Director of the Hoover Institution, the Thomas and Barbara Stephenson Senior Fellow on Public Policy, and the Denning Professor in Global Business and the Economy at the Stanford Graduate School of Business. Dr. Rice was Stanford University's provost from 1993-1999 and has earned two of the university's highest teaching honors as Professor of Political Science. She was the sixty-sixth Secretary of State of the United States from January 2005-2009, and the second woman and first Black woman to do so. She was the first woman to be Assistant to the President for National Security Affairs, from January 2001-2005 under President George W. Bush. Additionally, she served on President George H. W. Bush's National Security Council Staff, serving as Director, then Senior Director of Soviet and East European Affairs, as Special Assistant to the President for National Security, and as Special Assistant to the Director of the Joint Chiefs of Staff while an International Affairs Fellow of the Council on Foreign Relations.

Dr. Rice is the author and coauthor of numerous books, including *Democracy: Stories from the Long Road to Freedom*, *No Higher Honor: A Memoir of My Years in Washington*, and *Extraordinary, Ordinary People: A Memoir of Family*, among others.

Born in Birmingham, Alabama, she earned her bachelor's degree in political science, cum laude and Phi Beta Kappa, from the University of Denver, her master's degree in political science from the University of Notre Dame, and her PhD in political science from the Graduate School of International Studies at the University of Denver.

Photo credit: © Courtesy of The Gary Sinise Foundation

"I am a grateful American and I am grateful to God for calling me into this work."

—Gary Sinise

Gary Sinise

When I first met Gary Sinise in the fall of 2017, I had no idea how our relationship would grow in the years to come. I knew Gary from his award-winning films, television, and stage performances, but I would soon learn that there was much more to the man behind the actor. We had been introduced by a mutual friend, and now writer and speaker, Lieutenant General Rick Lynch.[1] We hosted an annual Veterans Day Service at St. Martin's to honor serving active military along with retired veterans, and General Lynch had been one of the featured speakers. The service often became a city wide event, and we used it as an opportunity to raise funds for the United Service Organizations, the USO.

For years, General Lynch had worked with Gary Sinise for the Gary Sinise Foundation, and General Lynch suggested we invite him to be a featured speaker. I did, and he agreed in the summer of 2017 to come for a service in the fall of that same year.

In late August 2017, Hurricane Harvey slammed into the Gulf Coast and brought devastation to Houston and beyond. For days, parts of one of the largest cities in the nation were literally underwater. To this day, I keep the voicemail I received from Gary on the heels of what became one of the worst disasters in Houston's history. Gary called to say how concerned he was and that he wanted to help, beyond the Veterans Day service we were hosting.

Within days, he was pulling together ideas for a fund-raising event for first responders in greater Houston who had damage to their homes. I raised my concerns about the cost for such an event and Gary immediately said, "There will be no cost. . . . I will bring my Lt. Dan Band, we'll offer a free concert, and let's raise some money!" The concert coincided with the St. Martin's event, and by the time it rolled around, Gary had convinced Grammy Award–winning performers Christopher Cross and Yolanda Adams to join him. The event raised over $100,000, which was passed on to ten families in Houston who had suffered personal losses during the hurricane.

In spending a few days with Gary, I also got to know of his deep faith, and how God had called him to more intentional service after the terrorist attacks of September 11, 2001.

Gary and I stayed in touch in the years after that concert, and when I learned that his wonderful and talented son Mac had been diagnosed with a rare form of cancer, and his wife, Moira, was also diagnosed with stage three breast cancer, our contact increased, and he and his family were in my daily prayers.

I was fortunate to visit with Gary at his Foundation, located in Nashville, Tennessee, which is where the following conversation took place.

Let's start with your mom and dad, . . . Mylles and Robert, and your grandparents, Vesta "Granma Betty," and your "Grandpa Dan." Somewhere along the way, your family stopped going to church. Was that a conscious decision on the part of your parents or something you think they just fell into because of the busy pace of their lives?

To be honest Russ, it's kind of hard to recall. I have vague little flashes of my mother combing my hair with Avon products to get me ready for church and Sunday school when I was about five years old. My grandfather came from a Roman Catholic family and grandmother was a Protestant—and from what I recall, there might have been a kind of division in the family—but attending Church, and belonging to a Church, was just not a high priority.

So, it is fair to say I was not brought up in a religious home as a young guy. In fact, when we moved to the Highland Park area of Illinois, I had a lot of Jewish buddies—but Saturday nights, they weren't available, and in the summers a lot of them would go to work at a kibbutz in Israel! They did go to Hebrew School and were faithful in attending services at the synagogue, and I suspect I was always kind of curious as to what all of that was about, but I never really went beyond curiosity. That was pretty much the pattern all the way through high school—so, no, no religion at all for me in a personal way in those days. All of that came later!

I think anyone who knows anything about you, or reads your works, would be struck by your brazen honesty and transparency. Your life reads a bit like the Bible—there are incredible stories, and dark ones. At one point you confessed as a fourteen-year-old, you had become a "thief, a liar, and a near-failing student," but at that point you really did not care.[2] Was there a connecting point for you in the disconnect from church, or faith, and what—today—you realized was a "dark path"?

Yeah, that's all true. As a youngster, I was kind of left to my own devices, and I got into a lot of trouble, and I really didn't care, . . . and I admit it. My mom had her hands full because we had a full house—my grandmother (her mother), and my aunt (her sister)—were both living with us, and Dad was looking out for everyone—which allowed time for a lot of mischief. But I believe in redemption!

One of the many significant things about your life are the people that had such a strong influence on you in your early life—your grandfather, Dan; your drama/theater teacher, Barbara Patterson; Officer Rash; even the lead in the Highland Park High School production of West Side Story, *Jeff Melvoin—who pulled you up from the chorus to receive your first experience of an ovation—it was here that you began to express a word that seems to define your life—grateful.[3] Can you say a bit more about those people and others?*

Let me start with my grandfather. We were all living on the South Side of Chicago in the early '60s, but when I was nine, Mom and Dad moved our family about forty-five miles north to Highland Park. So, growing up we would only see the grandparents every once in a while. So, I would probably not say that Grandpa had a strong influence on me at the time—because mostly I was afraid of him. He was an imposing tough Italian guy. He loved us all, but there was an old-school firmness. I recall one time as a kid: I used to play with matches, and on a visit to see the grandparents, I just about set their garage on fire and there was hell to pay! Grandpa was not happy. So while I was close to him, I mostly wanted to stay on his good side, which was sometimes difficult for this mischievous kid to do. But I tried.

And yes—Barbara Patterson—I just kind of bumped into her one day when I was in high school—when I happened to be skipping class. I was just standing out in the hallway, and she happened to walk down it, . . . and there we were. It was not that much of a stretch because honestly my friends and I kind of looked like gang members, which made us perfect for those parts in *West Side Story*. So she invited us to audition, and I got a part. I would say that was a moment of divine intervention because that was a moment when a lot of things began to come into focus for me. I was a struggling kid, and I began to see a possible purpose in my life.

In the middle of all of that, I got picked up by Officer Rash (his real name by the way) for selling some pot to someone who worked for the police department as a dog catcher. Being part of that play was really important to me, and I told that to Officer Rash. I got a stern talking to—and—a miracle as far as I am concerned—he let me go. I never sold pot again! And was able to focus on the play.

And yeah, I did not have a major part, only a few lines actually, but when the applause came, my buddy Jeff Melvoin, who was playing one of the leads and taking a bow up front, reached back and pulled me up to take a bow with him and the other lead actors in the show and I had that experience of an ovation for what I had done. I was so emotional that night, the play had changed me, and Jeff and the cast recognized that.

I have often thought whether or not I would have even stumbled into the theater world were it not for those people, those moments, those things.

Looking back, now, do you feel they were put in life's path by God?

What if I had not been standing there at that moment? What if Officer Rash had not let me off with a warning? What if I was not able to be in the play? I would guess I would have just kept playing around and getting into trouble. All of that set me on a different path. And I mean that moment—that set me on a course that turned into—you know—it turned into everything!

It's kind of like that feather that floats around in *Forrest Gump*. It just happened to land on me—on a day when I skipped class![4] Providence? It's quite possible. I mean we all look at things in our lives and just wonder if we took a right instead of a left, you know, whether we'd be in the same place we are now. Luckily, for me, I said yes to the right things at the right time. So, providence, divine intervention, yeah, because so many good things came out of all of that.

The "story" of your "Moira, sweet Moira" is simply remarkable. You have had tremendous ups and downs. You were engaged, then she broke it off; you got back together; began having your children—Sophie in 1988; Mac in 1990, and Ella in 1992—then came Moira's battle and eventual recovery from an alcohol addiction—which almost ended your marriage as well. Your wedding was not a religious service, there was no clergyperson, no fancy wedding rings—just vows exchanged in front of a judge with the Carpenter's "Close to You" playing in the background. But Gary, even in these days—prior to your deepening spiritual faith, you stayed committed to your marriage—often in a career field and world where broken marriage vows are as commonplace as the air we breathe. Can you say a bit more about "what" was the driving force in holding your marriage together?

Where we are is the fruit of a long journey. There were tremendous obstacles along the way that we have overcome, and to be honest, it was not always as strong as it ended up being in these last few decades. In those early days of marriage there were explosions and bombs going off in our relationship all the time—everywhere. You know, and we were just making our way through. We broke up and then got back together a couple of times during those early years. Young folks trying to find our way. We weathered a lot of storms.

Our journey was often a tough one, but you know we have been together now for nearly fifty years. If you look at the first part of the relationship, it was crazy—so crazy.

We first got together in 1976. While there were a lot of great wonderful times together, there were also challenges as sometimes she was going this way, and I was going that way. I was up and down, and her mom did not like me. But Moira saw something in me and was caught between her parents' feelings and her own feelings about me. At that time her parents and older sister would have preferred if she'd gone another way and forgot about me. But there was always something so strong between us. Even through those tough times our love for each other was clear.

At one point in the late '70s, we were going to get married, with a big wedding and all that. But, another test, as Moi decided she was not ready, and we didn't see each other for over a year. But as you said, the love was strong and in 1981 we came back together and got married in front of a judge one morning while I was doing a play at night. We didn't have rings, so I ran down to a Woolworths dime store in the neighborhood and bought a couple of cheap little rings. I think they cost $1.69 a piece. That ceremony took about four minutes and, as you mentioned, when it was over, the judge wound up a music box that played "Close to You" by the Carpenters. All of that—all of that and more—plays a role in who we are now and what our marriage has become. And when Moi and I think about all the things we have been through, we know we were just supposed to be together.

And then we had our beautiful kids, and that was really the beginning of our journey back into the faith, our faith, our Catholic faith. As they were coming along, Moi's participation in the Catholic Church became a huge, huge thing. While at first, I kind of followed along, as I consider it now, that gave us a grounding we had never known.

So those first years, and I mean the first twenty years or so, were just trying to figure stuff out. Our relationship, our parenting . . . But we hung in there, we worked through it all and these last thirty years do not look anything like the first ones!

And Moira—wow—she's just so special, so unique, and one of the most insanely hilarious people you will ever meet! That humor is so important. Still, after fifty years, she'll say something that just boggles my mind, and I find myself laughing for half an hour. Russ, we make each other laugh, and along with our faith in God that has been a key ingredient over the years.

Let me ask you about your journey into a deeper faith. Clearly something shifted with Mac's birth in 1990. I do not believe anyone could read about an epiphany you had at a traffic light in Van Nuys, California, and not be deeply touched. You were listening to the soundtrack from the Civil War epic, Glory, and you were overwhelmed with the circumstances of your life. Can you unpack that a bit more for me?[5]

Yeah, well, it was kind of like a scene from a movie. November 10, 1990. It was early in the morning, the sun just coming up. Mac had just been born, and I was heading home from the hospital to get some rest. I pulled up to a traffic light and I was just sitting there with this soundtrack playing. I was right there, at the stoplight, and I was thinking that Mac was healthy, and he was good, and we had been up all night. It was as if a camera was moving in and I was just overwhelmed, . . . and I found myself praying, thanking God, for the miracle of the birth of our beautiful baby boy. I would say that was among the first twinges of my faith awakening as an adult, but that was in the early '90s, and it would be a while before my faith became as central to my life as it is now.

In the same way a lot of people changed the direction of your life, the same can be said of Moira. It was an elderly French woman—a member of St. Michael's on the North Side of Chicago—who bumped into Moira when she was attending an AA meeting who told her, "My dear, you need to become a Catholic. You need to convert." Shortly after that, Moira decided she wanted to become more active in the church and raise the kids in Catholic school. Can you say more about that?[6]

In my book, you know, Moira and I decided to be pretty open about her problems with alcohol. We had some really dark times, and some of the worst were about six or eight months before her encounter with the woman at AA.[7] But Moira got sober and began her lifetime of recovery, and like a lot of people, found a lot of support in the AA groups.

But that woman (we never knew her name) really got her thinking. Moira's mother was Catholic and her father was Presbyterian, but going to church was not something that became a real strong part of her life early on. Kind of like my home, her family did not go to church on a regular basis when she was younger. But having recently found sobriety, she was doing a lot of reflecting and analyzing and searching and that day in the church, meeting the woman who told her she needed to become a Catholic, something happened, and it really got her thinking.

But she was ahead of you on the curve of becoming active in church?

Oh, yeah.

So, to some degree, she was like your first evangelist and really got you thinking more about your spiritual life and your walk with God?

Absolutely. I supported her decision, but initially I sort of reluctantly came along for the ride. When she made the decision to send our kids to Catholic school all I could really think about was my Catholic buddies who would tell me about their Catholic school days and how scary the nuns were! But I knew Moira knew what she wanted and when Moi zeroes in on something, she's going to do it.

But yeah, Moi led the way in all of that, and I remember thinking, "Okay, well that'll be your thing . . . you can do that." She entered two years of confirmation preparation classes called RCIA, Rite of Christian Initiation of Adults. It was led by a nun, . . . "Sister Bridget."

So, one day, Moi came to me and said, "You know, Sister Bridget wants you to come with me tomorrow." I ended up really liking Sister Bridget, . . . she was funny, . . . easy to talk with, but she really got to me that day. We ended up talking for three hours!

She got me to begin thinking about my faith, and so I started attending Sunday Mass with Moi and the kids. And then it began to become a regular part of my life. On an Easter Sunday, after two years of classes, Moira was confirmed into the Catholic Church. The kids and I stood with her, and I was so proud. But it was not a surface thing—it was deep, real.

Moira began attending daily Mass and I found that the church, and the school in which our kids were enrolled, began to really help us grow in our faith, and grow together as a family.

But as time went on, I started wanting what we were experiencing as a family, but I began to feel that I wanted it for myself as well. Moira and the kids did not know, but I had been meeting privately with the priest at the church we were attending. On Christmas Eve, 2010, I told them to dress up, because we were going out to dinner. And on the way, I pulled into the church parking lot.

They all looked confused and had no idea why we were there. I had set it up with our priest and he was waiting for us. We went into the church, and Russ, it was so special. In a small, quiet service, with Moi and my kids around me, I was officially confirmed into the Catholic Church.

We had come a long way, and God and our faith helped us through it all and I wanted to belong to the faith as Moira did. It meant so much to me at that moment to make that decision.

And like anyone who makes that kind of commitment, I suppose, I began to feel personally called by God to live more as He would have me live—to use the blessings I had received to serve Him in a more substantial way.

But yes, as you point out, my journey into a real personal faith, started with Moira's need and our dark time. I know, looking back, God used all of that to deepen me to be a better husband and father. Russ, she is my hero. She has been sober for twenty-seven years now. Due to debilitating arthritis, she has had so many surgeries on her spine, hips, and feet. Somehow, through it all, she has remained loving and optimistic. She is truly an inspiration.

I have often described those years before we came to faith, as an earthquake that shook our very foundation. But you know, as I wrote in my book, that earthquake helped us find the Solid Rock for our lives, and that Rock will never crumble, or fall.[8]

Another turning point occurred while attending a National Day of Prayer and Remembrance after the terrorist attacks of 9/11 at your local church in Malibu. Can you say a bit more about all of that?

Yes, *called* is a word I would use. President Bush had called for a National Day of Prayer on the Friday after the attacks.[9] And I remember that moment clearly. I went to our Catholic Church—Our Lady of Malibu. The church was so packed. There were people you would know—Martin Sheen was there, Ed Harris, but a lot of people you would not know. We were all crammed into this church and there was no room to sit, so I ended up standing on the side aisle. I was holding my daughter Ella's hand. She was nine at the time.[10]

The priest led us through the service. He said what a horrible week it had been for all of us. We were all living with those images of the planes flying into the Towers, the Pentagon, United 93 crashing in Shanksville, PA, the explosions, people jumping out of the buildings, and then the devastation that followed. Nobody could get those images out of their heads, you know.

And then somehow, I don't even know exactly what he said, Russ, but he said something and something in me shifted. I knew walking out of that service that my life was changed. I was going to take an active role in trying to get rid of this pain I felt in my broken heart.

It manifested itself in taking action—service to others, specifically for our service members. And that is when I started raising my hand to try and figure out what I could do. I wanted to play a role, and I felt like I was being called to do that. Putting it mildly, I did not know where this call was going to take me.

And then, Russ, I started thinking about the veterans of my own family differently than I ever had before. My grandfather in World War I, uncles in World War II, my dad serving in the Navy during the Korean War, and I realized I had all of these men in my life who had sacrificed so much, and I did not even really know what they did. That was the beginning of the work you see now in our foundation. And yes, well, it all began by walking in the door of my church, by praying, and by listening to this moment when God was calling me to turn from myself to service.[11]

You say that much of your own spiritual journey came to life in the midst of some of the darkest days of your life—your marriage—and yet God used that difficult season to make you a better husband, father and Christian—in which you began to really experience the joy of faith. In today's world, some resist walking through those kinds of dark times and choose instead to walk away. But you saw them instead as valleys that transformed you. How did adversity and faith work together to bring you to that understanding?

Making the decision to take my faith seriously, to walk in faith with our God in the Church . . . it gave me such peace. God calls us to serve others, and I began to feel to more and more fulfilled, you know. And it brought me joy as I realized it was giving me and our family a lot of strength, life-sustaining strength. And as I looked around, I saw it in the lives of other families—people of faith—and we began meeting so many of them that seemed to share that same sort of joy.

As you look back—you take tremendous stock in providence—and the way we respond to that can either lead us down wrong paths or right ones, but you believe you have been used by them to reach out to others for good. Isaiah wrote, "And when you turn to the right or when you turn to the left, your ears shall hear a word behind you, saying, 'This is the way; walk in it.'" (Isaiah 30:21). What counsel would you give to those who really want to bless the human family? How can they use their eyes and ears to listen more clearly to that "inner voice"?

Pretty simple—listen to that voice and serve others. That is what I've tried to do and what is the heartbeat of the Gary Sinise Foundation. Lifting people up.

I think very few people know how many times you have had brushes with death—from basically being evacuated on one of your USO tours, to a near drowning incident while filming a scene at the end of the fourth season of CSI, and then a near fatal car wreck in Washington, DC, in 2012, and yet here you are. Gary, all humility aside, do you think God is keeping you here to continue your service to others?

Well, I hope so, because I really think we are doing a lot of good things and impacting the lives of others in a positive way.

Gary, can we turn to 2018? This was a very hard summer—Moira was diagnosed with stage three breast cancer in June, and in August, Mac was diagnosed with the rare cancer, chordoma. It must have been devastating. How did your faith sustain you that summer?

I think one of the blessings in my life and service through the Foundation is having been involved with so much over the years where I have engaged with people that have really faced their challenges head-on and persevered and overcome. They seem to just put one foot in front of the other and keep going. And I've seen so many broken people over the years who have served and sacrificed for our country, and I have come to believe in some ways God was just preparing me, you know, for what we would face with our own family.

That summer, I had to just stop and ask, "What is going on here?" I've been one of the guys who's trying to help all these other wounded veterans, first responders, and also military families fighting cancer, and now I was facing this double whammy of a cancer battle. And as I began to think about all the people we had worked with—their resilience and how they faced their challenges—it inspired me to do the same. That, and our strong faith.

Your own life must have served in some way as an inspiration for Mac—for he pressed on—producing some incredible music. What did you learn from Mac during his battle—if that is the right word—with chordoma?

Oh, . . . Mac, I know he inspired me. I want your readers to know what a remarkable son Mac was until his very last day.[12]

A few years before his diagnosis, he was really going through a kind of dark time. He felt lost, and Moira and I invited him to come back and live with us. He started going back to church and you could see the changes in him. Then about a year after that, he got the cancer diagnosis.

You know there were drugs and treatments that helped Moira get to the other side of her cancer, but there were no reliable drugs for Mac. He had that initial tumor on his spine taken out and then about eight months later, it came back—and the radiation and the chemo, and honestly, we did not know if those would help—it was a crap shoot. There are no reliable drugs to fight chordoma. It is a very rare cancer, perhaps only ninety people per year are diagnosed with metastatic chordoma in the United States.

But Mac faced it with such strong faith. He would pray all the time. At night, before we all went to bed, we would circle up for prayer and Mac would lead us. One of his favorite prayer tools was St. Augustine's Prayer Book.[13] He also regularly read his Bible and Augustine's *Confessions*.[14] He read them and studied them over and over again. It was so positive for Mac, . . . really for the whole family. We actually began to take our theological questions to Mac!

As I look back, so many things helped him—I think if he had not come back to Church, had not begun to explore and strengthen his faith, not done all of that studying and reading, had not met with spiritual mentors, had he not had these things feeding his soul, I think he would have had a very different journey with his cancer battle.

And I just saw this amazing guy come to life. To me, Mac was a saintly guy, you know. And he would give me strength! Just watching the way he faced everything. And Russ, I was with him during the toughest stuff—in and out of the hospitals, sleeping in the chair next to his bed, one treatment after another—I saw him in intense, intense pain.

He didn't always share everything with me, because sometimes I think he didn't want me to know what he was fully experiencing, because he knew I was fighting so hard for him. After his death, I found on his iPad, almost a year's worth of photographs he had taken of himself—looking into the camera and you could see he was looking at the tumor on his nose, or the tumor on his eyebrow as they got bigger and bigger.

But if he wasn't in pain—or was not sick from the treatments—in those down moments, he was not a "why is this happening to me" kind of guy. Never. He was accepting—and I think that came from his personal faith in God, which inspired us in our own faith.

Moira survived her battle with cancer but continues to face chronic and debilitating struggles with arthritis, and your dear Mac left this life for the next on January 5, 2024. Gary, how has your faith helped you as you—literally—ministered to your wife and son over the last several years?

You know, Russ, I think Mac, it was Mac and Moira ministering to me. Not always in words but in action, in behavior, in acceptance, in faith. . . . Mac never let on to me that he was losing his strength or anything like that. He had his faith until the very end, and it was a strong faith, and that gave me courage and strength to continue to rely on my faith to help me through Moira's battle with cancer, and then Mac's battle until his death. And living through that was the most difficult thing I ever had to do, but my faith in God and our family, my beautiful wife and daughters, got me through it.

There are three "Lieutenant Dan" scenes from the movie Forrest Gump that I would like you to reflect on for a moment. The first is when wounded warrior Lieutenant Dan, who has lost both of his legs in combat during the Vietnam War, years later is on Forrest's shrimp boat, The Jenny, which ports in Bayou La Batre, Alabama. One night, a raging storm slams into the boat. Lieutenant Dan climbs to the top of the mainmast, curses and shakes his fist at the sky—yells out—not just at the storm, but clearly, he is venting his anger, grief, and rage at God, "You call this a storm? I'm right here ...!" Has Gary Sinise had moments like that?

Well, not quite as dramatic as crawling up a mast in the middle of a raging storm screaming my head off at God, but yes, yes there were times throughout this last five and a half years where I finally just let it out. Because you feel like you're battling uphill, and you are getting shot at from every side and you are just trying to stay clear of the bullets and the bombs raining down on you. And yet you have got to keep going. And there were times like . . . (*Gary pauses here and tears up*) . . . like there were too many bombs.

We reached this point where Mac was losing his ability to walk and stand, and I was just so incredibly frustrated. I was crying and upset, and I shouted at some family members and just left the room. I was trying to find some solution. We would have to lift him up, you know, to get him on the edge of the bed. That was getting harder and harder to do, because he was literally losing his legs. I felt like I was just banging my head against the wall, and I lost it that day.

So yeah, there were those days where I was just like "come on!" But those days would end, and I would draw on my faith, strap on the gear and go back into the battle.

In the scene after the hurricane, the sun is out, and Forrest's boat is the only one that has survived the storm. Lieutenant Dan seems to have finally released his anger and he flops back into the calm waters of the ocean, smiles and floats on his back out into the Gulf of Mexico. In a voice over, Forrest says, "He never actually said so, but I think he made his peace with God." Gary, have you made your peace with God?

Yeah, yeah, I have. You know after all of this, I cannot help but have questions, . . . just all kinds of questions . . . like "Is there anything else I could have done?" or "Why didn't I say this to Mac when I had the chance?"

There's no getting around what we experienced when you lose somebody like that. You lose a son or a daughter or anybody that you're close to . . . your heart breaks, . . . our hearts are broken. But I am at peace in knowing that Mac was at peace. His faith inspired my own.

What gives me comfort, peace, is knowing he was at peace at the end of his life. He was so motivated to finish his music. And he did it. He got to see his collection of work come together, and as you know *Resurrection and Revival* was produced and released shortly after his death, and then I found even more of his work, and we pulled together *Resurrection and Revival Part Two*. Those are incredible albums showing you how gifted Mac was. We sell the vinyl at the Gary Sinise Foundation website and all the proceeds go to support the work of the Foundation—Mac wanted that.[15]

The very end was so hard, but he wasn't in pain or struggling. I did not have to go to God in prayer and ask, "Please God make this stop, . . . there's too much agony. . . ." No, in the end, it was not a struggle. He left this life for the next and it was just—well—quiet and peaceful. The whole family was there, . . . terribly sad of course. But all that prayer, all that preparation, . . . it was an incredibly holy moment. God was really present with us.

I know you are faithful in your church attendance, what about prayer?

Moi is the prayer warrior in our home, she has her rosary going all the time, but yes . . . I pray daily. . . .

Gary, you have achieved much of what the world believes is of value—fame, wealth, success—perhaps beyond your wildest dreams. You have received an Emmy, a Golden Globe, have a star on the Hollywood Walk of Fame, and received an Oscar nomination. You have befriended people from all walks of life, been honored and recognized in innumerable ways. That said, what would you say to people of any age who believe these are the things that make life worth living?

These are not what ultimately bring joy. There's a quote in my book that is written on the wall of my Foundation, "When joy connects to mission a life of purpose begins to take shape." Until I understood that I was called to serve, that moment when I felt God was calling me to change the direction of my life, I was pretty much focused on all those things—getting the next movie part, making the money, building a career.

For me, there was a "preservice life," and that was all about me succeeding in my career, but then I was called to the service life—and that has given me a life of meaning and purpose.

Obviously, I am still very broken from our family's loss. One has a few choices after such grief. I could let that broken heart paralyze me, or I could let that service help heal my heart and inspire me to heal the hearts of others. All of that began for me in that church service after [9/11] and I believe for anyone who is ailing or dealing with a broken heart or is lost—serving others is a great healer for that. I am a grateful American, and I am grateful to God for calling me into this work.

Before we finish up—tell me more about the Gary Sinise Foundation, and what it has accomplished in these years since that call.

The Gary Sinise Foundation began on June 30, 2011. We now have over seventy-five staff carrying out the work, and since that time, we have received over $500 million in gifts to provide grants for necessary equipment and crucial training to first responder units across the country, serve warm meals to our defenders around the globe, provide critical support to our frontline heroes in times of natural disaster, and bring joy and music to our heroes and their families with concerts by Gary Sinise & the Lt. Dan Band, which we use to raise additional money for good causes, like we did back in Houston in 2017, but also to entertain our troops and their families.

How many concerts have you performed since 2011?

Five hundred eighty-five, nearly 600.

Tell me a little bit about your "Snowball Express."

Since becoming an official program of the Foundation in 2018, the Snowball Express program has served over 20,000 children of fallen military and first responder heroes and their surviving parent/guardian. What began as a once-a-year experience has since evolved into year-round programming to include intimate community events, empowerment workshops, and more, all culminating in the annual event held at Disney World just in time for the holiday season.

How many homes have been built by the Foundation?

By the time your book comes out, we will have built 100.

And now you are doing a lot of work to promote mental health initiatives for veterans?

Yep, through strategic partnerships with professional mental health organizations such as Boulder Crest and Warrior's Heart, the Foundation is honored to serve those heroes struggling with the invisible wounds of their service.

How would Gary Sinise like to be remembered?

As a guy who loved his family and tried to be a good dad, a good husband. I suppose I'd want to be remembered as somebody who learned from his mistakes, tried to make things better, and tried to—you know—give something back—simply as an expression for all the blessings God has given to me. I hope I am remembered as someone who was called, who responded and, with God's help, was able to make the world a better place.

GARY SINISE

Gary Sinise's stage, film and television career has spanned more than four decades. In 1974, at eighteen years old, he cofounded Chicago's Steppenwolf Theatre Company. He received nominations for Golden Globe, Screen Actors Guild, and Academy Awards for his portrayal of Lt. Dan Taylor in *Forrest Gump*, and earned the Best Supporting Actor Award from the National Board of Review and the Commander's Award from the Disabled American Veterans. Other film credits include *Apollo 13*, *Ransom*, *Snake Eyes*, *Impostor*, *The Green Mile*, *Mission to Mars*, and *The Human Stain*.

His most recent film and television work include, *I Still Believe*, *Good Joe Bell*, and the Netflix series *13 Reasons Why*. Gary has starred as Jack Garrett on the series *Criminal Minds: Beyond Borders*, and for nine seasons as Detective "Mac" Taylor on the hit series *CSI: NY*. Sinise is an Emmy, Golden Globe, and two-time SAG Award winner for his roles in *Truman* and *George Wallace*. He also received a SAG Award nomination for his role in *The Stand*.

For over forty years, Gary has stood as an advocate on behalf of America's service members. Beginning in the early '80s, he supported local Vietnam veterans' groups in the Chicago area, and since the '90s he has worked on behalf of the Disabled American Veterans organization, which he continues to actively support today. Following the attacks of September 11, 2001, Sinise's dedication to our nation's active-duty defenders, veterans, first responders, and their families has become a tireless crusade of support, service, and gratitude for all those who protect our freedom and serve our country.

In 2003 he formed the Lt. Dan Band and began entertaining troops serving at home and abroad. Over the years, the thirteen-piece cover band has performed hundreds of shows for charities and fundraisers supporting wounded heroes, Gold Star families, veterans, and troops around the world.

In 2011 he established the Gary Sinise Foundation with the mission to serve and honor America's defenders, veterans, first responders, Gold Star families, and those in need.

In recognition of his humanitarian work, Sinise has earned many distinguished honors including two awards from the Congressional Medal of Honor Society, the Bob Hope Award for Excellence in Entertainment, and their highest honor, the Congressional Medal of Honor Society's Patriot Award. In 2008, he was given the Presidential Citizens Medal, the second-highest civilian honor awarded to citizens for exemplary deeds performed in service of the nation. On April 17, 2017, he received a star on Hollywood Walk of Fame from the Hollywood Chamber of Commerce.

He is the author of *Grateful American: A Journey from Self to Service*, a *New York Times* bestseller.

Photo credit: © Suzanne Youngblood

"You can never have too much God in your life."

—Ambassador Nikki Haley

Ambassador Nikki Haley

I have long admired Nikki Haley because of her contagious optimism and steady hand of leadership in so many roles. Her wit and wisdom propelled her into the governor's office, the ambassador's chair, and as a leading contender for the highest office in the United States. She is also a devoted daughter, mother, and is married to an American serviceman.

As a woman of color, she faced discrimination during her childhood years. As she entered the world of politics, she was pummeled with criticism and falsehoods from her opponents and members of her own political party. She was called to lead her state through natural disasters, racial turmoil, and the tragedy of deadly school and church shootings. When the moment came for her to face down dictators and tyrants in other parts of the world, she spoke with clarity and boldness.

Yet, through it all, her reputation for being a person of character and integrity and honesty who met every challenge squarely put before her grew with each passing year.

But it was not just her natural gifts that enabled her to so capably guide the state, nation, and world she served, but her faith as well. As you will see here, Nikki Haley learned the lasting value of holding onto the grip of the One who was holding her all along.

For that reason and more, I was so pleased to have this conversation.

You have written and spoken publicly about the way in which your parents, your family, brought you up in a "spiritual way," and how much that meant, and still means, to you.[1] *Can you share more about that?*

Certainly! From the earliest age I can remember, God was part of the life of our family. It was, of course, part of my father's life as well, but my mother really pressed upon us the importance a belief in God. She found ways to insert God in every way she could. So, though we were Sikh, we went to every sort of Bible camp, vacation Bible school, or program for children around.

Mom wanted us to explore God. She would say, "Everyone has a different way of getting to God. My hope for you is that you find your way to God." Then she would put us in as many experiences as she could where God was the focus, regardless of the tradition or denomination.

So God was always part of the conversation. If something was going wrong in our lives, my mom would say, "God will take care of it." If something was going right, my mom would say, "You need to thank God for that!" So the knowledge and experience of a relationship with God was always present.

You were raised in the Sikh tradition of your parents, can tell me how you experienced God in that faith tradition?

Well, there was no Sikh Temple in Bamberg.[2] But it was important to my mom that my siblings and I had the experience of worshipping in that tradition. There was a small community of Sikhs, and they would meet every third Sunday in someone's home.

But that was not without its challenges. My parents and the teachers in our Sikh community would try and encourage us to speak only Punjabi from Friday through Sunday.[3] But my siblings and I just did not understand the language.[4] My parents did try and teach us, but we just could not get it.

Honestly, now, I wish we had learned, because I think we lost out of understanding some of the culture. But despite all of that, when we did go to temple, I could feel the Spirit of God and it was a holy experience for me, and even though I did not understand the words, I knew we were in prayer, and it was a holy experience for me.

I think one of the most powerful stories I have ever read was your telling of a life-lesson your mother, Raj Randhawa, offered. You were faced time and time again with prejudice and racial discrimination, not only as a Sikh, but as an Indian—as one with "brown skin," of which you have written and spoken over the years.

While growing up in Bamberg, a young boy came to the door, and while he might have meant well—his methods left something to be desired![5] *Can you share the end of that story in your own words?*

Yes, I love that story, but that fits within the larger story of the way our parents raised us to respect people of other faiths, and races. It grew out of their faith, and they passed that onto us in such a consistent way.

But it was hard being that "brown skinned" kid in a small town of 2,500. We were the only Indian family, and nobody really knew us or understood. My dad wore a turban, so we stood out even more. When my parents first moved there, I think most people were thinking, "Who are these people? Where did they come from?"

My mom was a teacher, and my dad was a professor. Together, they started a business and then we started up in school; but as they got to know us, all [of] the sudden everyone wanted to "save us." People were constantly trying to get my parents to convert to Christianity and trying to encourage our whole family to come to Bible studies and church.

So, as to the story, it was not uncommon that someone would show up at the door and want to talk about their faith, and give us a Bible.

So, yes, one day, this boy showed up and my sister Simmi answered the door. He was actually crying, and he handed her the Bible and said, "Since you don't believe in God, I want you to read this, so you don't go to hell."

Simmi did not know what to do with it, so she tucked it under her bed. That night, when my mom when to tuck her in, she found the Bible and said, "I want you to read this, . . . because there is truth in here, . . . there is good in it . . ."

And that's what she would do anytime someone gave us a Bible! That was her way, because they never wanted us to look at other religions in a bad way, they just wanted us to be confident in who we were and understand why it was that people were trying to come and save us.

But you all honored the local religious traditions in your own home as well, didn't you?

Yes. And every year, my mom would have us go through the traditions, so we did not feel left out. For instance, every Christmas, we would put up a Christmas tree and watch Christmas programs. We would honor the Christian traditions, because Mom did not want us to feel left out. We were different enough to what it [all] was, and they really did not want us to feel isolated.

But your parents and family had no problem living out their Sikh faith while at the same time honoring the Christian beliefs and traditions that were clearly the majority in Bamberg, . . . is that correct?

Right. That was the way they parented us, and it was important to them to honor our family traditions, but at the same time continue to educate ourselves about other belief systems. Key to that was that we were never to judge, because they passed on to us what they believed—that if you learn about other cultures, religions, traditions, then you'll better understand why people do what they do.

That sounds like the making of an ambassador at a very early age!

I have also been very touched by the way you and your future (and now present) husband, Michael, discussed your faith as you were dating. You went about a very intentional process, if you will, of discussing faith—and you both discussed a desire to have a "personal and direct" experience of God. Can you say more about that?[6]

You know, while we were dating, we knew we had different religions, but we justified in our minds that we could do both.

At first, I felt like it would be a betrayal to my parents for me to convert—I really did. My parents raised me well in a loving home, and I thought converting would be suggesting something negative about the way they brought us up.

And so when we first met, you know, before I had gone to his church or anything, we talked about it, and we talked about the similarities—we talked about how we both believed in only one God. We talked about how we were raised. And then I started going to church with him and I felt I was moving toward a different experience with God. I really "felt" it.

Michael and I always knew, if we were blessed to have children, that we wanted our kids to have two things—faith and a conscience. And we believed if we could just accomplish those two things, we would have done well.

So in the middle of all of that, I decided I wanted to convert, because we both wanted to grow in faith together, and do the same with our children.

Every now and then, we would go worship with my parents, because we wanted our children to have this experience with their grandparents in their own worshipping community. And we never wanted our children to look at others or their experiences in a bad or negative way. And, for me, I wanted them to know this is where I grew up and *how* I grew up.

It was all about being of one mind and one faith, and we believed this would better enable us to give our children those two gifts—faith and a conscience.

So then, can you say a bit more about your personal decision to become a Christian?

I put a lot of stock in Paul's words that Christians "walk by faith, not by sight."[7] In order for me to do that, my faith is something that has to be personal, in my heart. And there was no denying, when I sat in the church that day, the day I joined the Methodist Church, as a Christian, I was able to come to terms with the fact that you can make this choice, and it does not necessarily mean I was carrying out some act of betrayal against the way I was raised.

It was quite emotional, Russ. But I was being honest with myself, and I was being honest with God.

You know, I think that there's a time where you go through life, and you almost want to please God and impress God. There are times when you only want to talk with God about the good things in your life and the good things you want God to know.

And for me at least, I reached a point where I realized God knows me better than I know myself. So, there was no pleasing God anymore. No faking it.

And I understood that in order for me to deepen my faith, I had to be totally dependent on God, and I just knew in that moment, in that day, that the moment had come for me to completely open myself up to God and say, "Okay, this is the time I need to realize that my faith is being a Christian, by believing in the teachings of Christianity and becoming a follower of Jesus." And, at the same time, I did not believe, nor do I now, deny the way I was raised, but to be the Christian I was called to be.

And it was a Methodist Church, right?

Yes.

And what is your church home now?

Mount Horeb United Methodist Church—that has always been our home church, and let me say a little more about that. Even though we moved, and lived in different places, my relationship with my pastor became very important to me.

We got to know him, and he was constantly encouraging us. When I was governor, and then became Ambassador to the United Nations, he was constantly sending me Bible verses and reminding me that he was praying for my family and for me. And I always sought his counsel before taking a big jump.

I remember before I made the decision to run for president, Michael and I went and sat down with him to seek his direction and have him pray with us.

You cannot underestimate how important and powerful that kind of ministry is—being there, being present. It enabled us not to just have a relationship with a church, but a relationship with our pastor helped deepen our relationship with God. There is a real difference when your pastor encourages you or supports you in this way. So that place will be forever our church home.

What would you say to Christians today about honoring the religious traditions of others?

Don't judge, don't judge. That's the biggest, you know? It's like, you know, when my mom would say to us, "Everybody's trying to find their path to God." And I really do believe most people want to feel close to God, want to experience God, and we all do that in different ways—even we Christians, with all of our denominations!

The best way of reaching out with your faith is to help others. I think it is so important to live your life in a way that people want to be close to you and get to know you more. And then you know what happens? You begin to have conversations with them about their experiences and they can learn more about your experience, but again, never with judgment. When we were growing up, the sound of judgment pushed us further away. But it was the sound of love that brought us in.

I mentioned earlier that you endured tremendous racism and discrimination both as a family and as an individual. I do not know how many people might know that you were also physically abused by a caretaker in your childhood years.[8] And then of course, you faced so much opposition as you began to run for office—even from members of your own party, who told lies about you, your marriage, your positions.

A lot of people who might experience just one of those things might just get paralyzed and never be able to recover. But you experienced a myriad of challenges, and yet here we sit, and you have that smile, that optimism, that radiant sense of expectation. How did you emerge from that and become the strong, vibrant person you are?

Simply, my faith is what helped me through every challenge.

I was in college when I began personally coming to terms with the child abuse. My faith grew even stronger when the child abuse aspect really presented itself, and I began having memories, and I could not really put things together with what I was feeling. I had conversations with my mom and with my sister, which confirmed that it was real, that it did happen. When I was younger, it was something I would kind of push aside.

But then as I got older and began dealing with it again, it was a situation where, I just went to God with it all. I let my faith help me through it.

That is the same way it was with the races. All the races were difficult, . . . all of them were brutal, . . . all of them had hateful experiences.

But you know, through it all, my faith just grew even more. I kept thinking, "You know, when God's got you by your right hand, when things get tough, squeeze tighter."

I found I had to do that more with all of those challenges. And the tougher they got, . . . the tighter I squeezed!

The horrific killing of nine innocents gathered for Bible study at Emanuel African Methodist Episcopal Church on June 17, 2015, by white supremacist Dylann Roof was, I suppose, one of the most difficult seasons in your years as South Carolina's governor. How did your faith see you through that experience?

That was perhaps the one defining moment in my life. It was the first time there was a shooting in a place of worship in South Carolina.

I knew there was so much on the line and all I knew is that I didn't want people to suffer any more than they had. I did not want our response to be angry. I did not want riots. I did not want any form of hate.

You know, South Carolinians understood the complexities of the Confederate flag and the race issue. The rest of the country would judge us, which made it all more polarizing and more hateful.

So, I really felt called to try and keep the state calm and guide everybody toward loving each other. I wanted to press the point that we weren't going to let this horrible shooting and this killer of innocent people divide us by hate.

Part of that meant that I would attend every one of those nine funerals. All of them were open casket services, and I sat through every one. The pastor asked me to speak at each service, and I would go up and then just break down.

I could not even be strong for the congregation in the way I wanted to be.

And, well, it got to the point where I just could not stop crying. I would go out and do a press conference, and I would come back to my office, and I would cry.

I would go home, get in the bed, and I would cry.

Now, no one saw any difference in the way I did my job as governor of South Carolina, but people knew something was going on. I lost thirty pounds in the wake of that. Reporters wanted to know if I was on some new exercise program.

I did my job, but behind the scenes, Russ, I was struggling. I remember one night; we had a group of our friends over for dinner. One of them happened to be my doctor and, at one point, he looked at me and said, "How are you doing?"

And I just burst into tears uncontrollably. He said, "You have PTSD, and we have got to get you some help."

So, yes, I spoke to a therapist. And yes, they prescribed medication—and yes, those helped, . . . but at the end of [the] day, while those tools are important—

I remember one day, being so broken, and so sad, that I honestly . . .

Ambassador Haley has to stop in mid-sentence. She covers her mouth, drops her head and begins to tear up. She tries to speak again but can't. She apologizes, "I'm sorry, . . . I just . . ."

I tell her it is okay, and I understand, . . . anyone would understand. After a moment or two, she gathers her composure and says:

I came home, and fell to my knees and I said, "God, I can't do this by myself. . . . I need you to help me."

In that moment, what helped was not talking to a therapist, not taking medication, but instead, admitting to God that I was completely broken and that I needed help.

And from that point forward, my faith grew ten times. I have found, again and again, that my faith grows most in times of struggle. Yes, my faith is there in happy times as well, but there are those hard experiences you go through, and therapists, . . . and medicine, . . . and friends, . . . and essentially other people cannot fix [the problem]. There are things that only God can, . . . right? And that was that moment for me.

So, when you go through something like a presidential campaign and experiences, hateful things said or done, that is nothing compared to the kind of hate that took place in that Bible study at Emanuel Church.

You may remember that when Dylann Roof came into the church that night, he did not act like the other congregants, and did not look like them or sound like them, and they did not throw him out—they pulled up a chair and they prayed with him for an hour. And what did he do? He took out a gun and started killing people!

You move through that, . . . and you learn what hate is, . . . and you learn what love is, and everything seems small compared to that.

The Sunday before the church shooting, June 14, 2015, during a lot of racial division around the country, you called your state to a day of prayer for healing, and you have said also that you felt that played a spiritual role in the wake of the shooting. Can you share a bit more about that?

It was a time of tremendous polarization around issues of race—around all kinds of issues. Obviously, it is hard to comprehend why things like that hate-filled moment occurred, and even how a loving God allows those things to happen. But God did not drive that young man into that church, hate did.

So yes, I called for a day of prayer. I gathered a large group of pastors from multiple denominations and religions. We had no idea what would happen only days later, but I honestly believe in some way, it helped us get through it.

As horrible as that was, it became a sea-change moment in your state in the way racial division was faced and healed. A large part of that healing was your decision to take the lead on removing the Confederate flag from the steps of your state capitol. You said, "We are not going to allow this symbol to divide us any longer—the fact that it causes so much pain is enough to move it from the capitol grounds. It is, after all, a capitol that belongs to all of us."[9]

And you were inspired, in part, by President Barack Obama's remarks after the shooting in reference to the Confederate flag: "For too long we were blind to the pain that the Confederate flag stirred in too many of our citizens . . . by taking down that flag we express God's grace."[10] Share how you felt taking down the flag "expressed God's grace." Did your faith guide you in that as well?

Yes, but I keenly understood my fellow South Carolinians, and I understood that half of the state saw the Confederate flag as tradition and service, the other half saw it as slavery and hate.

My job wasn't to judge either side. My job was to get them to see a way forward and to do it together. And so it was not, . . . I never came out and said, "These people are wrong. These people are right." I very much respected everybody.

I told my constituents to believe what they believe. If they still wanted to fly it on their private property, that's their right. But we made the decision to move it to a museum—a place of history, where people could go see it if they wanted to see it.

But, as governor, I was going to lead people to see that we were not going to have it represent all of South Carolina in front of the statehouse.

And again, I would go back to that day of prayer. On the other side of the shooting and working through the decision about the Confederate flag, I believe those prayers helped, and I believe God guided us, because the end result of all of that is that moment spoke to South Carolinians—we did not have riots and protests. We had prayers, vigils, and hugs.

Before I get just a bit more personal, just a question or two more about how you have governed not only in South Carolina, but in your role as Ambassador to the United Nations, on behalf of the United States.[11] You have witnessed, firsthand, the hand of evil around the world. In your role as ambassador, you were particularly struck by the human rights violations in places like Cuba, Congo, and Venezuela. In what I will call the "comfort of American democracy," what you say are the dangers of that kind of evil?

When I was at the United Nations, I saw that when America spoke, the world listened. When America led, the world followed who we are as who the world wanted to be.

And to read and hear about the kinds of things that I saw is one thing, to see and sit down with people who experienced it is quite another. For instance, during my tenure, I visited the Democratic Republic of Congo, where battles between the government and armed local militias have plagued the country for decades.

But here is a place where horrific violence was occurring—babies were taken from the arms of their mothers and thrown into the fire[s], men were tortured and killed before their loved ones—the scale of violence is something that you really cannot even comprehend.

Every place I went, I would always sit down with the women—no other officials in the room—and we would have heart-to-heart talks. They were worried about their families, their kids, their way of life—everything.

And in these meetings, it only reminded me that everyone on this planet wants the same thing. They want to be loved. They want hope. They want their children to live better than they did. That want to know what good health is. They want all of those things. And, . . . they want to know what it means to live life without fear.

So, do you believe the United States has a moral role to play around the world when it comes to confronting that kind of evil?

Yes. America always has a duty to make the right moral decisions—not the right political decisions, not the right popular decisions, but what's really the right thing to do?

And I've always thought that we must fight for what's right. We must fight for what's moral, because the rest of the world is hoping we'll do that.

I believe we are what gives the rest of the world hope. So, when we say and do the right thing, the world still feels like there's goodness there.

And, whether it was seeing, you know, in Congo, where they used rape as a weapon of war; or whether it was seeing thousands of Venezuelans holding their babies in the hot sun [while waiting in line] for hours just to get the one meal they might get that day—in the same place where they were killing zoo animals just to get food, . . . they speak to you, and they speak to humanity, . . . and they call for a response.

I will say—in the middle of these horrible stories there was good at work. In every one of these challenging areas . . . there was a church—of some denomination, any denomination—that was doing their best to give people hope.

That is why morals, faith, religion—all that works together to bring us through the challenges. When it comes to humanity and how we are called to live with one another—there are no borders to who we should love and for whom we should care.

You have to stand back and try not to think of it in terms of countries, but instead, I think we are called to want as much for everyone as we want to ourselves.

And so yes, I think that is what we are called to do as individuals, but it is also something America is called to do.

We cannot solve all the problems of the world, but our Lord said that to those who have been given much, much is expected.[12] America is the wealthiest, freest, most richly blessed country in the world, and if we believe in those words, much is expected of us and we should do all we can to alleviate the suffering of all of God's children.

I am good friends with one of your former constituents, Clark Gillespy, who was the president of Duke Energy for South Carolina for many years.[13] He shared that as hurricanes approached South Carolina during your gubernatorial years, you would call him personally to make sure Duke was prepared for whatever may befall your state. Let me share what he said about you and then ask you a question on behalf of both of us: "Nikki Haley leads and speaks from faith. It is clear to me that she draws on a Higher Power for her decisions. She is an incredibly humble person and yet she does not have to be. She makes things happen and is driven not by populism, but by the right thing to do. She has strong convictions, and she is right on the issues—every single time, despite, at times strong opposition. Where does that conviction come from? What role does her faith play in that process?"

Clark gives me too much credit. He was great to work with. Well, you know, every decision I can remember making was always with God. I can honestly say, in every situation, I have talked to God through the whole thing. And so what I do believe yes, you can have faith, but God calls on us to do the right thing too.

Part of being a human is to realize, part of the reason we are put on this earth by God, is to make a difference. God is not going to do everything for you.

So it is a kind of partnership with God, in which you try and honor God with the decisions you make.

For me, it always goes back to what my parents would say to me, "The best way to appreciate God's blessings is to give back."

And so that's why I do what I do, and the driving force behind it is God. My goal always is to find ways to lift others up, . . . ask the right questions.

How do you make them safer? How do you make them stronger? How do you make them more hopeful? How do you be honest with others?

And that last one—being honest—that means being truthful, and that means saying the right thing—even at times when it's not comfortable.

So, yes, to circle back—I always do my best to invite God into every decision I ever make.

Before your inauguration as governor, there was a prayer service in Trinity Episcopal Cathedral in Columbia, South Carolina, and you have said that one minister in particular spoke "directly" to you: "With the help of God, you can change political history."[14] How has God helped you "change political history"?

You know pastor, I think that people like to say changing political history is, . . . "being the youngest governor in the country," or "being the first female governor in South Carolina"—those kinds of things.

But changing political history is when you change lives.

You know we had so many crises in South Carolina during my tenure—[from] a once-in-a-1000-year flood to a school shooting to a church shooting to major storms and hurricanes.[15]

Helping people in times of crisis, to me, was what mattered the most.

You know, at the UN, when I fought for people who could not fight for themselves—especially with regard to human rights, that is what it means to help people in challenging times.

To me, that's really the change you want. Real leadership reveals itself not in the good times. The good times are easy—right? It is in challenging times that you are really called to step up to the moment.

When faced with tough times, you can curl up in a ball and go in the corner because you are scared—or you can decide to step up and do the right thing—tune out all the noise and just take God with you (or let Him take you with Him!). I think that is what matters and that is what changes history.

I think one of your favorite sayings is "Let's get excited!" You begin talks in that way. What "excites you" about your faith journey?

There's a lot to be excited about. There's a lot to be hopeful of. And I think sometimes people need to be reminded to get excited. There's still good in the world. There are still things that we can be excited about.

And another of your sayings that is a favorite of mine is "You can never have too much God in your life." Can you say a bit more about that?

Well, you can't [can] you?! God is what makes everything better. And I think that when you struggle—have God; when you celebrate—have God; when you wonder—have God. You can't have too much God in your life. If God is with you every step of the way, you still need more of Him. I mean, it's the way I look at it. More God—in every part of life!

What does your prayer life look like? Any other spiritual disciplines?

Every morning, before I touch a phone, before I look at anything, before I do anything, I read my devotional. It was for years, *Jesus Calling*.[16] Now it's *Jesus Always*.[17]

I read the devotional, and then I say my prayers in the morning.

Then, I talk to God throughout the day like a constant conversation.

And then when I go to bed at night, I always thank God for the day, and for allowing me to live in it.

I intentionally go through every blessing that I had with God and thank him for all that He has given me; then I end with people who I feel need my prayers—if someone is sick, or family.

Honestly, at night, sometimes when I was exhausted, running for president, I did not have a lot of hours. I still offered my prayers but often would fall asleep in the middle of saying them!

But I always made time for that devotional time and that prayer time in the morning.

When I knew we were going to have this conversation, it reminded me of something I started to do when I was little, but I still do it.

As children, we used to say an Indian version of the Lord's Prayer. Once I committed it to memory, I started, every time I went up steps.

Here I am, at 53 years old, and still to this day, every time I go up steps, I'm still saying the Lord's Prayer.

This prayer has become such a part of my daily routine and it helps me invite God into every aspect of my life.

I am always going up the stairs somewhere, and so I am always praying.

It may seem silly to someone else, but not to me. Any time I can make that connection—as often as I can make that connection it helps me—it gives me strength, it gives me hope, it gives me peace.

Now let me land where I have in these interviews—despite your many, many challenges over the years, you have still achieved incredible influence, success, power, fame—what would you say to those who might believe those kinds of human achievements are all that matter?

I wouldn't have made it without faith. And you know, it's easy to look at the accomplishments, but what I would want is people to look at the challenges. You know, those? Yes, faith is what got me through those accomplishments, but faith is what got me through the challenges that led to those accomplishments.

That's where my faith carried me. When I did not know which way to turn, or what decision to make, God would show me the way.

God gave me everything I have, and I have tried to honor God with those gifts.

I know God has me by my right hand, and I am holding onto His.

I would say to anyone who does not think they need God, or faith in God in their lives, that for me—I simply I cannot imagine my life without God.

Life is so much easier with faith; life is so much more peaceful with faith.

Faith and belief do not mean a life without challenges and heartbreak, but I just cannot imagine going through those without faith and without God.

Like I say, . . . "You can never have too much God in your life," and that has certainly been true for me.

THE HONORABLE NIKKI HALEY

In 2010, at age thirty-eight, the Honorable Nikki R. Haley was elected the 116th governor of South Carolina. She was the youngest governor in the country and first minority female governor in America. She is the only female governor in South Carolina history.

During Governor Haley's tenure, South Carolina was a national leader in economic development. Known as the economic "Beast of the Southeast," the state's unemployment rate hit a fifteen-year low, it saw over $20 billion in new capital investment, and her administration announced new jobs in every county in the state.

The people of South Carolina decisively reelected Haley in 2014. Two years later, *Time* magazine named her one of the 100 most influential people in the world.

In 2016, President Donald Trump nominated Haley, age forty-five, as the US Ambassador to the United Nations. In that role, she served as a member of the President's Cabinet and on the National Security Council.

After serving in the Trump administration, she founded Stand For America and Stand For America PAC.

At age fifty-one, Ambassador Haley ran as a Republican candidate for president while her husband was deployed to Africa. In 2024, she outlasted thirteen other candidates and became the first Republican woman to win a presidential primary. She continues to fight for limited government, fiscal responsibility, and a strong foreign policy that keeps America safe, has the backs of our allies, and holds our enemies to account.

She currently serves as the Walter P. Stern Chair of the Hudson Institute and as the Vice Chair of Edelman Public and Government Affairs.

Ambassador Haley is married to Major Michael Haley and has two children. She is a two-time *New York Times* best-selling author of *With All Due Respect* and *If You Want Something Done*.

Photo credit: © John Russo

"I'm not on my way up, I am on my way out! And I want to go on the record...! I am repeating myself, but it's worth repeating. God,... He is more and more at the center of my life. I just want to do God's will...."

—Denzel Washington

Denzel Washington

As I began this project, one of the people I most wanted to interview was Denzel Washington. Not only had I watched his television work and films from his earliest days to the present, but many of his roles deeply moved me and gave me cause to think about the way I was using my life to glorify God and make the lives of others better. Open your streaming service and watch any—and I do mean *any*—of his films and you will step away changed.

But beyond his acting career, I have been touched by various commencement speeches he has given over the years and his inspiring and thought-provoking insights from his book, *A Hand to Guide Me*.[1]

It had been several months since I had written him with an interview request, and since I had not heard back, I had surmised my request had landed in what I often affectionately call "File 13" (the file to nowhere!). Several months later, Laura and I were hosts to a church group taking a historic tour of, among other places, the beaches of Normandy. One night, on a break between some dancing to some '80s hits, I looked down and had a missed call. It was from Denzel Washington. (But he left a message.)

"Reverend Russell, Reverend Levenson, I should say. God is truly amazing. This is Denzel Washington, I got your letter, and your book.[2] I am on my way Malta to shoot a film—as you probably know, the Apostle Paul spent some time there.[3] As God would have it, I will be back in the fall, and I look forward to the opportunity to witness my own faith. I'm going to take your book with me and read it and know that you will be hearing from me.

I'll keep your information, I don't text or any of that kind of stuff, but I'll get back in touch with you. Okay, God bless . . ."

It did take a while for our schedules to align. But he would call occasionally. One day, after several months had passed, I noticed it was his birthday, December 28, so on a lark, I called, and he picked up the phone.

I started to introduce myself and he said, "I know who this is, I have you in my phone!" I told him I did not want to pester but just wanted to wish him a happy birthday. He said, "You're not pestering me. I am sitting here with my lovely wife, listening to gospel music and reading from the book of Jeremiah. What do you think that means?" I said, "I don't know, what does it mean?"

He said, "It means we are going to do that interview!" He went on to say something that held a lot of insight about this work I had begun, "There are a lot of people in my business that are not that open about their faith, because they are afraid it might have some [negative] impact on their career, but I'm not on my way up, I am on my way out! And I want to go on the record!"

Mercifully, by God's grace and with the help of Denzel's agent, things came together, and I was blessed to meet this wonderful man in his agent's office in the summer of 2024. When he came in, I addressed him as "Mr. Washington," and he quickly said, "No, come on man, . . . Denzel, give me a hug."

That hug, mercifully, helped relieve the moment of being star struck. Before we began the interview, we chatted just a bit. He reminded me that his father was a preacher, and at one point he said, "I've thought about becoming a preacher—I'm not going to act forever."

And I thought to myself, "If ever there was a man prepared to speak before others about God, here is that man."

Before I jumped in, it was Denzel, not the retired Episcopal priest who said, "Hey, why don't we start with a prayer." And that we did.

When did you begin to experience God's presence in your life?

My name is Denzel Washington Jr., and my father, Denzel Washington Sr., was a preacher. So I grew up in the church. We had to go to Sunday morning services, prayer meetings, and all that kind of stuff. As a kid, I really did not want to go, but if I had to say, being there certainly opened the door for me to experience God.

In your book, A Hand to Guide Me, *you open with that wonderful quote from Proverbs: "Train up a child in the way he should go, and when he is old, he will not depart from it."*[4] *Who were the earliest "trainers" in your own faith journey and in what ways did they help you understand and grow in your faith?*

My mother and my father. My father was a hardworking man—worked four or five jobs, and it seemed to go from one job to another. But his work ethic and his consistency and faithfulness really had an impact on me.

After my parents broke up, my mother had a boyfriend who was also a really good businessman. So, I really learned a lot from both he and my mother about how to run a business. My mother ran her own beauty parlor.

In your commencement speech to [graduates of] the University of Pennsylvania, you said, "I try to give myself a goal every day. . . ." What is your goal today?[5]

To do God's will. I started the day with a good buddy of mine, Michael Harris, who at one point was one of the biggest drug dealers in America, but after he was sentenced, he really turned his life around.[6] He was pardoned, released. We are really good friends, and he is a completely different person. I think getting together with Michael this morning was what God wanted me to do.

This morning, we were talking about the same thing . . . what do we want to do with our lives, and I told him that I just want to go home, be at peace with the Lord, and do what He has in mind for me in my days here on earth.

I know I've been blessed beyond measure, and I want to use my abilities for the glory of God. You know, there's nothing more I want. I don't want anything material, . . . I don't want money, . . . I don't want things, . . . I just want to do God's will, and I want to help other people.

In your commencement address to the graduates of Dillard University, you made a remarkable statement—"True desire in the heart for anything good is God's proof to you sent beforehand to indicate what is already yours." Can you say a bit more about that?[7]

Yeah, it is one of my favorite sayings. I read it years ago in one of my devotional books. The thing about that desire is that it is a gift of God. You cannot earn that desire; God places it in you as an invitation to walk into the relationship that is already yours for the taking. It's grace, it's a gift, and it reminds us how much God wants to guide us.

Well, that's a good lead into my next question. So, in that same address, you did not pull any punches with regard to your counsel to rely on God, . . . your opening salvo was "Put God first in everything you do. . . . Everything I have is by the grace of God. . . . It is a gift. . . ." And then you went on to say, "I have been protected. . . . I have been directed. . . . I have been corrected. . . ."[8] Can you give an example or two wherein you feel you have been . . . protected by God, directed by God, and corrected by God?

Well, they all kind of come together in different ways. It's an ongoing process. But as to being protected, in my years as a kid, I had been caught doing things I should not be doing—*busted* is a better word. Half the time, I was protected without knowing it. My three closest friends when I was age fourteen, all got busted, but they went on to serve time—probably a hundred years between them.

I had been busted, but I didn't serve a day, and it is not because I wasn't doing what they were doing; I was, but I was protected. Going to prison was not God's plan for me. Being protected is something I have learned about through my faith in God. I no longer worry about how I am protected; I just know that I am, and I trust in that.

As to being corrected, that is still going on! But it means I must be in tune with the Lord. I must be asking Him, "Alright Lord, what are you telling me? Which way should I go? What should I do? What should I not be doing? What should I learn from this?"

Which, of course, leads me to get directed. When I am asking for correction, I am also asking for direction. In following that pattern, I have come to see more and more God's plan for me, which for the first sixty-nine years of my life has worked pretty good . . . so far. Things could change! But whatever happens, I just want to do God's will.

One of the things that strikes me about you is your humility. Even today, meeting people here in your agent's office, everyone has said what a great person you are, not because of all you are known for or have achieved, but because of who you are—approachable, genuine. I guess it is hard to speak to humility, but do you see a relationship between humility and your faith?

You have to guard your ego. I mean, here you are interviewing me, so it could be all about me, so all of that lends itself to a kind of path toward building up your ego. But I think part of being an authentic human being is being humble. I am not telling you, the preacher, anything you don't know, but I think when you are in tune with who you are—a child of God, and realize that everything comes from God—well, then that leads to gratitude, which takes the focus off of you and puts it where it belongs—God!

Can I fold together an important moment and an important quote . . . ? The moment—you have spoken about several times, and written about—March 27, 1975, the day when Ruth Green wrote down that prophecy about your future. Can you share that again for me?[9]

I have told that story a lot, but it was almost fifty years ago. I was twenty and working in my mother's beauty parlor. And here comes one of her customers, Ruth Green. She writes down on a piece of paper her prophecy for me.

But her prophecy was not that I was going to go back to college, or be an actor, or famous or rich . . . no, she wrote, "Boy, you are going to travel the world and preach to millions of people. . . ." Ruth did not even know how to spell the word prophecy, so my mother helped her with that and my mother added *Reverend* . . .

I did not understand it at the time, and I was thinking, "Who is this crazy woman?" But now, now I understand it. The Lord has given me the opportunity to get to the ears of a lot of people, and now I am talking more and more about my faith, as we are doing right here.

You had a lot of different doors open to you in this way, and it incarnates, in a way that moment when Lesra reads the opening words of Rubin Carter's first letter to him in your film, Hurricane, . . . *"He who bemoans the lack of opportunity, forgets that small doors may at times open up to large rooms. . . ."*[10] *For those who will read this book, how does a person keep their "antennae" tuned in to the Ruth Greens they will encounter, . . . to the doors that might open into larger rooms? And why do you think God puts those kinds of things in front of us as opportunities to receive—rather than just handing them over without our asking?*

That is a good question, but a simple answer. Prayer, right? I mean, I don't want to use clichés here, but prayer. Honest conversation. Honest, truthful, one-on-one conversation with the Lord.

You have received a lot of earthly recognition—ten Academy Award nominations, two Oscars, nine Golden Globes, your Tony for Best Actor in Fences, *. . . and yet, I read your mother once said, "Man gives you the award, God gives the reward." But nevertheless—you have gotten a lot of those awards. Are all of those awards gifts of God? What do they tell you about our Lord and His work in and through your life?*

Here's the deal. They are a gift from God, but they're not an admission fee to God. You can't get closer to God based on what you have done. You have to lay all of that at His feet.

Do people come to God when everything's great? When have they achieved a great many things? When are they at their best? Few people do, right? When you get a billion dollars, that's not usually the point when someone says, "I think I will follow the Lord now!" Why do you think that is?

Denzel turned interviewer for a moment, and I said to him that I love a quote of Augustine that I read many years ago: "There's an unsatiable hunger in each of us that God alone can satisfy." And he said . . .

That's right, we are hungry in that way and God understands that, but we often miss that point. We think money's going to fill that, or prestige. . . . And the more we get, the more we realize those things do not do it. So we feel we need more. But only God can fill that place, . . . can meet that hunger. Only God.

Sidebar . . . you have had some incredible roles, . . . including Rubin Carter (The Hurricane, *1999); Steve Biko* (Cry Freedom *in 1987); and Malcom in* Malcom X *(1992)—do you have a favorite role?*

Ha! When I used to get asked what my favorite role was, I would say, "The next one!" That's kind of like saying to a preacher, "Of all the souls God has helped save, do you have a favorite?" And your answer would be, "The ones I haven't helped save yet!"

I am not comparing making movies to the work of God helping to save souls, but you know, in every role there is potential—to make a real difference, so I consider that so much more now.

A lot of people define themselves by their "roles" (mother, doctor, realtor, actor, artist) or by what they have (wealth, possessions, influence, etc.), . . . but you have said (UPenn address), "The chances you take, the people you love, the faith you have, that's what's going to define you. . . ."[11] *Can you share how you have been defined by those chances, people, and faith?*

Well, I would switch that around now, and I would put faith first. I mean that's what I've learned, in terms of taking chances. I can only speak for myself of course. I have been blessed. Other people tell me God has blessed me with great ability as an actor, and then they say, "He's not really taking chances," because of the talent God gave me.

I have had pretty steady work for forty years, but I guess early on, I realized as an actor, the only power I have is to say, "No, I just can't do that part." And you know, there were some parts I just couldn't do. I had some good representatives who helped me with that.

But faith has played a big role in helping guide me through all of that.

I love your words, "If you pray for rain, you've got to deal with the mud." When have been some moments where the "mud" has shown up in your life and how have you dealt with it?

A lot of what happens in this industry has to do with the attention you get. And of course, there is negative attention and positive attention. And if someone is getting more positive attention than you, well, when you are trying to climb your way up, there are others who are going to try and pull you down … That's just human nature really. But some of those who are trying to pull you down can be devious and despicable and you can spend your whole life trying to either win those people over or push them away and, in the end, you find you really can't win that fight. There's always going to be somebody poking you here and there and so again, I find I just have to give all of that to God.

But you know too, there are good things that can come out of mud! Fame is filled with mud, but ultimately good things can grow out of that mud. You pray for rain, yeah, you get the mud, but with a little sun, with a light, with the right seeds, some really great things can grow. That's pretty simple.

Like I said a minute ago, the older I get, really—the simpler life gets.

In what ways?

I am repeating myself, but it's worth repeating. God. He is more and more at the center of my life. I just want to do God's will. Wherever that leads me, and I start there, every day. I don't want to make any more money. I don't care about winning Oscars. I don't want to have any more things. I don't need God to give me any more of those things. I don't even need those things. I want God to be in charge of everything and take me where He wants me to go, and I'll go that way!

How has that played out in the roles you choose to play?

When I am presented with a role, I don't try to convince myself God's talking me into it by thinking in the back of my mind, "I really need the money, but the Lord is doing this for me!"

No, the older I get, the less time you have for things. There is only a finite number of movies I am going to make. So as for whatever else I am going to do, the quality and commitment and the integrity and the focus—all those things become more and more important.

So at this point, any endeavor is important. I don't want to waste time. To go back to that "protected piece." I know I am protected and hopefully as I take steps, God's light will reveal what is right for me or what is not.

You work in a vocation where lasting marriages, and perhaps I should say—fidelity, is the exception, not the rule—but you have been blessed to be married to Pauletta for forty-one years. How has God worked through your marriage?

Ha! Well, [again,] when you pray for rain, you have got to deal with the mud! That's my answer! In our case, Pauletta put up with more mud than I did. I was dealing with the mud outside the home, but she was dealing with the mud inside the home.

And now, I have a lot of friends who have been married a lot of times. I have some friends who really blew it at some point, but God was always in it. I know He gave me the right woman. He sent this woman to me. So, I am going to do what now? Start over!? I'm too old for that. My wife is an incredible gift of God to me. I think realizing that is so important in marriage. God brought us to one another, and we are living into His plan for us.

Denzel, you are a man of prayer—and you have told others that in times of blessing you get down on your knees every morning and thank God for your many blessings . . . grace, mercy, understanding, wisdom, parents, kindness, peace, prosperity . . . I am reminded of St. Teresa of Avila's wonderful words, "Souls without prayer are like people whose bodies or limbs are paralyzed: they possess feet and hands, but they cannot control them. . . ."[12] *So, how does prayer strengthen your day-to-day life?*

It forces me to listen. No, I take that back, not forces me, but it helps me to learn to listen, . . . because I am a talker!

Do you have a particular place where you pray?

I have a little place in my room where my Bible is, but I pray all the time. I'm praying all through the day.

Do you and Pauletta pray together?

Yes, . . . we do.

Say a bit about where you worship, when you worship, and what worship does for you?

When we are in Los Angeles, we worship at West Angeles Church of God in Christ, and when we are in New York, we worship at the Kelly Temple Church of God in Christ in Harlem.

Mr. Washington, you have written, "We are, all of us, the sum of our influences...."[13] How has our Lord influenced you?

In every way. In every way.

Our faith, as you have so eloquently said, is not just about sustaining the person in the mirror, but about giving ourselves to others. As you have written, "Being successful means helping others...."[14] Can you say a bit more about that as well?

All the blessings, all we have received, comes from God.... And if it comes from God, it is a gift, and if it is a gift, should we not use it, share it, be generous with it? At this stage of life, the most important things to me are my faith and my family, and what I want to do more than anything is to put God first and help others. Real success? Helping others.

Let me try and land the plane here. I have asked this question of everyone for this book: People will look at Denzel Washington and I think most would say, "He has it all—money, fame, influence, power..." What do you say to those who think those are the most important things in life to have?

What is important is not what you have on the outside; what is important is what is on the inside that will help guide you as to how you are going to use those things on the outside. One of my favorite verses is: "For everyone to whom much is given, from him much will be required; and to whom much has been committed, of him they will ask more."[15]

Whatever we have comes from God; and we are called to honor Him with those blessings.

How would you like to be remembered?

I don't care about that kind of stuff. I never even thought about a question like that. *(I confess, at this moment, I thought I had run the risk of blowing this interview! Then he said . . .)*
  I mean, the easy answer is, a man of God. A man of God.

Okay, I'll take that.

Ha! Ha! Lord said, "Shut up."

Man of God . . . Anything else? (I ran the risk of pushing a bit! And it was worth the nudge!)

Just as important as saying a man of God, is the process, the development that comes from God—that does not come from wealth, it does not come from fame, it does not come through the Church, it doesn't even come through the pastor . . . it comes from your personal conversation with God; it comes from your encounters with God.

Can you tell me about such a moment?

Well, let me think about it, because there's not one day, but the date that comes to mind when you ask me that was one day when I was worshipping at the West Angeles Church of God in Christ, and, . . . I made the decision to walk down the aisle, to be prayed over. And, I was filled with the Holy Spirit, just this powerful presence moved over me and in me, and I was overwhelmed.
  When I look back on it, I think I was a little embarrassed at the time, because I was slobbering and crying, and I was just a mess.
  And they took me in a back room, and I just remember thinking, "I just got filled with the Holy Spirit. . . ." And man, I never told this story before, but it seems like people were coming all around me, and it felt like I was literally being lifted off the floor.
  It was powerful, but it was at a time in my life when I was not ready to commit fully, because I was still wanting to party and take life on my terms, do things my way.

Here I go, but repeating myself, now it's much simpler. The older you get, it is easier, because you let go of all the stuff and you just cling to God.

* * *

That seemed like a good place to end. We talked for a bit more, and he was kind enough to ask me what "else" I planned on doing in my retirement years. He let me know it was "okay" to come back with more questions and then we prayed together before I left.

Now, Denzel Washington has spent his life telling good stories, and while the story is not over, let me end with a good one.

Five months after this interview, on December 21, 2024, days before his seventieth birthday, Denzel Washington was baptized at the Kelly Temple Church of God in Christ in Harlem, New York. In the background, before being lowered into the baptismal pool in the church, Nina Simone's spirited hymn "Take Me to the Water" was heard throughout the church, and Denzel was singing along.[16] *I watched the service and was very touched. I knew I wanted to ask him why he made that decision, so I called and left a voicemail and requested a brief follow-up to our initial conversation.*

A week or so later, he called about three in the morning. He was heading off to rehearsals for a multi-week production of Shakespeare's Othello, *in New York. He told me he was putting in eighteen-hour days, but he said when he came up for air, he would be calling me back. As usual, he made good on his promise, and we scheduled the follow-up.*

It would be a few months after the baptism, but on a beautiful winter morning, we had a follow-up call. I asked him to tell me why he chose to be baptized at that time.

Let me begin at the end. They presented me with a "license to minister" at that service, and that was a surprise to me. I am undertaking some study before I am ready to take that on.

But what happened is that I got up early on Saturday morning and decided to drive over to where I grew up, in Mount Vernon, but I went through Harlem. And I decided to go by the church that my mother grew up in.

When we got there, I noticed the door to the sanctuary was cracked open. So, the Lord said to me, "Go on in there!" I went in, and I sat in the back, and they were having a program for their students who were going off to college, and they were giving them scholarships.

By the time that was over, I was giving out scholarships! *(Denzel starts laughing.)* They moved me up front, and I said a few words, and then I told them I would give them a certain amount of money each year for this scholarship program. So that was that day, and I sat with Bishop Blake, who was visiting there.[17] And after that service, we got together in his office, and we were visiting. And after all of that, my heart led me to be baptized where my mother went to church.

And that is the Kelly Temple?

Yes, the Kelly Temple. It was founded in 1939 by the Reverend Otha Miema Kelly.[18] In fact, I think my father preached there, and that is where my mother first saw him. My father's first wife died, and, in fact, Bishop Kelly thought my father was a good choice for my mother, and they got married in 1947. . . .

I want to share some of the things I have written down that are guiding me as I stepped into this new year, . . . here are a few of them:

"We don't get to heaven by what we know, we get to heaven by Who we know."

"Far better to stand with God and be judged by man, than to stand with man and be judged by God."

I'm stealing those from somebody . . . I didn't make them up! But that's where I am at and I just want to get closer in my walk—daily, staying in the Word.

You know, you live long enough, and you bang your head up against the wall, you eventually stop and figure it out and realize you can open the door! *(Denzel laughs again!)*

I shared with Denzel how touched I was by what he said after he was baptized, and so, with his permission, I share that with you here, his very moving words to close out this reflection on his spiritual journey.

Once Denzel had dried himself off, (for it was a full immersion baptism!), he quietly and gently walked to the pulpit and offered words of thanks to the church, to those gathered, to his wife, Pauletta.

Then he spoke a beautiful word of hope to the congregation that I want to share as I close out these wonderful and inspiring insights Denzel so willingly shared.

I let him know that I planned to close out this chapter with his words after his baptism, and fitting, and hopeful, and inspiring words they are.

"God has done a lot for me, but He will do a lot for anyone who trusts in Him. It may not be being an actor or someone famous, but with God, the sky is literally the limit, and there's no limit to the sky.

"I believe God is good all the time. I believe God is with us when we are not with Him.

"I believe God is for us, when we are not for Him.

"He watches over us, when we don't watch Him.

"He protects us, when we don't protect ourselves.

"He gives to us when we don't deserve it.

"So, I am thankful. I am thankful for all God has given me in my seventy years. I am thankful for my loving, faithful wife.

"To God be the glory for all these things. That's what matters most. And in the end, I just want to be in that number, when the saints go marching in!

"Amen!"[19]

DENZEL WASHINGTON

Denzel Washington is a native of Mt. Vernon, NY, and graduated from Fordham University, where he majored in drama. He spent a year at San Francisco's prestigious American Conservatory Theatre before beginning his professional acting career. Since then, Denzel's unforgettable performances have garnered him two Academy Awards, three Golden Globes, and countless other awards.

Denzel received his first Academy Award for the historical war drama *Glory* (1987) and his second for his portrayal of the corrupt cop in the crime thriller, *Training Day* (2001). Denzel won a Tony Award for his performance in *Fences*, during his return to Broadway in 2010.

In 2016, Denzel starred in the critically acclaimed film adaptation of August Wilson's *Fences*. In addition to producing and directing the adaptation, Denzel reprised his original Tony Award–winning role alongside Viola Davis. The film received four Academy Award nominations, including Denzel's for Best Performance by an Actor in a Leading Role.

Denzel returned to the stage in 2018, when he starred in a revival of Eugene O'Neill's *The Iceman Cometh*, which was directed by George C. Wolfe. His performance garnered him a Tony Award nomination.

He also starred in Dan Gilroy's *Roman J. Israel, Esq.* (2017) for which he received multiple Best Actor nominations.

In 2016, he was selected as the recipient for the Cecil B. DeMille Lifetime Achievement Award at the 73rd Golden Globe Awards, cementing his legacy in Hollywood. He most recently was honored with the AFI Life Achievement award, one of the highest honors for a career in film.

Denzel recently produced *Ma Rainey's Black Bottom* (2020) for Netflix, directed by George C. Wolfe with cast including Viola Davis, Chadwick Boseman, and Colman Domingo. The Warner Bros. thriller *The Little Things* (2021) starred Denzel alongside Rami Malek and Jared Leto.

Denzel also directed *A Journal for Jordan* (2021), starring Michael B. Jordan, and helmed the Joel Coen–directed *The Tragedy of Macbeth* (2021) alongside Frances McDormand, for which he received an Academy Award nomination for Actor in a Leading Role.

Denzel produced *The Piano Lesson*, which began streaming exclusively on Netflix in 2024, and starred in *Gladiator 2* from director Ridley Scott, which also hit theaters in 2024. Most recently, Washington will star in *Highest 2 Lowest* from director Spike Lee and has made his long-awaited return to the stage in *Othello*, alongside Jake Gyllenhaal.

Photo credit: © Holly Reed

"I know there are a lot of atheists in the world who say they don't need faith in God. But I'll tell you, Bill McRaven does, and I need it more every day—it has been my saving grace!"

—Admiral William H. McRaven

Admiral William H. McRaven

In my years in ministry, I have been fortunate to be around people from virtually every walk of life. I have also been on planet Earth long enough to know not everyone has admiration for those who serve in the various branches of the military. If you happen to fall into that category, you might be tempted to turn to the next chapter but let me plead with you to resist that temptation.

I grew up in a home that understood the value of the protection afforded by those who served in our nation's armed forces. My father was a second lieutenant in the US Army, and after a season of active duty, he served in the reserves for several years.

For whatever reason, as my vocation in the priesthood unfolded, God placed me in parishes that benefitted from the counsel and wisdom of retired veterans. For five years, I served in Pensacola, Florida—the home of one of the largest US Navy bases in the country. On the Sunday closest to Veterans Day, it had been my practice, wherever I served as rector, to recognize and honor the veterans who worshipped with us, and on Memorial Day, to do the same for those who gave their lives for the cause of democracy at home and abroad.

On these occasions, I would typically invite a veteran, or someone who was active in the military, who also was a Christian, to come and participate in our Veterans Day services. As the years grew, my list of heroes grew, and I came to hear incredible stories of courage, sacrifice, service, and valor.

I had heard speeches by Four Star Admiral William McRaven, and I had read his works. Most who heard his speech to the 2014 graduating class from the University of Texas have said it will go down as one of the best commencement addresses in history. And most Americans will also know that under the direction of President Barack Obama, as the ninth commander of the United States Special Operations Command, he supervised the operation that resulted in the death of one of the worst terrorists of the present generation, Osama bin Laden, in 2011.

So, when I invited Admiral McRaven to be a guest speaker at one of our Veterans Day events at St. Martin's Episcopal Church, I quickly learned that this would not be a one-off, as we stayed in touch from that day to this. As the years increased, I read more of his books and listened to more of his speeches. And with each new story of courageous missions, near-death experiences, a battle with cancer, and life lessons from commanding untold numbers of troops under his command, my admiration only grew.

To say Admiral McRaven is one of my heroes, would not do him justice—he is much more than that, and over time, perhaps what I have come to admire most is his humility and his unwavering faith in God and God's purposes.

If you are one, like me, who appreciates and understands the role of the military in our nation's history and its protection to this day, or if you are a skeptic, read on. I think you will find what I have found—a true American treasure.

Let's begin by giving you an opportunity to tell me a bit about your religious upbringing and what role it played in your home?

Though my parents were in the military, I was born and raised in Pinehurst, North Carolina. My mother grew up in the Methodist Church, so the family followed her lead and so we worshipped in the Methodist Church. We did not go every Sunday, but we did go once or twice a month. And to be honest, our attendance was sometimes dictated by where there was a football game on that my father wanted to watch!

That said, my father and mother were very spiritual. They were both deeply faithful Christians, but men of the era did not really wear their religion on their sleeve. My mother grew up as a student of the Bible and that was her practice when we came along. So it was my mother who really formed and shaped the faith of my two older sisters and me. She was shaped by her faith as a child, and it was important to her to pass that on to us.

But then you met, fell in love [with] and married Georgeann, who was Roman Catholic. How did that change things for you?

Yes, when Georgeann and I married, in 1978, my mother told me she had the greatest respect for the Catholic faith, but she really wanted me to remain a Methodist. But when I saw how the Catholic faith shaped Georgeann, it really spoke to me. She could not be a better example of the Catholic faith. I had agreed to raise our children as Catholic, and so we worshipped together in that way.

You know, Russ, when you're around people who practice their faith, who believe in their faith, and you see that they are good and noble and honest people, you can't help but be impressed by their religious foundation. And this was true of my wife who wore her faith so graciously and humbly. I never knew a more faithful practicing Catholic than she, so it was easy for me to take those steps and after I retired from the military, I became a Roman Catholic not just in practice, but in name as well.

There are obviously some differences in doctrine and spirituality between the Methodist Church and the Catholic Church, but over time, I just had no problem making the move, and I was really fed spiritually by the homilies, the way of worship, and of course, the sacrament of regular Communion.

Was there a specific moment in your faith journey that really impacted you? Was there a specific person, other than your parents, who played a significant role in your spiritual life?

I never had a big epiphany. Of course, all the layers played a role—being raised in the church, a child of faithful parents, being taught to read and believe in the Bible.

But I will tell you what probably influenced me more than anything, joining the Fellowship of Christian Athletes when I was in high school.[1]

During my participation with them, I traveled to Estes Park, Colorado, on two occasions as part of their FCA Athletes Conference. And they brought in these great speakers, who were Christians, [such as] Tom Landry and Roger Staubach.[2] Those two trips really solidified my belief as a young man. But in the years that followed, my beliefs have just become stronger and have been reinforced again and again.

Prayer became very important to me, and whenever I had down time, I prayed. And my understanding of prayer grew. I came to realize that my prayers were not always answered like I would have liked, but those things I had prayed for worked out. For instance, I could not see God's hand a lot of times in the moment, but when I began to step back, I could see how the dots connected, and I realized God's hand was at work, in my life, and I feel very, very fortunate in my life to be led and guided along the way by His hands.

It is an understatement to say that you have experienced the dangers of military engagement. How has your faith sustained you in those times?

The roots of my faith run deep, because I was brought up in it, and so I never really questioned my faith. And when things got difficult, I would rely on that faith. You know, I would pray a lot, I would look for guidance, but I also had, well, they're not epiphanies, and maybe they're little, minor miracles. So I've had a number of near death experiences, and a couple of them have kind of reinforced that faith.

For instance, in 1995, I was the commanding officer of SEAL Team 3 on the West Coast.[3] And I went out to observe a training mission up on the central coast of California. When I arrived, a large storm had been raging, creating these giant twenty-five-to-thirty-foot waves that were coming into this harbor where a couple of our boats were. These were thirty-two-foot boats that we called rigid hull inflatables—think of it as a kind of big, rubberized boat that could carry about ten to twelve guys.

I saw one of these boats getting ready to go out into this monster surf. So I turned to one of my SEALs and said, "Take me over to talk to that young lieutenant who's in charge of that boat." When we got over there, I said, "Hey son, what's your plan?"

And he goes, "Well, we are trained for weather like this, and we have been counting the waves, and, while there's a certain timing to it, we know how to go around the break water and push out of here."

So I said, "Okay, strap me in, . . . I'm going with you!"

I did not have a dry suit on, and the water was pretty cold, and he tried to talk me out of it, and I just said, "No, I'll be alright."

So we get strapped into these bolster seats and take off. The plan immediately diverted. Instead of going around the waves, the guy driving the boat goes right into it. At about twenty feet, we go straight up—we were airborne for about four seconds then we came down on the second wave. Another wave—bigger, about thirty feet, and up we go again. The kid guns it, which is the right thing to do, and this time we are in the air for about five seconds (I am counting!). And when we hit, we hit in such a way that the engines are knocked out.

So here we are, the boat is stopped and here comes the third wave—and it's probably fifty feet high. The boat basically stands right up and just completely dumps us all back over into the water.

I am now trapped under the boat and completely tangled up in what we call a shot line.[4] I cannot breathe and I'm probably twenty feet below the surface. And I remember thinking to myself, "Well, I am never going to see Georgeann or my children again."

It was like slow motion and there's no way out and then, all of the sudden Russ, I am free, and I shot to the surface. Of course, I was now caught in the next set of waves, but the SEALs that were nearby and saw the boat get dumped come in and they rescue me. I need to add, they received the Navy Marine Corps Life Saving Medal—which is the highest award you can get in peacetime.

But the point of that story was that there I was underwater, completely trapped. And I can tell you, Russ, there was no way out of this. I mean, no way—outside of a miracle, and I think that is what it was.

One of the things about the business I was in is that you have a lot of near-death experiences. A parachute doesn't work, or you're almost hit by a round, or [an] explosion goes off. And to be honest, you don't spend a lot of time thinking about it, because it's just the nature of your work, and if you worry about it or overthink it, then you're not going to get back out in the field again. So you're just like, "Okay, I almost died today, but I didn't, okay. We go back to work."

But this one was a little different, because, yes, I didn't die that day. But what I couldn't intellectually get through was the fact that I was completely bound up underwater. I had been trying to untangle it. This rope around my neck was getting pulled tighter as the boat was pulling away, and I am getting ready to black out, and then—I'm miraculously free.

Of course, at first, I am thinking, "Okay, how did that happen?" Because I'm trying to rationalize this. "Did the boat turn? Did the rope around my neck and my hands and my legs suddenly untangle?" But I knew it did not happen that way. So there was a reinforcement of my belief that the hand of God somehow reached down and untangled me that day. I tell people that what happened was miraculous, however you want to describe "miraculous."

But I need to say—it was not an epiphany moment for me, because I have a deep faith. It was not like "Oh my gosh, there is no God," and then "There is a God!" No, I've always known there [is] a God—and there He was again, helping me in that moment.

That leads me directly to my next question. You have obviously seen a lot of horrible things in your work around the world. Has any of that tested your faith or diminished your faith or made you question your faith?

No, because, you know, I have out of my faith, I have a particular belief about good and evil in the world. Part of this, I believe, is that God lets us make our own decisions. We have free will. And we have free will to do good things. We have free will to do bad things, and when we take the right course, we are doing what God calls us to do, and vice versa.

Of the many things for which you are known, perhaps toward the top of the list is your commencement speech for the University of Texas, which subsequently you expanded and published as a best-selling book—Make Your Bed: Little Chings That Can Change Your Life . . . and Maybe the World. . . ."[5,6] *Of the "little things," you begin with the call to "start your day with a task completed." And then you go on to unpack how the first thing you did when you rolled out of "the rack" was to begin the process of making your bed. More to the point, you suggest that the "sentiment of cleanliness and order applied to every aspect of military life."*[7] *How might such "order" apply to one's spiritual life?*

I will answer that by telling you a little story. In 1978, I first got command of my first SEAL team called "Underwater Demolition Team 11." With the exception of a few of the guys and me, almost everyone there was a Vietnam vet.

So when I got there, I had a conversation with the command master chief, in which I said, "Hey, look, you know, I'm going to try to earn the respect of these, you know, battle-hardened warriors out here. What do I need to do?"

He said, "Well, I think there's four things you need to do. First, you need to work hard . . . come in early, . . . work hard. Stay late. Come in on the weekends. You may not be the smartest, the brightest, the best SEAL, but if you work hard, they'll respect that."

"Okay, check."

Then he said, "Learn the business of the business. Learn about how to pack a parachute and how to scuba dive."

"Okay, check."

Then he said, "Then learn to be a good teammate. SEAL teams are much like a football team. You got a locker room, you got playbook, okay, be a good teammate."

"Check."

But then he said something that threw me off a little bit. He said, "You need to be a good person . . . Because if you're not a good person, . . . if you go out at night . . . you drink too much, you womanize, . . . if you do things you should not do, when you come back in the next day, you will bear the burden of those decisions, and you won't be focused on being the best SEAL you can be."

So, all of this answers your question about "cleanliness." Of course, we are all human and we all make mistakes. We all do things we wish we hadn't done. But if you keep your life as clean as you can then you don't bear the burden of the bad decisions, and you're much more likely to do things better and better. You're going to be better at your job. You're going to be better at your relationships. You're going to be better at everything if you have a clean and orderly, religious life, a faithful life. I mean, doing good is important. It has a value to it, and the more good you do, the better you will feel, the better you will be able to do the things God calls you to do without being burdened by straying into those things you know He does not want you to do.

Let me stay with that just a bit, because in a very practical way you do make a connection between making one's bed and faith, writing, "Nothing can replace the strength and comfort of one's faith, but sometimes the simplest act of making your bed can give you the lift you need to start your day and provide you the satisfaction to end it right."[8] Can you say a bit more about that? What might it mean to you—regarding your own spiritual journey, to end the day right?

I begin and end each day with prayer. It was an absolute necessity when I was in combat. Days rarely go well. You lose soldiers in combat. Inadvertently, civilians are killed. Somebody's yelling at you about something. Days are hard in combat, and days are hard in life.

The end of the day gives us the opportunity to reflect and ask, "What could I have done better?" But prayer also allows me to realize that, yes, there are difficult problems out there, but when I pray, it reminds me that there is Someone who can help me with whatever problems I am facing, because I can't solve them all.

Prayer turns me back to God and allows me to invite Him to come into my life and help me resolve my problems or give me the knowledge I need in a particular situation, or the strength to get through the tough times.

Russ, when you are a combat leader, you are looking for someone to give you the understanding and strength to get through the difficult times. Who are you going to trust? Yourself? No, turn to God. So, in faith, and through prayer, you get what you need to face the troops. As a combat leader, you're the one that has to talk to the families whose kids have been killed. You're the one who has to make the hard decisions. Prayer, for me, has been vital in those situations.

In July of 2001, you endured a harrowing brush with death in a parachute accident—your pelvis was separated, tearing the myriads of muscles that connect your pelvis to the rest of your body—this was after falling 4,000 feet. You describe an out of body experience wherein you "heard yourself" screaming.[9] Can you tell me more about that? Did you have the wherewithal to pray or cry out to God in that moment? I know there were surgeries and procedures and a long season of recovery after that. How did you rely on your faith during that time?

Absolutely, but I always rely on my faith. So that parachute accident was not an epiphany per se, but there was a little bit of the miraculous there.

Tangled seems to be an issue with me . . . but yes, . . . I made the jump and immediately got completely entangled in my parachute. Then, I had a midair collision with another serviceman. I was spinning head down. The reality is, the parachute probably should not have opened at all, but when it did, it tore me apart. Having said that, as I mentioned earlier, you know, this was kind of the price of doing business.

By that time, I'd been in the military or in the SEAL teams for about twenty-five years, and I had had a lot of brushes with death.

When I hit the ground, I knew I was broken up, but I also immediately knew I was going to be fine; somehow, I was going to get through this. Unlike the boat accident, where, in my mind, it was miraculous, because there was no way I should have been able to untangle myself at that point in time, in the case of the parachute, I've seen parachutes in bizarre situations open the way mine did.

But despite all of that, I had to turn to prayer. And like all tough times, you just pray your way through it. Really, I prayed a lot for my family then, because I could see they were worried about me.

How long was that recovery period?

I was only in the hospital for about a week, but because they had to pin me and plate me and all that sort of stuff, frankly, I had trouble in the hospital. I got this thing called "Sundowners Syndrome," which is where you go a little crazy looking just straight up at the ceiling [for hours and days on end].

So I got out of the hospital, and then they moved a hospital bed into my military quarters. At the time, I'm a Navy captain—I'm referred to as the Commodore. I'm in charge of all the SEALs on the west coast.

So I had a lot of doctors [who] work for me; so they kept a good eye on me. They come over every day, you know, check on things. But it was, you know, several months before I was able to kind of walk again. It was probably a year before I could walk well. And I did, because 9/11 happened. Soon after that, I went from that job being the Commodore in charge of all the SEALs to the White House in October of 2001—and my parking space was about half a mile from my office—so my physical therapy was to take a long and painful walk from my car to my office! It was probably a year before I could run again.

You learned of the importance of friends during that time. A lot of people will say that success is the fruit of personal willpower, talent, and labor—that people pull themselves up, but you have written, "Make as many friends as possible, and never forget that your success depends on others."[10] *Why is that so important?*

Part of this is how you're raised. But my mother and my father were very sociable. They had a lot of friends, and I saw the value in that.

    I sometimes tell my SEALs: Life is like being in a little rubber boat. We are in this boat with lots of other people, and we need to work together to paddle the boat. And the point of the story is, I don't care if you are the biggest, the fastest, the strongest, smartest SEAL in the boat, you can't paddle it by yourself, and here's the point—you can't go through life by yourself. Somebody's going to have to help you when you fall, somebody's going to have to pick you up, dust you off, and tell you everything's going to be okay. So, get out there and make as many friends as you can, have as many colleagues as you can, accept the goodwill of strangers, because you just can't get through life by yourself.

Let's talk about another major challenge in your life. While serving in Afghanistan, in 2011, you got a call telling you that you had chronic lymphocytic leukemia (CLL). In what is called the "great faith" chapter of the New Testament, the author of Hebrews wrote, "Now faith is the assurance of things hoped for, the conviction of things not seen."[11] *And the Apostle Paul writes that "hope" is one of the "fruits of the Spirit," evidence of the Spirit of God living in and through someone.*

    I once read the words of W. T. Purkiser, a [Church of the] Nazarene pastor, "The future belongs to those who belong to God. This is hope."[12] So *after your diagnosis you talk a lot about the power of hope. One of your physicians had nothing but bad news, while another brought you immeasurable hope.*[13] *Your "punch line" to this experience was pretty simple—"I found in my travels around the world that hope is the strongest force in the universe."*[14] *How did your faith strengthen your hope through that experience?*

I have a hope that comes from my experiences. I have seen the worst of humanity and the best of humanity. For instance, parents [who] will do anything to take care of their children in a war zone; you see enemies forgive each other when they realize they have more in common than their differences.

I have traveled to over ninety countries around the world and witnessed people from different religions work together for a great good. So, during despair, in the midst of the poverty, in the midst of war, in the midst of everything that's bad, invariably, you will witness incredible nobility, this incredible humanity, and that always gives me hope, in spite of all the ugliness. I think it pleases God to look upon us and despite all the bad things He sees, He also sees that we are capable of loving others.

If we focus only on the evil and bad things going on around us, it could certainly lead us to despair, but hope pulls us out of that.

One time I was visiting soldiers at Walter Reed Hospital, and came into the room of a young man who lost both his legs, one arm and part of his other arm in battle.[15] I could not imagine what he must have been feeling and, Russ, he looked at me and said, "Sir, I'm twenty-four years old, I'm going to be just fine."

I thought to myself, "Here is this twenty-four-year-old man, he's a quadruple amputee, and he's just told me he's going to be fine!" Well, if he can be fine during this incredible tragedy, then no matter how bad my day is, I can find a way to be fine.

That young man gave me hope. If you want to look for bad stuff, it's not hard to see. Sometimes you must look a bit harder to see the good stuff, but it's out there, and God will use it to give you hope and it is important that we never lose hope![16]

I suspect most people connect your name to Operation Neptune Spear, May 2, 2011, which brought about the killing of terrorist Osama Bin Laden, but you also were the commanding officer who helped bring about the capture of

Sadam Hussein on December 13, 2003, and the rescue of Captain Richard Phillips on April 12, 2009, through the synchronized killing of three of his Somalian captors. You have acknowledged in speeches and in your writing the importance of the power of love in overcoming evil and hatred in the world, but you have also written, "As I hunted bad men around the world, I did not always have love in my heart. To each man God has given special talents. Mine seemed better suited to exacting justice than to offering mercy."[17] Has your vocation as a soldier ever been challenged by your personal faith?

Russ, it's a difficult circle to square or square to circle. I'm a soldier, you know. I was trained to protect, trained to defend, and when necessary, trained to kill. I have had to unfortunately dispatch hundreds, if not thousands of people, who are given the same task. I haven't always gotten it right, and it is something that you think about all the time in combat.

Nobody normal wants to kill innocent civilians. Certainly, I didn't want to, but on occasion civilians were killed. Because in the nature of war, you have the frictions of war. You think you've got it right; you don't have it right. And you must end up living with that.

But you know, there are times when I realize that I can protect people. I witnessed in Afghanistan and Iraq truly evil people in the world. I said a moment ago, as good as and as hopeful as I can be, there are evil people in the world, and sometimes you need the soldiers to take care of the evil people so that the good people can continue to be good.

And I'll be honest and say, I do not know how I reconcile that with my faith. All I can do is pray that I get it right as often as I can, and do, also pray that God forgives me when I get it wrong. Because I hope that God can see in my heart and realize that I'm trying to do the right thing.

I am keenly aware that when I kill someone, I am also violating one of the Ten Commandments, but I hope that I'm doing it for, you know, that greater good.

And I must leave it up to God to judge me.

Admiral, one of the things I love in your speeches and in your writings is when you talk about all the different kinds of people you have encountered in the ninety plus countries to which you have been. There are Christians, around the globe, perhaps well-meaning Christians, who suggest that any other religious expression is void of truth. In other words, you have spent a great deal of your adult life around people of other faiths, particularly Muslims. From your experience of working alongside those of the Muslim faith, what might you say to those who might say, Islam has nothing to offer us.

A moment of true confessions here—obviously, I'm a Christian, right? I believe in Jesus Christ and ascribe to the teachings of Christianity. But intellectually there is absolutely no way I can think of a loving God that will not take care of the Muslim children, the agnostics, all of those [who] aren't Christians.

God will take care of them. It is God's job to decide how they live out their faith in their own tradition—whether they be Jews, Christians, Muslims, Hindus, Buddhists, or whatever. God will judge as God will judge, and it is not up to me to do that.

Of course, I do believe Christianity is the truest of religions. I absolutely believe that Jesus came to die to forgive us for our sins.

But I also believe we worship a loving God, and I simply believe God's love is far more expansive than we know. I believe God created us all in His image, as His children and God is going to take care of His children!

So my belief is that I am called, as a Christian, to treat everybody with respect until they prove otherwise.

As to Muslims, specifically, I have met some wonderful Muslims, and I have also encountered some who were trying to kill me. And I suspect some of them could say the same thing about me.

So just to nail the point home, it is not my place to judge, I'll leave that up to God.

Just to expand on that a bit, I have heard you tell a remarkably moving story about having to meet with a Muslim father, whose adult civilian sons were killed by soldiers under your command. Can you say a bit more about that?

As I have said, the nature of war sometimes is you don't always get it right. And we had a mission that went terribly wrong. It was, in fact, a disaster and it was the worst civilian casualty that I had seen in my time of war. It was heartbreaking.

What happened is that my men came upon two Afghan men whom they believed to be Taliban, because they had guns and tried to engage my soldiers. My soldiers killed them, only to find that they were Afghan police.

Two women were also inadvertently killed, because they were behind a door and the rounds went through the door and killed them both. It was just horrific, and there was no other way to put it. My heart broke for the father of these two men, and I believe one of the two women was actually his daughter as well—just horrible.

As the commanding officer, as a Christian, and as a father myself, I was compelled to travel to one of the provinces in Afghanistan where the father of these children my soldiers had just killed lived—and to personally apologize to him.

There were a lot of people who thought I was a little bit crazy and some who were not happy with me at all. But it is what I set out to do.

Before this meeting, I talked with an Afghan general who worked for me and I asked, "What do you think I should say to this father?" And he said, "The father will forgive you." And I responded, "How?" And he said, "The father will forgive you, because this is what we are taught in Islam."

And then he said something very wise, Russ, "He will forgive you, because it not only takes away your burden, but it takes away his burden as well, and the burden of anger and desire for retribution that he might bear."

I remember thinking, "Well, that sounds great, but, but not every Afghan I've dealt with wanted to forgive me."

I traveled with some of our Afghan allies, to a small village in the Paktika Province of Afghanistan.[18] We walked into a room I would describe as a kind of city hall, and there were perhaps 200 very angry Afghans, and outside the room there were many more.

Try and picture this—as I sat down with the father and one of his sons, I am completely surrounded by very angry Afghans, and his son was probably the maddest of all. He had nothing but hatred in his eyes for me. I was honestly worried that he would pull out a knife and kill me right then and there.

I was sitting with a mother who was translating my words for me to the Iman who was then telling the father what I was saying. The father looked like a typical Afghan—he had a long beard and was wearing Afghan garb, but he just looked beaten. This tragedy had taken its toll on him, and he would not look me in the eye.

I said, "I'm a soldier and my home and family are a long way from here and I miss them." I told him that I could not imagine what it would be like to lose a member of my family. And then I said something like, "I do believe this—you and I both worship a loving God, a forgiving God." And then I asked for the father's forgiveness.

Then there was a bit of a pause, and the Imam is talking, and then the father and son began talking and I could see that the son's temperament changed.

He turned and spoke to the Imam who turned to me and said, "We will have no more hatred in our hearts for you."

My faith called on me to apologize, and his faith called on him to forgive.

It's actually a living parable. In your book, The Hero Code, *you remind your readers that as Christ hung on the cross, he prayed, "Father forgive them, for they know not what they do."*[19] *But your suggestion is that forgiveness is one of the most Christlike gifts we can offer, writing, "The hardest things any hero can do is to forgive."*[20] *How has this understanding of forgiveness been informed by your faith?*

I do think that's the case. In that book, I began by writing about courage and wrote that I agreed with Winston Churchill that courage is the most important of all qualities—because it guarantees all the other qualities. If you are not courageous, then it is hard to be humble and honest. But I ended the book with the importance of forgiveness, because at the end of the day, I think true heroes are those that can find a way to forgive.

And you know, Russ, I think that really speaks to the time in which we are living because we seem to be so slighted and hurt by every little thing, and a lot of anger comes out of that.

We need to find our way back to the power of authentic forgiveness.

Heroes get it. They say, "I've got it. You made a mistake. You're forgiven." And then they move on—that's what true heroes do!

Do you have a favorite scripture?

This is going to sound a bit strange. But it is actually Jesus's words from the cross, when he cries out "My God, my God, why have You forsaken me?"[21]

But the reason it sticks in my head is if you were going to make up a story about God on earth, you would not use those words. You would tell a story that says the reasons Jesus was up on the Cross.

But instead, here we witness the human side of the divine Jesus, who basically is saying, "I have done everything you wanted, why have you forgotten me!"

It testifies, for me, of the truth of Jesus's Crucifixion, and that means a lot to me.

And I like Jesus's teaching on prayer in Matthew's Gospel, where he tells his disciples, "Is there anyone among you if your child asks for bread will give a stone? Or if the child asks for a fish will give a snake? . . . How much more your Father in heaven gives good things to those who ask Him!"[22]

Which, of course, teaches us how to pray and how to receive from God.

I know you attend church, you read the Bible, can you tell me about your prayer life?

(Admiral McRaven laughs.)

I pray a lot. I talk a lot to God, throughout the day. It's not just getting on my knees before I go to bed. It's kind of a constant dialogue. Which is important to me because that makes me feel a personal connection to God, which I want all the time.

I do pray at church. I do say my prayers before I go to bed. And I pray when I need guidance or inspiration from God.

I know how important Georgeann has been as your life partner. Is it forty-six years? Do I have that right?

Yes, very good, forty-six going on forty-seven!

You have said that she's helped you with your faith. How do you share your faith together?

We have had just a fantastic marriage, but there have been tough times—we've raised three kids, we've gone through the hardships of life—siblings die, parents die. And when you go through things like this, you cling to each other.

We talk about our faith, and it is our faith that has helped us get through those tough times. We do pray together.

One of your life lessons, for lack of a better phrase, is that "man is worthy of this world." Can you say more about that?[23]

If you look at the world we live in, there are horrible things that happen—crime, war, violence, but if you strip all of that away, there's an awful lot of good in the world.

Like I've said, I think I have seen the worst of humanity, but also the best of humanity, and I believe most men and women try to do good. When you see that, I have to believe that man is worthy of this world.

God has given us this world, put us here and called us to be the best we can be. Yes, we stumble every day and make mistakes, some of them are horrible atrocities. But I try and focus on the good, look for the good, because I think in the end, the goodness will outweigh all the evil.

In his book, *The Heroes of History,* Will Durant recalls all these incredible stories.[24] He tells his reader that we tend to focus on the atrocities of history, forgetting that there are millions of people going about their daily lives doing good.

And so I believe that to be true. I have traveled to so many places and met so many good people—so I think in the aggregate, man is worthy of this world. If humanity wasn't, we probably wouldn't be here!

On May 27, 2015, you were asked to give the commencement address to the University of Texas Southwestern Medical School graduates, and among the qualities you said was necessary, was "faith." Not faith in themselves or their skills alone, but something greater than themselves. I would suspect you believe that is a call to everyone, regardless of their profession—but why is such faith so important?[25]

So, yes, I had a young man that worked for me at SEAL Team 3. He had been in Iraq and, at the time, I was stationed in Germany.

I had a short break, and it was my practice to go and visit the most seriously injured soldiers, who were usually medevacked from Iraq or Afghanistan to Landstuhl Regional Medical Center—this huge military hospital complex not too far from Luxembourg.

So a friend of mine, [named Mike,] who had worked for me, had been seriously wounded and transported to this hospital. I went up to see him.

Russ, he had been shot twenty-seven times. Fifteen of those rounds penetrated his body armor and pierced his body. Before I go in to see him, I see one of his nurses and I ask her how he is doing.

She says to me, "I've been working in this hospital for years, and I have never seen anyone this badly wounded—this shot up and he's actually going to be okay."

And I immediately began to thank her and the doctors.

And she says back to me, "It had nothing to do with us."

Her point was, his healing was beyond their capabilities, that his healing came from the hand of God.

I think it is important for doctors to understand that those patients in their care will present them with things that are beyond their medical skills, and that's where having faith in something bigger than their own skills takes center stage.

Another powerful story.

So we come to a question I have asked each person in this book. What would you say to someone who says, "Admiral William McRaven has power, influence, fame, success—isn't that enough? Why do I need faith? Why do I need a relationship with God?"

I know I am very blessed right now. Russ, as you know, I mean, since I've retired, things have gone well for me, and I do have a lot of material goods, and I could not care about any of them.

Maybe it's just growing up as a military officer where you didn't have a lot, you know. I mean, military pay is not great. You learn to live on what's important, and here are the most important things—your family, your friends, and your faith.

If you don't have faith in something bigger than yourself, it's really hard to tackle the troubles that come your way. I have lived through very difficult times in my life and in my career. And I have got the best wife and family in the whole world. I have got great friends.

But there often come those times, when you really need to call on something, some power that is bigger than you and your own little world. And that realization comes from my faith in God, to whom I turn for guidance, inspiration, and strength.

I know there are a lot of atheists in the world who say they don't need faith in God. But I'll tell you, Bill McRaven does, and I need it more every day. It is my faith that has gotten me to this point in life. I cannot guarantee that it will happen for everybody in the same way—but it has been my saving grace!

ADMIRAL WILLIAM H. McRAVEN

Admiral William H. McRaven is a retired US Navy Four-Star Admiral and the former Chancellor of the University of Texas System. During his time in the military, he commanded special operations forces at every level, eventually taking charge of the US Special Operations Command. His career included combat during Desert Storm and both the Iraq and Afghanistan wars.

As the Chancellor of the UT System, he led one of the nation's largest and most respected systems of higher education. As the chief executive officer of the UT System, McRaven oversaw 14 institutions that educated 220,000 students and employed 20,000 faculty and more than 80,000 health care professionals, researchers, and staff.

Admiral McRaven is a recognized national authority on US foreign policy and has advised Presidents George W. Bush, Barack Obama, and other US leaders on defense issues. He currently serves on the Council on Foreign Relations (CFR), the National Football Foundation, the International Crisis Group, The Mission Continues, and ConocoPhillips.

Admiral McRaven graduated from the University of Texas at Austin in 1977 with a degree in journalism and received his master's degree from the Naval Postgraduate School in Monterey in 1991.

He met his wife, Georgeann, while they were students at UT Austin, and they have three grown children. Admiral McRaven stays active with his writing, speaking, and board commitments.

Photo credit: © Cameron Powell

"I don't know if it takes falling apart to be found, but I really feel found...."

—Amy Grant

Amy Grant

Most students of the culture would agree that the birth, if not the golden age, of contemporary Christian music began in the late 1960s to early 1970s. Over the years that followed the genre grew, as did the number of artists. B. J. Thomas, Sandi Patty, Evie Tornquist, Andraé Crouch, Al Green, and . . . a bright-eyed, faith-filled teenager named Amy Grant.

A few years after Amy came on the scene, I became quite serious about my faith, which I nourished with the help of mentors, Christian friends, Bible studies, prayers, and Christian music. I listened liberally to all of the artists mentioned above, and that included Amy Grant.

Laura and I were fans of Amy way before we ever met her, and that admiration continued into and through her transitions into secular music. Without going into the particulars, I was a bit stunned when, many years later, she accepted my invitation to come and perform at St. Martin's in Houston, as well as speak to a community-wide gathering of women about her own faith and family journeys. I think it is safe to say, that from that point on, Laura and I were blessed to consider Amy a friend.

Over the years that passed, we learned that the person you see on stage and screen is actually the same person in quiet conversations of two or three. There were times when we asked for prayers for one another over this matter and that. In the summer of 2022, we were in the midst of making plans for a return visit to St. Martin's, when [Amy] had a major bike accident. She was riding down a large hill, hit an unforeseen pothole, and was tossed from her bike to the ground, suffering, among other injuries, a severe concussion. At first, she had hoped to snap back, and we even landed on a date for her visit to Houston. But, after a few months, it became clear to Amy and those around her that her full recovery would take longer than hoped for or expected.

It would be over a year before she did make that return visit to St. Martin's. Her concert was a smashing hit and ended with a standing ovation. That evening, when it was over, we briefly spoke about a talk she was to give the next morning, once again, to hundreds who gathered to hear her in the church's parish hall.

"How do you want this to go?" she asked me.

"However you want it to go! People are just thrilled to have you!" I said, then added, "You have an hour if you want that long."

She laughed and said, "I can fill an hour!" Then, with the innocent honesty of a young child, she said, "I am still recovering a bit, and I may call you in the morning and say, 'Let's do this a different way . . . you ask questions, and I can answer them.'"

"Whatever you want to do," I replied.

"Is it okay if I bring my guitar?"

"I think folks would love it!"

"I don't know if I'll sing, but holding onto it makes me more comfortable."

She did bring her guitar. She did talk for an hour, without notes and without questions and answers. And she did sing a bit, and she reminded everyone why her star shines as brightly in her sixties as when she inspired others with her first major contemporary Christian hit, "El Shaddai."[1]

Since that time, our friendship has grown, and in pulling this work together, I knew I had to include a conversation with Amy. We met in her Nashville home, prayed, and talked and, well, she even sang a bit! After we caught up and spent some time talking about her ongoing recovery from the bike accident, she joked that she was still in the healing process and that "we're all in this, and we're just doing the best we can!"

Is there a moment to which you could point when you began experiencing God's presence in your life?

In some ways, that's a hard question to answer, because I can't point to one moment, but instead, many. Music was at the heart of it, though. I grew up in a church that had a lot of hymn singing. I remember standing next to my great-grandmother and hearing her sing. She was a short woman but had a wonderful alto voice. To be honest, I can't recall one sermon I heard in my growing up years, but music really shaped my understanding of God.

Beyond the music, nature. I was the youngest of four sisters and we spent a lot of time playing outside. We loved spending time in the undergrowth on the hillside where we lived, which was on the backside of my grandmother's farm. I liked to create these little forts—habitats to really be drawn into nature. I had always been so curious about God.

But it was out in nature that I felt, and feel, the presence of God. I have sometimes felt like everything in nature is like a secret pointing back to God and when I experience connectivity to nature, I also feel like I am experiencing the divine.

When I really started to grow in my faith, I found myself offering what I will call a "wordless prayer," and often it was God's creation that would inspire that.

What role did your parents play in shaping your faith journey?

Well, like I said, we were a churchgoing family, so it was something my parents modeled for my sisters and me, but I love the way my mother communicated faith and God to me, in such a loving and gentle way. The way I heard it explained by her, and have come to believe, is that faith is just a never-ending journey. We're always growing, experiencing, changing.

One of the things I love to do is plant seeds and watch them grow. That's been a great metaphor for how I understand my faith.

You were baptized on a Sunday night in May of 1973—the spring of your seventh-grade year—and you have described that as a celebration moment—being "forever transferred from the kingdom of darkness to the kingdom of light."[2] Knowing we are going to talk about the evolution of your faith journey—looking back on that moment—how would you describe that moment—was it an actual profession of faith? Is that when, as we Christians say, you invited Jesus into your heart and accepted Him as Lord and Savior? Or was it something different than that?

Well, I really had already accepting Christ into my heart, but I wanted to get baptized. We were attending the Church of Christ at that time, and once someone professed their faith, you got baptized; so it is what I chose to do. But the baptism was scheduled for a Sunday night, and it happened to be the same night the local Episcopal Church youth group was sponsoring a dance.

The baptismal area was behind the pulpit, and I think the pastor could tell I was worried about getting my hair wet and messing it up before the dance, and he said something like, "Don't worry about your hair." But, I WAS worried about my hair! But of course, that's the way seventh-grade girls on the way to the dance think, regardless of baptism! But I did so love God, and it was all part of the continuum of my faith.

You have shared the story about a particular moment in your friendship with Sarah Cannon (Minnie Pearl) when she asked you if you knew the most important crayon in the coloring box—and while you were trying to figure it out, she said, "Black, . . . without black everything appears flat, . . . without black there is no depth" (p. xvii).[3] Amy, can you say a bit more about that—generally? (I'll get to specifically a bit later.) Just generally—how do you believe our darkest times add depth to every other experience?

Let me back up a bit. Years ago, I was spending a day with a fantastic blues artist named Kevin Moore.[4] We were headed over to one of his friend's houses for a recording session when the friend called and said, "Don't come over, don't come, my wife has just asked me for a divorce." He was hysterical, and I said to Kevin, "We're not going to your friend's house, . . . his life is in turmoil now." And Kevin said something powerful to me. He said his wife had just given him the gift of a long, hard look in the mirror. And I remember thinking, "Whoa."

He was saying that someone can have this tumultuous moment, where things happen that kind of bring all of life to an immediate stop, and you are given the opportunity to take real stock in your life and start assessing what has been and what is.

That is exactly the way I felt when I had that bike accident. At that moment, my life really simplified. Before it happened, I had been thinking there were some changes that I knew I needed to be making in my life. I don't recall this, but the friend I was biking with said that when we stopped at the top of the hill before the accident, I was actually saying, "I'm spread too thin, and I don't know how to make these changes in my life."

Then—well, bam. I am in the hospital, in the ICU actually, all banged up. And while I don't remember this either, my friend told me one of the funny things I said: "I can't believe I still have all my teeth." But then she told me that I said, "I needed this."

All of it really helped me tune into stories of tragedy that come with life lessons. I'll give you an example.

I was watching Oprah Winfrey, and she was interviewing a man who had been on her show a lot. He was a kind gay man, and his partner died in that horrible tsunami.[5] He said, on that day, his life changed forever. But he went on to say even though it was tragic, he also experienced the beauty of human nature when so many people began to reach out and help.

So, well, yes, . . . most of us don't have to live too long to experience something awful, but there is often good imbedded in it somewhere. The older you get, you find life has both—tragedy and beauty, and they are often connected in some ways.

I really think all of that becomes clearer as you get older . . . and you begin to see the end of life, which of course makes everything more precious.

It's funny, because in talking with my children, they see all of life through that youthful lens, a generation younger than me—and I think, "Well, when they get to my age, they're going to see it." It really doesn't make sense for me to try and tell them what the road looks like from here, because they are not here yet.

You wrote a lovely, thought-provoking poem entitled "Who Am I," which includes the lines "Who I am . . . does it matter anyway . . . Who I am . . . And what I've learned along the way . . . Who I am . . . changes a little every day. . . ."[6]

You have written about looking in the mirror and seeing some gray hairs, a few wrinkles and you consciously choosing to accept the passage of time. You've also written, in a culture that worships youth and beauty, the process of aging is not the feel-good experience everyone is looking for. What would you say to the forty-, fifty-, and sixty-year-olds who may read this and be battling against the passage of time?

What you think matters when you're young, does not matter when you are older. It's about that simple. I mean, age just beats it out of you. You can't stop the hands of time. You look ahead at what aging might bring and think, "I'm not going to celebrate that! I'll never celebrate my first gray hair, or those bags under my eyes, or my aging skin." But, you know, you can either look at it that way, or come to the point where you decide, "Maybe it's better just to make friends with myself."

More importantly, what would you say to younger adults, even teens—who get swept up in that whirlpool?

Honestly, I think it would be better to reframe death for every person, you know. Because when you are younger—everybody's figuring out what they are going to do for the summer . . . or graduating . . . who's getting married . . . who's having a baby . . . but at my age, every week somebody we love has passed away. And I mean *every* . . . week.

And as I was facing all of that, at some point in the last year, I just said to myself, "I am going to reframe this, because none of us knows where the end of the line is. . . ." What to say to young people? "You are made in the image of God, so let's figure out what really matters and be very intentional about the way we live our lives."

*Your first record came out in [1977]—*Amy Grant, *and it's safe to say your vocation as an artist, songwriter, and singer basically exploded. Where did you see God's hand at work in those earliest years of your career?*

Well, Russ, you know, I was a hard worker, and this may surprise some of your readers, but I never dreamed of being a singer. There were always better singers than me in the room. But doors started opening up for me, and I walked through them. But I never had an end goal, just one door at a time.

My passion is probably not what a lot of people think it is either. My passion has never been singing. Instead, I love creating spaces that allow people to see life differently. And that can be a camp for kids or, yes, on a stage. But in all of those settings—a song, a story, a get-together, a concert—sometimes, suddenly people see themselves differently, and that opens the door to see other people differently. And a lot of times, once that happens, people see God differently. It is about opening up spaces of creativity and hospitality that bring people together—THAT is my passion, and music just happened to be my primary tool in doing that.

But as your career started taking off, was Jesus sort of your cheerleader?

I think the way I experienced Jesus during that time was just to be grateful. I realized it all came from him. Regardless of whatever environment I was in, it all was working together where I felt I was getting to know God better, and realizing I was "known" by God. It was just—well—God, in everything.

Amy, you have been so transparent about one of the hardest seasons of your life—your separation and divorce from your first husband and father of your first three children, Gary Chapman.
    As someone who has walked with perhaps hundreds of folks through a divorce over the years, I have my own perspective on how and why divorce is sometimes the best way forward—but how have you come to see that in your own life? Was there a "straw" that was the "last straw," or was it a series of things, moments? And, despite how difficult it was, did you experience our Lord in that season?

I think during that time of my life was the most profound game-changing season for feeling the presence of God. It was not, of course, the first time I felt God's presence, but something happened to me when I went through divorce that I had never before experienced.
    Yes, I had fallen in love with another man. And no, we were not having an affair. But at the time, I had three children, everything was becoming overwhelming. I remember walking out of the back of our home, a big, beautiful farmhouse, and I just fell down on the dirt.
    I mean, my face was in the grass and dirt, and I began to weep. I was crying and crying and crying some more. I remember thinking at the time, "How many lives am I ruining?" And I said, "God, I'm so sorry." And—well, whew, I cannot even explain it, but all the sudden God covered me—completely, it was like this blanket of calm, and peace.

It was like, "Okay, I've fallen off the cliff by myself," but then, in that moment, I realized I was not alone.

That was one time, but there was another when I was out in Los Angeles. On the outside, a lot of things seemed good. Work was going great.

But on this trip, I was sitting in my hotel room all by myself, and I was listening to a cassette (which tells you how long ago it was!). My first marriage was never easy, in fact, it wasn't from the beginning. And I was sitting there listening to this music, thinking about how hard my marriage had become.

I decided to just be really still and quiet and I tried to imagine myself crawling up into God's lap. And it was as if I was there long enough to really let my fears come out. And again, all of the sudden, I just burst into tears. And again, I was asking myself, "What are you doing?" I again started thinking about my children and wondering if my kids were going to be destroyed because of divorce.

And then, I experienced an almost audible voice, three words, "I've got them." It was profound.

When you knew your marriage would likely end, you felt compelled to tell evangelist Billy Graham because of the times you had played at his crusades, and because of your own personal relationship. He said something very poignant—"God is always at work in our lives, even when we take the long way home."[7]

Yeah, and he was right. That's true about a lot of things. My kids have had their own challenges growing up, and when they get themselves in trouble, I try [to] say things like, "It's a long haul, if you spend your life trying to amuse yourself." But sometimes you just have to figure that out on your own.

Now, looking back, before the divorce, I had all kinds of things happening that felt a long way from where I wanted to be. But honestly, they were things that helped tune my ears in a way that I could listen to God.

It's not always easy for children of people who live in the public eye like you have, how has that played out in your home?

That's a great question. I love getting to sing for people, but that is not how I identify myself as a human. How I identify myself is by believing, . . . I am alive, . . . I am a child of God, . . . and I am an appreciator of the world.

I want to feel a sense of purpose, and I want to experience creativity with my fellow man.

But I was very intentional about not bringing my work home. I don't have any of my old records around the house. My kids don't normally come to my concerts except our annual Christmas concert in Nashville—so they know me as singing Christmas music. For instance, my youngest daughter doesn't even know a lot of the other songs I sing, because I did most of my recordings before she was born!

Not too long ago, she cracked me up, because she came to one of my concerts and, afterwards, she called me up and said, "Just in case you need reminding today, you are so cool! You're amazing! You are so freaking cool!"

But I am thinking in the back of my mind, when I recorded a lot of those, it was about thirty years ago, that's a chapter in the story of my life, but it is not at the core of who I am, and it's not what we sit around and talk about at the dinner table.

Praying for children is a full-time job for a parent. How do you pray for your children?

You know, my main prayer for my kids is to say, "God, find them the way you found me. Lead them into the faith the way you led me."

You and Vince married in 2000, and it was in this relationship that you say you experienced authentic love. That, alone, is a life lesson about how to live as a married couple—but how did you see God's hands in the birth of your relationship with Vince then and now, some quarter of a century later?

There was a day when I was unloading a bit on him, and he responded, "Amy, . . . I love you. . . . I can't say I always understand you. . . . What I can say is that I welcome you. I welcome you and whatever you bring to the table is enough."[8]

Kindness.... Kindness goes a long way. And Vince is kind. I am a talker. I love processing with words and Vince is such a quiet man. We talk more now than we ever did, and that took a long time. But he was welcoming of me from the beginning, and I think early on, I was critical of him. I wanted him to be different than the way I was experiencing him, and I did not realize what I was doing.

I wanted Vince to be all the things I had projected onto him—and, I guess a lot of couples do that. But I do think if you have been married before, as I was, you try and project all the things you want onto your new spouse. And one day Vince said to me, "Someday, you'll wake up and realize who I am *not*." And that was an important moment for me.

When I finally stopped looking for all the things I had projected onto him—that were not really him at all—things I would never find, I was able to discover who he really is and all the wonderful things he brings to our marriage, well that brought about a beautiful change.

So I guess that's my advice—love the person for who they are, not for who they are not—and, well, be kind. Vince sure is kind to me.

When you were in your forties, you wrote that "the beauty of being in the middle of life is the vantage point it provides."[9] Now—roughly twenty years later, in your early sixties—what beautiful things are you learning by this season of life?

I don't want to sound silly, but it is not the big things in life, but the little details of life that make me want to lean in. Can I tell you a story?

Of course.

So, we were somewhere out in Arizona, and I was singing with the symphony. We were traveling by plane, not a tour bus, which means a hotel room, and it also means we're not schlepping all of our gear everywhere. Later, this van is going to pick the band up and take us to rehearsal.

So, I have a little coin collection, which I keep at home in one of those gigantic plastic jugs—pretzels or something came in it. I was inspired to do that by the book, *A Tree Grows in Brooklyn*.[10] The mother in the book had a tin can, and she would toss coins into it, to save, in case they had a family emergency.

But when I was waiting in that hotel room, I decided to go through my backpack, my purse, my pockets, and my luggage and put any coins together to take home. I gathered them all together, and tossed them into this little jewelry pouch, a little bag, and I cinched it up tight and threw it in my backpack.

Before we get picked up, I put on only what I am going to wear that night and grab my backpack.

Here's where your question comes in about leaning into the little things. I am more intentional about staying open to what God might do at any moment and in any particular situation. So I am trying to stay open to ways God will show up and I am watching, and I am listening.

Now I know this seems like such a tiny thing, but here you go. So we get out, and we're walking to the back of the concert hall, and this man comes up with his daughter. I don't think they are homeless, but they do look slightly disheveled. And he says, "Excuse me, I don't want to bother you, but my daughter and I need bus fare."

Somebody in our group said, "I have a daughter, and I know how important this must be," and she opened up her purse and handed him a $5 dollar bill. He said, "Thank you so much, but they only accept coins."

And by then, I realized why I tossed my bag of coins into my backpack. I pulled out that little pouch and told him it was full of coins, but I did not know how much was in there, so maybe he should count it out first. He did, and, well, it was the exact amount of the bus fare.

So, the older I get, a big question for me, at least, is: "Am I listening to God? Is there something I need to know? Is there something God wants me to do?"

And the more I listen, the more I experience stories like that one I just told you!

The older I get, the more I want to feel a sense of purpose, and I want to experience connectivity with all those I encounter.

You have confessed—you want to be led by Jesus in your life, but you find that hard—because you do not relax enough and tend to push back against directives. When do you find it most difficult to follow?

It's probably not so much "when," as it is "who." I'm just not a good follower in general, so a lot of who I am just tends to push back on someone else taking the lead. But I do believe God knows where he wants to take me and that He'll get me there, regardless of me!

Can you share a bit about your prayer life? When, where, how do you pray?

It's different every day. I don't have a regular time and place, every day. Some days I roll out of bed, and I hit my knees. Sometimes it is with words, and other times just sounds.

A lot of times when I pray there are all kinds of pictures going through my head, and I don't have enough words to wrap around them, so what I do is just bring all those thoughts into the presence of God—that's the way I prayed today.

Sometimes it feels like I am praying without ceasing and other times just when the Spirit moves me. My hunch is someone's prayer life is like most things in life, it changes over time, . . . it certainly has for me.

I have kind of an underlying mantra—"Holy, Holy, Holy is the Lord God Almighty, Who was and is and is to come."

Of course, I pray for my kids. Mostly, for them, I ask the Lord to give them somebody who will make them feel loved and cared for.

Life does get in the way. Let me tell you about an important life lesson on prayer I got from my first mother-in-law. It was back in the early '90s and I was having a lot of music success. At the same time, I had a young child. One morning we were sitting around the coffee pot, and I told her, "I don't think I've said a succinct prayer in two weeks. . . . I'm just exhausted."

And she said, "Amy, sometimes it just takes one good prayer."

I asked her, "Will you tell me that prayer?"

And she said, "Just pray: 'Lord, lead me today to those I need and those who need me and let something I do have eternal significance.'"

So that's a prayer I pray often!

Any others?

Yes, I like to pray, "Let me receive what you have to give me."

What about other spiritual disciplines?

I love the Scriptures. There have been times in my life when I really have studied them intently. I developed this habit of committing to memory a few specific Scriptures that remind me of the whole picture.

I thought about this before we got together today because one of my practices is actually singing the scriptures. I remember about twenty years ago, one of my managers asked me, "What do you want to do musically?" And I said, "All I want to do is put Scripture to music."

So, do you have a favorite verse?

I do! Can I sing it for you?

Of course.

Like today, this morning, as the day began, I started singing in the shower. *(Amy sings now.)* "In the beginning was the Word, and the Word was with God and the Word was God. . . .

"He was with God in the beginning. Through him, all things were made. Without him, nothing was made that has been made. . . .

"And in him was life, and that life was the light of men. . . .

"The light shines in the darkness, but the darkness has not understood it.

"There came a man, who was sent from God. His name was John."[11]

You know, knowledge about something is not relationship with something, and learning the Scriptures in this way, memorizing them, singing them, brings them to life for me. They are not just words on a page, they lead me into a deeper relationship with God.

A lot of people feel like—if one becomes a Christian and faithfully follows the Lord—says their prayers, goes to church, reads the Bible—then everything else in their life will run smoothly—they will be "blessed." The worst expression of this theological bent is probably the prosperity Gospel, but if ever there was a poster child for one who has faithfully given their life to our

Lord, and, at the same time, suffered a number of blows—it is certainly Amy Grant, particularly over the last few years.

The pushback and character assault after your divorce, your mother's death in 2001, your father's death in 2018, your unexpected heart surgery in 2020, your bike accident and traumatic brain injury in 2022, and your throat surgery in 2023. One of those challenges is enough, but you have had one after another—and yet—here you are! Still smiling, . . . still singing, . . . still believing, . . . still trusting. I heard you interviewed after one of these moments, and you said that even the most awful and worst of life's tragedies can have redemptive qualities within them. Here is where, I think, you can really help the readers of this book. What would you say to others who walk with our Lord and yet experience tremendous heartache or tragedy?

So these experiences have allowed me to do more than just think about what we believe; instead, they have actually deepened my relationship with God—all of these things we have been talking about—prayer, the kindness of others, trusting in the promises of God's faithfulness, in the Scriptures—these have helped.

But I'm still a rascal. I have my doubts and weak moments like anyone, but I keep at it and God is faithful.

Learning to practice gratitude, for everything, has become more and more important for me. After my bike accident, I am retraining my brain, but there have been so many helpful people along the way—doctors, friends.

Years ago, a good friend of mine, Ruth, was diagnosed with cancer. One day, after she had been going through all the treatments, I went to visit her. She looked beat up, had lost all her hair.

And she said, "Amy, as awful as this has been, I'm grateful for the gift of cancer. The experience of being weak, having to depend on others, has made me grateful for every piece of my life, even the hard suff. I am grateful for my family, for my health, . . . if I could bottle it up and give it to you to drink, I would. I don't know how much longer I have—months, or years, or decades—that's okay, because really the uncertainty of life makes every day a gift."

I see now, even more, the wisdom in her words.

Your distillation of the Good News of the Gospel hits the nail on the proverbial head: "The real work of Jesus is forgiveness. It is not our good behavior that puts us in right standing with God. No one is that good. But instead it is believing in and receiving the work that Jesus did on the cross on our behalf."[12] *Amen to that. How has that understanding brought healing to your own life?*

All of us tend to see life through our own lens, which tends to make us want to just operate out of our own self-interests. But God is faithful, and we are all living under the wings of His mercy and forgiveness and that helps me be patient with myself when I am not perfect and, well, it allows me to be more open to other people. I remember there were times in my life when I would think on Jesus's words, "Father forgive them, for they do not know what they are doing." And I would pray, "I hope you spoke that over every person."[13] I believe Jesus did, and that's good news for me, . . . it's good news for all of us, because who does not need mercy and forgiveness?

And now we come to the point of this interview and this book where I ask all this question. In the world's eyes, and by the world's standards, Amy Grant has achieved fame, notoriety, success, wealth. You count among your friends great actors, singers, and more than a few of our presidents. You have Grammy and Dove nominations and awards, and most recently, were honored at the Kennedy Center. But what would you say to those who believe that these are the things that make life worth living?

I guess I do have a lot of those things—maybe I have all of those things. I would say that they are not what make me feel alive, because what does allow me to experience the fullness of life is all of those intimate relationships and exchanges in life—even the wordless exchanges.

I'd have to say, I don't know what it would feel like every day wondering if my children would be fed or have a roof over their head. I don't have a terminal disease at this point in my life, so I am not facing that.

When you ask me that question, what I can speak to directly is that I do know that is the kind of list a lot of people say to go for—but all of those things are like a shiny bell that rings for just a minute. But they are not an answer to any deeper longing. They are not the answer to any deeper connection or purpose. It's not different than the dopamine hits people get from getting a thumbs up on [their] social media pages—and it lasts about that long.

Did you just come up with that?

Yeah, I did, because I mean when my life was the most public and I was at the pinnacle of my career, singing to the largest audiences is when I was the most lost and lonely. It was when I was falling apart. I don't know if it takes falling apart to be found, but I really feel found. I think that in my own moments of crises, those became the events that significantly built my trust in God.

AMY GRANT

Amy Grant's career spans more than forty years and stretches from her roots in gospel into becoming an iconic pop star, songwriter, television personality, and philanthropist. With three multi-platinum albums, six platinum albums, and four gold albums, her total career album sales have exceeded $30 million and over one billion global streams. Grant's chart success has been consistent throughout her career with six No. 1 hits, ten Top 40 pop singles, seventeen Top 40 Adult Contemporary tracks, and multiple Contemporary Christian chart-toppers. In addition to her six GRAMMY® Awards, Grant has earned twenty-six GMA Dove Awards (including four Artist of the Year Awards) and has been awarded a star on the Hollywood Walk of Fame, as well as the Music City Walk of Fame, and the Nashville Songwriters Hall of Fame.

In 2020, the T.J. Martell Foundation—the music industry's leading nonprofit to fund innovative medical research focused on treatments and cures for cancer—honored Grant with the Tony Martell Outstanding Entertainment Achievement Award at their annual Honors Gala. Most recently, The John F. Kennedy Center for the Performing Arts included Grant as one of their five distinguished honorees to receive the 45th Kennedy Center Honors for lifetime artistic achievements. In 2023, Grant toured in seventy cities across the country and released her first new music in a decade, starting with the single "Trees We'll Never See" (March) and "What You Heard" (April). Grant released *Lead Me On Live 1989* in October 2023, which is a full-concert documentation from the 1988-1989 Lead Me On Tour. Grant finished the year with two Christmas tours, including dates with Michael W. Smith, as well as the annual Christmas at the Ryman residency with Vince Gill, which celebrated over 100 headline shows at the Ryman, the first co-headliners to mark this incredible milestone.

In 2024, Grant toured the country playing thirty-three shows in the spring, including two headlining shows at the Ryman Auditorium over Mother's Day weekend. She released the long-sought-after *Songs from the Loft* album, (originally released in 1993), for the first time on digital formats. This past fall, Grant released an "Expanded Anniversary Edition" of her classic album, *House Of Love*, with never before heard tracks and remixes and recently finished a twenty-plus show headlining tour featuring many songs from *House Of Love*. Grant will finish the year with the annual Christmas at the Ryman residency with Vince Gill, featuring songs from their recent *When I Think of Christmas* album. Grant is also writing songs for her next musical project to release in 2025.

Photo credit: © Courtesy of the author

"Fear not, I am with thee...."

—Isaiah 41:10

The Honorable James A. Baker III

It would be impossible for anyone to consider the monumental shifts in the tectonic plates of international and national civic, political, and military policies of the 1980s and 1990s without, at the same time, lifting up a person who was at the very center, if not taking the lead, of those decisions that changed history. Few people in American history have held as many prominent roles in American government as James Addison Baker III.

Serving as the lead architect for no less than five presidents' campaigns, Secretary Baker served as US secretary of the treasury under President Gerald Ford from 1975 to 1976; as tenth White House chief of staff under President Reagan from 1981 to 1985; as US secretary of the treasury under President Ronald Reagan from 1985 to 1988; as secretary of state under President George H. W. Bush from 1989 to 1992, and as the sixteenth White House chief of staff under President Bush from 1992-1993.

As I have shared with you in the preface, my relationships with those throughout this book vary in their depth—some I have known only recently, but some I first met decades ago, and such is the case with my counselor, my friend, my mentor, and my brother in Christ, James "Jimmy" Baker.

From my teen years on, I was always keen to study politics and the machinations of government, which also meant I was tuned into who was in elected and appointed offices, regardless of their party affiliation.

I had long admired Secretary Baker from afar, so you can imagine how I felt when I saw him emerge from his motorcade that had pulled up and stopped on North Columbus Street, just outside of the Churchyard of historic Christ Church in Alexandria, Virginia.

As part of my seminary training, I served Christ Church for two of the three years of my studies. Among the many duties of the seminarians on staff was to walk the grounds and buildings before and between worship services to make sure things were in order.

In all honesty, when I saw Secretary Baker, my heart skipped a beat—he did not know who I was, but I certainly knew who he was. "Good morning, Mr. Secretary," I offered.

"Good morning," he said with a smile and outstretched hand, "I am here to attend the baptism of my grandchild."

I knew there was a private baptism service being held between worship opportunities that morning, so I pointed the way, and after thanking me, he went on his way.

That would be the last time I had any interaction with him, until some sixteen years later. I had just been called as the fourth rector of St. Martin's Episcopal Church but was still finishing out my post as rector of Christ Church in Pensacola, Florida. My cell phone rang, and when I picked it up, without introduction, I heard, "Hello, is this Russ Levenson?"

"Yes, it is."

"This is James Baker, and I wanted to welcome you to your new post."

"How are you?" (I uttered the only words I could think of at that moment that caught me completely off guard.)

"If I were any better, there would have to be two of me to enjoy it all."

I had no idea that once I settled into my new position at St. Martin's that Secretary Baker would not only be someone to whom I turned for advice and counsel, but along with his wife, Susan, he would come a close friend.

In my book, *Witness to Dignity: The Life and Faith of George H. W. and Barbara Bush*, I have written in more detail about the many ways in which my relationship with Secretary Baker and our forty-first president, George H. W. Bush, also a member of St. Martin's, overlapped—including the moment when both of us were kneeling in prayer at the bedside of President Bush when his life ended.[1]

But I learned so much more from Secretary Baker as we worshipped together, prayed together, took long walks, and had long talks on his ranch in south Texas. I recall one time when we sat whispering on a chilly morning in a deer blind in which he allowed me to pepper him with questions about all the work he had done for five of our US presidents, his role in the end of the Cold War, the liberation of Kuwait, and so much more. His words, "there would have to be two of me to enjoy it all," seemed to invite a thought: "There must have been ten of you to accomplish all you did!"

By the time of this interview, I had lost count of the number of times we had visited privately together, many of those times in prayer—in which I saw displayed his reverent devotion and commitment to our Lord and his faith.

At the time of this interview, he was recovering from a fall down the stairs, which resulted in the fracture of his L1 vertebra, and months of recovery and rehabilitation after major back surgery. Though ninety-four years of age, he did not skip a beat and was looking forward to his ninety-fifth birthday, which he hoped to spend in Africa on safari!

But as you will read, throughout all of nearly ten decades of life, God has been a source of comfort in times of need, strength in seasons of extraordinary challenges, and guidance to serve in the many roles life has afforded him.

Over the years in your speeches and in your writing, you speak openly about your parents—and have described them as "austere" and "strict disciplinarians."[2] What was their approach to Church and the faith in your childhood years?

Well, it's true that both of my parents believed in discipline and order and in following through on the promises you made—completing the job. My dad was so strict with us that some of my friends and I nicknamed him "the warden." That said, he was the best father anybody could ever have had, but he did expect us to toe the line. Mom was a little bit different in the way she went about her parenting. She kept telling me, "Jimmy, you've got a wonderful legacy, and now it's up to you to live up to it." But in all honesty, my mom is the one, Russ, that kept me on board with my faith and spirituality.

Mom was—for a number of years—a Christian Scientist. She made sure we went to Sunday school here in Houston. I don't remember much about it, but she made sure my sister and I were always there! At home, my mom routinely read Psalm 91 to my sister and me, and this was a particular comfort when Dad was overseas in the trenches of World War I.

But I'd have to say it was mom who kept me—well, who most kept me—focused on my faith and on religion. Was she a practicing Christian Scientist? I honestly do not know, because we went to plenty of doctors growing up, and I know that by the time of her death, she was no longer connected to that branch of religion. So, despite her participation in the community of church, I do not think she took fully to their doctrine.[3]

Can you recall a moment, or a season, when God became more than a word for you? Was there a gentle or more profound epiphany about faith in your younger years?

Well, I don't remember any "shazam!" type moment. I really do not. My faith has strengthened me since I began as a student at the Hill School. Chapel was mandatory every day—you didn't skip or you got in big trouble![4] But that is really where my faith began to crystalize. In the beginning, I thought it would be terrible to have to "go to church every day." But after the first year or so there, I really began to enjoy chapel, and I think the other students found that to be true as well.

You joined St. Martin's Episcopal Church in Houston, Texas, following your first wife and mother of four boys, joining first as a baptized member on October 31, 1961, and then going through confirmation classes and being confirmed as an Episcopalian on May 24, 1964. What drew you to the Episcopal Church (perhaps besides Mary Stuart!)?

When I met Mary Stuart, I had been attending a Presbyterian church, but when we married in 1953, I had decided she was a much better Episcopalian than I was a Presbyterian! And my father's sister, my aunt, and a number of family friends attended Palmer Memorial Episcopal Church in Houston, so for a while we attended there. But once Mary Stuart and I got married in 1953, and we began to build a family, Mary Stuart really wanted to raise our boys in the Episcopal Church, and so we eventually began going to St. Martin's. I actually attended membership classes with my lifelong friend, George H. W. Bush, and became a confirmed member on May 24, 1964.

Mary Stuart seemed to have deep faith that sustained her, especially after her diagnosis with cancer and as she approached her own mortality. You have said that her faith was a source of comfort and courage as she faced her own death. How did her faith impact your own?

That's correct. Her faith was a great comfort to her and frankly to me, even though neither one of us wanted to burden the other with the knowledge that she wasn't going to get well. We just did not talk about it much, and that was the approach we ended up taking with the boys. I am not sure to this day if that was the right approach, because her death came to them as a huge shock. After her death, her father actually got a little upset about the fact that I did not share more with them.

But Russ, I didn't share how sick she was with anybody other than George Bush. There was some hope that I would run for his congressional seat, but I could not because of Mary Stuart's illness.[5] And, I desperately didn't want it to get back to her that she was going to die. We just did not discuss it. I think she knew it, but her faith was a great strength to her, and because it was to her, it became so to me.

I tell people all the time, she showed me how to die. She was very brave, . . . very brave. You know, she would say, "Oh, I don't feel good" or "I hurt," but she was really strong at the end. In fact, she even designed a home we built on Green Tree Road in Houston—your road—which she never got a chance to live in.[6]

I was able to take her over to the house before she died. It was about two-thirds finished, and I took her in a wheelchair. I wheeled her into that beautiful living room that she created with a fireplace, and she really liked it, but never got a chance to live in it, and I regret that.

And, honestly, I regret the fact that God decided that she needed to go. But she had great strength and great dignity at the end, and that's why I say she showed me how to die.

When she was first diagnosed with cancer and then, of course, after her death, did you feel or experience the comfort of God?

Well, yeah, it is my faith that kept me going through that difficult time, and I believed, and believe today, that she's up there in heaven and that I am going to see her again. I really believe that.

I need to add that I was totally unqualified to deal with her death, in part because I was unqualified to deal with my four boys on my own—they were hellions! They were ages seven to fifteen, and I would come home in the evening, and the caretaker would be there, and they would be running her ragged all day and she couldn't do anything, so I would just retire to my library and have a strict drink. . . . I mean a stiff . . . stiff drink!

Though it is hard to read, her November 29, 1969, letter to you, which you found after her death, addressed to "My dear sweet and loveable Jimmy," ended with "God and I will watch over you and the boys and keep you safe." While I know her death was devastating to you and your sons, did you experience her presence in this way? Did you feel she and God together, perhaps, were "watching over you"?[7]

Absolutely. Every time I think about that letter, it's hard. It's really hard. I mean, that's also part of why I say she taught me how to die—how brave was that?! Writing to me in great detail about her impending departure. I mean, it was a lovely letter, and I read it occasionally still, and I break up every time I read it.

And at the end of that letter, she wrote, "Don't be sad. Rejoice and come to me someday."[8]

Yes, she said "come see me," but she did not say "come see me soon." And she also wrote that the boys will be fine because "they're half you." Russ, that's on her tombstone: "Rejoice and come to me."

I went out there recently, because her birthday was May 7th, and it was also around Mother's Day. Every time I go out there, it's a solid, sad experience. But God has helped me through it and has helped me in so many ways.

You have been fortunate not only to have one love of your life, but two. Though she grew up a Roman Catholic, Susan Garrett also found her way into the Episcopal Church and St. Martin's, and like Mary Stuart, her faith is a very important part of her everyday life. I once heard you say that one of the first sounds you heard in the morning was Susan's knees hitting the floor for prayer. That is a beautiful portrait, but again, how has Susan's own faith impacted your own?[9]

As we talk about my faith, I can only say, "Boy, look at my wives." Susan had, and has, a deep faith. But you know, the first rector of St. Martin's, Tom Bagby, was old school, and because Susan was divorced, he would not marry us! So we chose to get married at First Presbyterian Church in Houston, but that did not give me cause or reason to leave the church, where our faith was being nourished. As the years went on, Tom was very kind to Susan and me. But I will say, I always regret that we did not get married in the Episcopal Church because that is where I really committed to our Lord and the faith.

And yes, . . . Susan begins her mornings in prayer and her faith is strong, . . . strong, . . . strong! And it has been throughout our marriage, probably a lot stronger than mine, but it has helped me. If I am honest, I have had my doubts along the way, and I don't know a Christian that has not had some doubts.

I remember you told me that shortly before his death, George asked you if he would see his daughter, Robin, in heaven.[10] And that's the way I feel. I want to know if I'm going to see my parents, Mary Stuart, and other loved ones who have gone on.

But, because I believe in Jesus Christ, and his promises, I do believe I will go to heaven. I don't know what it's going to be like. Will we all be going up to sit on a cumulus cloud? How old will my loved ones be? But I do not have any doubts about life after death, and those reunions, because of my personal faith.

One of the favorite quotes of your lifetime friend George H. W. Bush is his remark the day he was sworn in as vice president, "Who'da thunk it?" But you have gone on to say the same of your own vocational track—serving six American presidents and serving in three senior government positions. Looking back now, what role, if any, do you feel God played in the remarkable historic moments in which you played such an important part?[11]

Well, I think God played a humongous role in it because—first of all—I never intended to have a second career in politics or public service. And with the help of George Bush and others, I think God directed me there. To have run two campaigns against Ronald Reagan and then be asked to be Reagan's White House chief of staff!?

Every year now, since George has been gone, I go up to College Station and I take flowers up to his grave site and I put them there, with a little note that reads, "Heffy, who'd of thunk it?"[12] For example, when I was asked to run George Bush's campaign for president, everyone kept asking me "What are you doing?," because we really did not have a snowball's chance in hell of winning. At the time, Texas Republicans wanted John Connolly to be president, but George was my friend, and he was so well qualified.

How could all that followed have happened were it not for God's guidance and my faith in Him? Sometimes, I still cannot believe it. For instance, I never contemplated being secretary of state of the United States![13]

In her senior years, when she was in her mid-nineties, my mother used to ask me, "Jimmy, darling, now tell me what it is you do?" And I would remind her, "Well, Mother, I'm the secretary of state of the United States of America." And she would say, "You don't mean it?" and I would say, "I do mean it, Mom." And she would always respond, "Well, you know if you father had lived to see this, he would have never let you go into politics or go to Washington."[14]

I didn't have the heart to tell her that would not have mattered. I had practiced law for twenty years with a good firm and had a great experience, but the second career was very meaningful to me. I never even dreamed that I would have that position and particularly during a time when the world changed, fundamentally, and we got a lot of good things done for our nation and for the world, as a consequence of that. And again, I would say God's hand was part of that, and my faith was crucial.

I think it is fair to say that a strong foundation of moral principal guided you in your decisions and leadership during some of the most important moments of American history—the end of the Cold War, the Strategic Arms Reduction treaties, the end of Apartheid [in South Africa] and release of Nelson Mandela, decades of attempts to wage peace in the Middle East and, of course, [Operation] Desert Storm. Were these efforts also driven by your faith? And frankly, looking back on any of these moments or others, where did you see God's hands at work, either through you or in the initiatives themselves?

Absolutely, I needed God's help, during all those years—particularly when I was Reagan's chief of staff. I did not have a lot of friends in the White House at first. All of the Californians resented my appointment. I was not with his campaign in the beginning and a lot of people did everything they could to take me out—it was a brutal time. In fact, at the time, I was approached about serving as the commissioner of major league baseball.[15] But Edward Bennett Williams, who owned the Washington Senators baseball team told me, "You're not going to do this Jim, because President Reagan's going to call on you to serve in his cabinet."

And, I thought, "Well, there's very little chance of that happening—and even so, it would not be a key position like secretary of state"—but then it happened, and I can tell you God's hand was in it. Let me give you an example.

In the midst of the beginning of the end of the Cold War, I invited Eduard Shevardnadze to my ranch out in Jackson, Wyoming.[16] In those days, officials of the Soviet Union were not allowed to go more than twenty-five miles away from their embassy in Washington [DC] or the UN office in New York.

We spent two or three days out there and we got a lot of good work done—we got a lot of arms control done. At the end of the day, we had a big dinner. I gave Shevardnadze a pair of cowboy boots, and I told him, "Mr. Minister, I want you to have these. Back in Texas we wear these when we're walking through the barn, so we don't get any water on any of our nice shoes." But then he said, "I have a gift for you," and it was a large enamel and metal Russian-made plaque with an image of St. George defeating the dragon with the words, "Good defeats evil." And he said, "You see, Mr. Secretary, even we Soviets are changing our world view—good is defeating evil."[17]

Let me hover on Desert Storm for a bit. I know that you and President Bush took great pains to gather the evidence that atrocious human rights violations were being carried out in the wake of Saddam Hussein's invasion of Kuwait. Am I accurate in saying that because of your faith, you and the president not only believed that would be a just war, but consulted with religious leaders prior to the beginning of that war?

Both the President and I came to that conclusion. Of course there are some wars that are just, and some are not, but we were absolutely convinced that this was to be a just war, given what Iraq had done and how it had been precipitated, but more importantly how the occupation unfolded. We may, or may not, have studied specifically Augustine's just war theory, but the decision to go to war was a moral one and a just one.[18]

You also consulted with clergy, including the presiding bishop of the Episcopal Church at the time, Edmond Browning?

Yes, well, here we were, two Christians, two Episcopalians—one the president and the other the secretary of state—to tell him why we were supporting this war. It was more like an alliance of two like-minded countries, and we felt it just. The presiding bishop was a pacifist and opposed the war, but once we launched it, Browning did call the President to offer pastoral support.[19] And we had the support of Billy Graham and the pope.[20] Having those conversations with key religious leaders was important to the president and to me.

A fellow member of St. Martin's told me that he recalls being struck one particular Sunday when he came into the church early and saw you on your knees in prayer before the worship service. Soon thereafter, Desert Storm was launched. Do you recall prayer as being a source of guidance and strength in seasons like that?

Yes, yes, I do. It was and remains a source of great comfort to me. I prayed often during my time in Washington because we were always confronted with problems and issues that come to the present but never have simple answers. And I wanted to make sure that we were on the right side of the issues we took on, and prayer helped guide me in that.

Mr. Secretary, as you look back on your life, when, and/or how have you most experienced God's presence in your work and family?

I look at my life and consider all that God has given me, and how could I not believe? How could I not have faith. And Russ, you know this better than anyone, but it is amazing how many times you pray and the prayer is answered. When that happens it is not just luck or coincidence.

Tell me a bit more about your "Runner's Bible"?

My mother gave that to me many years ago, and I read it every single day. It is a collection of verses from various places in the Bible, under various topics. While I take reading it seriously, it was put together intentionally as Bible verses for those "on the run." I take about a quarter of an hour or so to read every day.

I will tell you, when I was in Washington and was facing so much opposition at times, and so many thorny issues, it was of immense help to me. One of the verses I read over and over again was Isaiah 41:10 (NKJV), "Fear not, I am with thee." It was God saying to me, "don't worry, don't fear, just believe." And my response would be, "God I believe you're going to take care of this, . . ." and He would take care of it![21]

And I'll just say it again—come on, look at all the stuff we were able to accomplish in those years I was serving President Reagan and President Bush—how in the world could we have done all of that without God's help. It was a tremendous privilege to serve in that time, and I believe God put me where I could best use the gifts He had given me.

But I would add, God has richly blessed me with all of my wonderful children and grandchildren. When Susan and I were first married, blending my four boys and her two sons and daughter was hard—not all the children were happy about our marriage. Of course, together, we were blessed to have a daughter—Mary Bonner Baker. But we stayed at it, said our prayers, and we turned many of those challenges over to God in prayer. Today, I am happy to say we all get along and our children—all of them—are doing quite well. That, too, is a real blessing from God.

In our seventeen years of friendship, I have known you and Susan to be "regulars" in church, how does the experience of worship strengthen your daily life?

Well, I attend church because it is what the Bible tells us to do! And it strengthens me. I don't think going to church is a one-way street. I believe God's going to help His children regardless of their faith, but if you are in a canoe, it helps to have a paddle! And for me, church helps me live this life and strengthen my relationship with God.

Do you have a regular time that you pray? Or is it as the "Spirit moves you" so to speak? Or is it a little of both?

It's a little bit of both. Morning is when I read and meditate on those verses from *The Runner's Bible*. But I pray at other times. Of course, Susan and I pray together, before meals, and other times, particularly when we have a sickness in the family or a death, . . . but she's far above me on the prayer scale!

You have said you feel closest to God when you are out of doors, especially on your ranch, Rockpile, near the south Texas town of Pearsall. Can you say a bit more about how that experience impacts your own faith journey?

Yes, whether I am walking on the property or sitting in a deer blind, I really feel God's presence. I love God's creation and when I look on it, it strengthens my faith, because it is hard to look at it and doubt God's existence. How could Creation happen, if not by God's hands? That's just the way I am. So when I really want to get alone with my thoughts and spend some time with God, I go out to the countryside, where I am by myself in the midst of His handiwork—that's when I really feel alive.

Of course, you and St. Martin's played a key role as both the president and Barbara Bush left this life for the next. You visited with them several times, prayed with them, and of course you were with the president at the time of his death. At the same time, both privately and publicly, you seemed to have a firm confidence in life after death. You told the president early on the day of his death that he would be going to heaven, and in your remarks at his final funeral in Houston, you offered the words, "We rejoice, Mr. President, that you are safely tucked in now and through the ages with God's loving arms around you."[22] *You have said this kind of farewell to a lot of your loved ones and friends, but has your belief, or faith, in life after death increased with years, or has it always been part of your spiritual DNA?*

I will say again that I absolutely believe in life after death, but like most believers, I still have a lot of questions about what that life will look like. In the meantime, I want to live life to the full while I am here. I would add that I pray every day, Russ, that I keep my marbles, because I think the saddest thing in the world is to see somebody who was vibrant and alive deteriorate mentally. I do not want to be a burden to my family in that way. I don't ever want that to happen. I understand that our bodies begin to deteriorate—particularly when you fall down fourteen stairs and break your back! I understand our physical bodies begin to deteriorate, but I do not want my mental capacities to diminish.

We have talked about your own journey through death's door to the next life many times. You have even specifically taken me to the place where you say you will be "planted." But you seem not to have any angst or fear about that moment. In fact, you often talk about it was a smile and a bit of humor. Is that, also, a fruit of your faith?

You know where I am going to be buried, I have taken you there and shown you the spot! I do not fear death. How could I? If I have faith, how can I fear that? I have faith, so I do not have fear. When you believe what the Bible tells us and what Christians believe, which I do, there is nothing to fear when this life ends, for it is only the beginning of a new life!

How would you like to be remembered?

I would like to be remembered as somebody who took on a lot of tough jobs and did them well and finished them.

How has our Lord helped you in that?

He has helped me finish a lot of those jobs! All of them, frankly!

What advice or counsel do you have for those who are drawn more toward fame, power, or success than they are to matters of faith?

They are fleeting, . . . they all go away. Shortly after I began as White House chief of staff for President Reagan, I was in my car and driving through the gate on the north side of the West Executive Avenue.[23] From that vantage point, I could actually look down Pennsylvania Avenue. And on one particular day, I recognized a person who was walking along by himself—and it was one of my predecessors. There was no band, or military vehicle, no pomp, no ceremony or anything else. And it was as if God was reminding me in that moment, that what I was experiencing—this moment in the very center of power not just in the West, but in the world—it was temporary, and fame and fortune are fleeting.

In the end you give all of those things up. You know they may be fleeting, but fate is not. The time we are given is beyond our choosing, when we are born, when we die, but what we do with that time is so important, and for that, I have had to turn to God again and again. You know, I quoted President Eisenhower from his inaugural address, "We must be willing, individually and as a nation, to accept whatever sacrifices may be required of us."[24]

In the end we give up everything this world has to offer, because ultimately, we belong in the next world, so as 41 used to say all the time, what matters most are our friends, our family, . . . our faith. That's what lasts forever.

THE HONORABLE JAMES A. BAKER III

The Honorable James A. Baker III had a career in public service and politics that stands unparalleled. He is the only person to serve as Secretary of State, Secretary of the Treasury, and twice as White House Chief of Staff—for Presidents Ronald Reagan and George H. W. Bush. Starting in 1976, he led an unprecedented five presidential campaigns for Presidents Reagan, Bush, and Gerald Ford.

Secretary Baker is considered one of America's most effective Chiefs of Staff for his work under President Reagan. During that time, the President reduced taxes, loosened regulations and help re-ignite America's economic engine. As Secretary of the Treasury under Reagan, Baker played a key role in the Tax Reform Act that simplified the nation's tax code and the Plaza Accords to stabilize global currencies.

During his tenure as Secretary of State, the Cold War ended peacefully, the Soviet Union dissolved, and democracy spread across the globe. Secretary Baker lay the diplomatic groundwork for the unification of Germany, forged the unprecedented international coalition that forced Saddam Hussein's troops from Kuwait, and designed the 1991 Madrid Peace Conference.

Secretary Baker's public service continued after leaving the government. He founded the James A. Baker III Institute for Public Policy at Rice University, was Personal Envoy of the United Nations to seek a political solution to the conflict over Western Sahara and was Special Presidential Envoy to restructure Iraq's sovereign debt.

He is a senior partner with the law firm Baker Botts. He and Susan Garrett Baker have eight children.

Photo credit: © John Filo_CBS

"I feel that I have been called to make a difference—not by achieving fame, or money—but by responding to God's call on my life."

—Jim Nantz

Jim Nantz

If you are a fan of golf, basketball, football, or any other sport that finds its way to your television screen you will likely know the face and the unmistakable voice of Jim Nantz.

My friendship with Jim Nantz began through our shared relationship with and admiration of President George H. W. Bush. Shortly after coming to St. Martin's, I was asked by President Bush to offer an invocation at the re-dedication of his presidential library on the campus of Texas A&M in College Station, Texas.[1] Jim was the master of ceremonies for that event, and his jubilant optimism and wonderful personality served as the perfect lead, and backdrop, to the events of that day.

He did not know me, as the old saying goes, from Adam, but he treated me like we were old friends. Our paths crossed at other times over the years, primarily around events organized by President Bush, but Jim was never hesitant about staying in touch and when I asked him to consider writing a foreword for my book *In God's Grip: What Golf Can Teach Us About the Gospel*, he did not hesitate.[2]

We met at Jim's new home in Nashville, Tennessee, and after talking sports a bit, Jim warmly welcomed the opportunity to talk about his faith.

I love what President Bush wrote about you—"Spend ten minutes with Jim and you will know the deepest currents that shape who and what he is. . . ."[3] *What are those "currents" that have shaped you? Have they changed over the years?*

I think everything I've achieved in my life starts with my faith and my family. My mom and my dad were deeply rooted in their faith and raised us with a focus on religion in our everyday lives—we went to church, we prayed before meals, and we said our prayers at night before bed.

They taught us to treat others the way you want to be treated—and to be kind. They also encouraged us to explore the world around us—meet fascinating people, watch them, learn from them. Identify what makes them special and consider what qualities they have that you would want to exemplify in life.

Being mentored by others has played a big part in my life, and it is why my life has taken the course it has. I have had so many special people that put their arm over my shoulder and lead me in the right direction. Whether it be 41,[4] or Arnold Palmer, and many others.

Yes, through these generous currents of positivity, mentoring has been a profound part of my life. To name just a few—my golf coach Dave Williams,[5] who was a deeply committed Christian, Ken Venturi, Arnold Palmer, and Jack Nicklaus. There were also many of my broadcasting heroes—Jim McKay, Jack Whitaker, Dick Enberg, Chris Schenkel, Keith Jackson, Pat Summerall—they all took the time to be invested in my career and guide me. They were giants in my life, and they figuratively took my hand and led me. They were giving of themselves beyond what was necessary for them to do, . . . doing it out of the kindness of their hearts.

What was the religious life of your childhood home?

My mom was Baptist, and my dad a Methodist. We moved around a lot when we were young. I was born in Charlotte, North Carolina, and because of my dad's job, we moved several times. First to New Orleans, then California, and onto New Jersey (perhaps the longest stint in my younger years, we attended a Reformed Church in Colts Neck, New Jersey). Ultimately, we ended up in Houston. But it is fair to say we worshipped in a lot of different Christian churches over the years.

Though you have lived—and continue to live—a remarkable life—from Super Bowls, to the Masters, to the Final Four—you seem not only surprised to some degree by all you have achieved but remain remarkably humble. Your father encouraged you to reach for the stars and you seem to understand that you defied the odds in so many ways. In short, your "calling" so to speak, is as much a gift as it is the fruit of your own sweat equity. How have you seen God's hands guiding your journey?

Well, the man that showed me the importance of humility more than anyone else was 41 (the 41st US President, George H. W. Bush). He lived that every day.

Many years ago, when 41's son, George, was considering running for Governor of Texas, we were all together at an exploratory event in New York City. Famed jazz musician Lionel Hampton[6] was there. Hampton was in a wheelchair at that stage in life, and I noticed that without missing a beat, 41 walked right over to Hampton and dropped down on one knee to talk with him. That night, at the dinner after the event, I said, "Mr. President, I saw when you greeted Lionel Hampton that you dropped down to one knee instinctively . . . can you tell me about that?" And he said, "Jimmy, you should never make anyone feel like they have to look up to you. Everybody should be on the same level." Russ, it was an amazing thing to have witnessed.

A big part of humility is not taking the things you have been given for granted. I have had the chance to broadcast seven Super Bowls, thirty-two Final Fours, forty Masters, and that is everything I dreamt of as a young boy. It was my childhood dream, helped by a lot of nurturing and love from my parents and my sister, Nancy.

I am not saying I did not work hard for it. There was a lot of borderline obsessing in my early teens as I began to compulsively think about pursuing my dream of one day working for CBS Sports and covering the great championships of American sports. No one was going to outwork me, but I did not want anyone handing me anything. When I look back at all the remarkable things I have been able to do, with the perspective of hindsight, you begin to see that the things that matter most often are the little things, a touch of kindness, going out of your way to help someone else, and of course the most valuable tool to learning—listening!

But, at the same time, I know these have been blessings from our gracious God, and I do not take that for granted, and am grateful for each and every one of them.

You once wrote that there is "perceived power and then there is real power."[7] What, for you, distinguishes the difference in the two?

The impetus for my writing that was, again, my relationship with the Bush family. They had "real" power, but they did not exercise it in everyday life. They did not flaunt it. They were just real people. And then there is the corporate world—I'm sure it's similar at most every major company. Management moves on, CEOs come and go, but when they have the throne or they're sitting in the biggest seat, it's interesting to watch the way power is wielded. I'm not trying to minimize being the leader of a major corporation in America, but on one hand, I got to watch up close and personal how the former leader of the free world—who had real power—and then compare it with those who held these temporary positions in the business world. Oftentimes there is just a real disparity between the two.

For 41, I think it was not a planned thing, it was a subconscious thing. I remember many times going out to dinner with him—and there was the presidential motorcade with Secret Service agents in an SUV in front of us, and behind us—but 41 would rush out to the car and try to squeeze into the back bench seat because he did not want to inconvenience his guest—me! Think about that. And he was eighty at the time!

Then there was this time when we went to a quaint ice cream shop in Ogunquit, Maine. There was a long line of people and when they saw the president, they tried to wave him to the front of the line—he would have nothing to do with it.

President Bush would never play that card—cutting in line was not in his DNA. He always exuded real power. Perceived power plays that front-of-the-line card all day long.

You have also mentioned a time when you were on the red carpet being interviewed after the film Tin Cup *was released, in which you had several scenes. You recall that the trappings of the moment gave you the impression that it revolved around "who you were," but not "what you were."*[8] *What I have noticed when you interview people is that you are intent on getting at the "what" under the "who." What would you say to those who say—in fact—what matters most is "who," not "what?"*

In today's world, a lot of people want to be around the "who," but not really the "what." What that person really is on the inside, with all the surface stuff taken away. I was at the premier of that film and saw how much of that was going on—entertainment crews getting interviews with the most popular people, . . . the right moment to be dropped off on the red carpet, . . . the right place in line to draw the most attention, and I realized how superficial it was. I get it, that is all part of the movie business, but when I conduct an interview, I want to go below the surface.

I think that comes from working as a storyteller and telling other people's stories for a living. I get uncomfortable when I am the story. Russ, most people have no idea that I'm interviewed fifteen to twenty times more than I am interviewing someone else because there are podcasts, sports radio shows, there are media press conferences before big events like the Super Bowl, and I know what it feels like to be constantly on the hot seat.

But when I'm doing the asking, I work hard to shine a light on other people's stories, and I really like positive stories. I want to be able to frame a moment for someone—especially those triumphant moments that do justice not just to who they are—but what they are, deep down.

Jim, when did God become more than a word to you? When did you first experience God's presence in your life?

I think He becomes more [than] a word, you know, in my life with every passing year. Not that I just started when I entered my sixties, but a realization of God has been ingrained in my life. . . . I have always had God in my heart.

But I think I've become more disciplined with my relationship with God—in terms of prayers and thoughts—the older I get. I know a lot of that ratcheted, up to a whole new level when I became a father. I wanted my kids to have the same foundation my parents gave me—so it has been important for me to take them to church, to worship together, introduce them to the Gospel, and to say our prayers together at night.

When do you most "experience" God's presence in your life today?

I experience God most in the morning. I begin most days in prayer, but sometimes I am up, I bolt out of bed and run off and miss a day or two. I feel off base, out of sorts, if I don't start my day with prayer.

I would guess a lot of believers grapple with prayer—"Am I doing it the right way? Are my prayers being heard?" But it is important to me. A lot of my prayer time is given to gratitude—grateful, grateful, grateful for so many things.

You began a regular "ritual" in 1986—after the death of your mother's father, Bronze Holland Trull—an intentional moment of prayer and meditation whenever the US national anthem was sung—about ninety seconds—to bring to mind gratitude for the blessings of your life. Is that something you have continued through the years?

Absolutely. I think of it every time. My grandfather on my mother's side, Bronze Trull, died on May 18, 1986. He was a World War I veteran. He was from Charlotte and came back to North Carolina after the war, had four kids, raised them in a two-bedroom, one-bathroom house.

After the War, he worked as a delivery man for Sunbeam Bakery. He did that for years.

He was a proud patriot, and as I watch the national anthem each week at my NFL games, I think of him. As the anthem is played, I use that time as a moment of prayer and gratitude not only for my country, but for the people in my life. It's a discipline in my life—a time to pray and give thanks.

When your dad was diagnosed with Alzheimer's in the summer of 1995, your first inclination was to "fix it." When you realized that it could not be "fixed," how did that impact your soul?

At the beginning, I always thought I could fix it, . . . that I could figure out a way to make things okay. I am not a good "fix it" guy around the house, so if a light bulb goes out, I'm the wrong guy for that job. But I always felt like I could figure out a way to save my dad. But then I ran into the unfixable disease of Alzheimer's.

So, how did your faith help you when you realized you could not fix it?

You know, my dad was so central in my life, and it was really, really hard to see my father—who was invincible in my eyes . . . and realize he is actually going to die, that I am actually going to lose him. I know that was a fear I had as a young boy—my mom or dad dying, when I was a toddler or pre-teen or whatever. But then I had to come to terms with it.

How did my faith help me? You know, the power of prayer helped. Asking to be led, being open to try to grow and learn from things and pleading, in prayer, for peace for my father. Asking God to help us all make the best of this situation.

The story of your relationship with your father is simply inspiring—he was not just your father, but your friend, your traveling companion, your life coach—lots of men do not have that relationship with their father, nor fathers to their son. I think it is fair to say the kind of relationship you shared was rare by today's standards. What was the glue that made it work so well?

The reason I titled my book *Always by My Side* is because Dad was just that. He was the "glue." He was there for me, and I wanted to be just like him. He was my role model—my first and most significant role model. And like any kid, I watched him closely and learned from him. I realize now, having younger children, they watch everything! Now, I've got three beautiful and wonderful children, and they love their daddy—and I thank God for that.

My dad was not only my cheerleader, but also my mentor, and he had great wisdom. I can still hear my dad saying to me, "Your voice gets heard by a lot of people. Make sure they hear your voice that encourages them to make a difference."

And so when your father died, you allowed his death to inspire you to make a tangible difference. Can you tell me more about that?

Yes. Right after Dad's passing, I began to have discussions with Houston Methodist Hospital about collaborating to create the best state-of-the-art Alzheimer's clinical care and research institute in the world. The book did quite well and generated a lot of awareness. At first, I did not know what to do with my newfound platform, but then I realized, "It's right in front of you, Jim." So, we created the Nantz National Alzheimer Center (NNAC), named after my dad, in Houston. I took all the proceeds from the book, and I gave 100 percent of it to start the center.

Since 2008, the NNAC has grown into a world-renowned clinic and research center. When my dad got diagnosed, we had no treatment that would improve his symptoms. Now, for the first time in history, patients who are diagnosed with Alzheimer's have access to drugs that can give them hope, manage and slow the progression of the disease, and give families more time with their loved ones. The NNAC played a big role in the clinical trials that brought these new drugs to market. And it's not just pioneering research that makes the NNAC special, it is also about the team. We have an incredible full-time staff who take a comprehensive approach to patient care. We have raised tens of millions of dollars and in the last few years we have seen fantastic results.

Russ, I love what I do in the sports world and could not have dreamed I would have all the experiences I have had. I'm at an age now where I realize what I am really called by God to do. I have been given a mission—to defeat the opponent that defeated my dad. I believe, of all the things I do, that is the real reason the good Lord put me on this earth.

While you clearly shared the care of your father with your mother Doris and sister Nancy, your devotion was unrelenting. What would you say to others who face a similar journey with a loved one? Why is it important to "be there," even if it seems like the loved one has slipped away?

He was there for me, . . . he modeled that for me, and so I wanted to be there for him. Mom and Nancy carried the heavy load, and they wanted to be there for Dad too. Of course, I traveled a lot during those years but always made it a priority to be with him as much as I could. And when I was there, I talked to my father a lot. I felt like he was hearing everything I was saying.

Regardless of his reactions, or lack thereof, I talked to him as if things were normal. And when I was not with him, I would call and there would be a lot of one-way conversations when the phone was put up to his ear and I would just ramble on.

I could not bear the thought of losing him, but in the thirteen years between his diagnosis and his death, it was impossible not to think about staying connected with him every possible way. I worried a lot about my dad, but it really, truly was the strain of saying goodbye over and over again, thinking every time I was with him, or talking with him, that it could possibly be the last time. So, being there as much as I could was so important and I think it meant a lot to him.

You were there with your dad when he left this life for the next on Saturday, June 28, 2008. I confess that I have been with a number of people at the time of their deaths, and it has only deepened my faith in God and in what rests beyond the door of death. How did you draw on your faith in that moment?

Faith is so important to get through those moments. John Wooden, who had an incredible career, was the head basketball coach for UCLA for almost thirty years, including during the Vietnam years and when there was a lot of strife in our country.[9] One time when I was paying a visit to his home, he said that he always wanted players who had faith, because faith helps you through the challenges of life, and he was right. When he said that, I thought instantly of my dad. I try to live my life in that way.

When you gave one of the eulogies at Arnold Palmer's memorial service, you acknowledged the grief, but also encouraged those attending and watching to remember that though he was no longer physically present, his legacy and life lived on—within their hearts—and that he had, in fact, "gone home." You have said something very similar about your father—that though he is not here with you, in some way, in the words of your book, your father is "always by your side." When do you most experience his presence?

There's a backstory there that is really important to me. Arnold and I got very close in the years after Dad's death. We did so many speaking engagements together and I would be the *Q* (questioner), and he would offer the *A* (answer). He liked for me to join him at countless corporate events where we would hang out, have a meal, do some social things together. There was an age gap between us, but he treated me like a son.

In 2004, as my dad was dying, I was struggling with a very big decision in my career. I had been offered an opportunity to host a network morning show. This forced a decision to stay on the path I had been walking, which was my childhood dream, or to make a sudden change and enter the news space of network television. I told Arnold that it was difficult to decide which option to choose because even though my dad was alive, he wasn't able to articulate or fully understand what I was going through and could not give me the advice I needed. I told him I so desperately wanted to talk to my dad and get his insights.

Arnold took his hand and thumped it right on my chest, saying, "You don't understand . . . he's right here. Your dad is right here. He has been talking to you the whole time. Go with your heart because your dad is right there." Arnold was right. Dad's voice was already in my heart, and again, as I have said about Dad, he was always by my side.

Jim, do you have a favorite Bible verse?

Yes, I Corinthians 13—the "love" chapter. Paul's reminders about what real love is, and what the most important attributes are—faith, hope, and love. In the end, the greatest of them is love. Those are the things that keep your life centered. You have to have those, even in moments of despair, because they will see you through.

Jim, you have been invited into the homes of tens of millions of people during your career—with that optimistic smile, amazing energy, and words those of us have come to love and welcome, "Hello friends, Jim Nantz here . . . !"

The "hello friends" greeting came from trying to send a coded message to my father. I open every broadcast with "hello friends." My dad had so many friends and I wanted to honor that, so I began saying "hello friends" as a way to reach out and let him know I was thinking of him.

In that flicker of a second, when you come on television, there's an anxiety or anxiousness to get it right, to be calm, to do well. There are millions of people on the other side of that lens. I can't see them, but they can see me. So, "hello friends" allows me to train my thoughts toward my dad in that moment of nervousness. It's calming as I see his face smiling back at me when I look into the camera.

I think it is fair to say you learned so much from your father and really took to heart his belief that the true measure of a person's life was not in terms of success, but whether or not he or she lived a life of significance. So now we come to the real question of this book. You have, in fact, achieved much of what the world believes is success—fame, notoriety, wealth—but what would you say to those who believe that's the ultimate goal in life—that is what is most important?

Boy, you know, it's the old Rubik's Cube of how do you define success? I'm not sure that any of the three you just mentioned means a successful life. Let me quote again our mutual friend, 41, who used to say that a successful life cannot be defined unless it includes service to others.

My parents loved me so much and I loved them, and as long as they were alive, I wanted to make them proud of what I did with my life, and now that they have gone, it has morphed into making my children proud. As I said, I feel that I have been called to make a difference—not by achieving fame, or money and all that, but by responding to God's call on my life. I wanted to be a sports commentator for CBS since I was a little boy, and I have been able to do that, but I have been called by God to come on this planet and help find a cure for Alzheimer's, and by God's grace and with His help, I am getting to do that—and that is the most important kind of success.

Perhaps without knowing it, you have just quoted Mother Teresa, who used to tell others that as children of God, we are not called to be successful, we have been called to be faithful! And that is what you are doing!

Thank you—I can only do that drawing on the inspiration of others and with God's help. . . . Being faithful is far more important than being successful.

JIM NANTZ

CBS Sports Commentator Jim Nantz, the four-time Emmy Award winner and five-time National Sportscaster of the Year, joined the CBS Television Network in 1985. He currently serves as the lead play-by-play announcer for the NFL on CBS, including the Super Bowl, and the lead anchor of CBS's golf coverage, including the PGA Tour, the Masters, and the PGA Championship. In February 2024, Jim called his seventh Super Bowl in Las Vegas, which was the most watched telecast in history with over 120 million viewers, and on January 12, 2025, Nantz called his 500th NFL game on CBS.

His storied career also includes covering NCAA Division I Men's Basketball through 2023. In 2007, Nantz became the first commentator in history to complete the rare broadcasting trifecta—calling the Super Bowl, NCAA Men's Final Four, and the Masters all in a span of sixty-three days. He repeated this trifecta in 2010, 2013, and 2016. In 2019 and 2021, Nantz completed an even rarer quintet, calling the AFC Championship, Super Bowl, Final Four, Masters, and PGA Championship in a span of 120 days.

Nantz received the Lifetime Achievement Award from the Broadcasting+Cable Hall of Fame in May 2023, the PGA of America Hall of Fame in November 2023, and he was inducted into the National Sports Media Association Hall of Fame in December 2021. He was honored in 2019 with the Arnie Award and in December 2018, Nantz was inducted into the Sports Broadcasting Hall of Fame. In August 2011, Nantz received the Pro Football Hall of Fame Pete Rozelle Radio-Television Award—the youngest recipient ever of this award. Nantz also was honored by the Naismith Memorial Basketball Hall of Fame as its youngest recipient of the Curt Gowdy Media Award in 2002.

On January 19, 2011, Nantz returned to his adopted hometown of Houston to team with Houston Methodist Hospital at the Texas Medical Center to create the Nantz National Alzheimer Center (NNAC). The NNAC is dedicated to funding innovative diagnostic discoveries for early and accurate detection of Alzheimer's disease and other dementing illnesses in hopes of one day finding a cure. Nantz's father, Jim Nantz Jr., himself a former college football player and lifelong inspiration to his broadcaster son, suffered from the ravages of Alzheimer's disease for thirteen years and Nantz chronicled his father's story in the instant *New York Times* bestseller, *Always by My Side*.

Nantz, along with wine industry veteran Peter Deutsch, CEO of Deutsch Family Wine & Spirits, formed the Deutsch Nantz Alliance (DNA) to produce an artisanal Sonoma fine wine brand named The Calling (thecallingwine.com). His wines have won accolades from *Wine Spectator* and *Wine Enthusiast*. In 2024, Nantz was recognized by *Wine Spectator* as a Wine Star for his achievements in the wine industry.

Nantz graduated in 1981 with a degree in radio/television from the University of Houston, where he was recruited as a member of the golf team. In May 2001, he received an honorary doctorate of humane letters from his alma mater, becoming its first former student-athlete to ever deliver the commencement address and be bestowed an honorary degree at the university.

Photo credit: © Jennifer Almquist

"To believe in God is just to admit the truth."

—Sam Waterston

Sam Waterston

I have admired Sam Waterston's work since I first saw him in some of his earlier films—Nick Carraway in the 1974 adaptation of F. Scott Fitzgerald's *The Great Gatsby*; the affable Peter Willis in the science fiction thriller *Capricorn One*; and the American journalist Sydney Schanberg the 1984 Oscar-nominated British film *The Killing Fields*, a horrific retelling of the Khmer Rouge regime in Cambodia.[1] And I suspect, like most of you reading, I was impressed by Sam's portrayal of District Attorney Jack McCoy on television's longest running crime drama, *Law and Order*, for 19 years, until his retirement from that show in February of 2024.[2]

I knew from my own reading that Sam was also an Episcopalian, so on a long shot, during my tenure as rector, I invited Sam to come to St. Martin's in Houston in December of 2012 to participate as a reader in a number of celebratory and worship services we were hosting.

I am still struck by our first meeting. He was staying at a hotel not far from the church and we agreed to meet in the lobby to visit for a bit before I took him to the church to review the program for the next few days. He got off the elevator, rounded the corner, and offered a big smile and outstretched hand. He was wearing jeans and a dress shirt, and we jumped right into conversation. Sam was not asking for any fee for his time with us and after I told him how thrilled I was that he came, I asked what prompted his decision. He smiled and said, "You would not leave me alone!"

I wrote a good bit about that first visit in my book, *Witness to Dignity: The Life and Faith of George H. W. and Barbara Bush*.[3] It was clear during those few days that Sam had a deep and sincere faith. Once we parted ways after that weekend, we stayed in regular touch for the next decade. He and his wife, Lynn, were always warm and welcoming in our correspondence, which always ended with "Love, Sam."[4]

Now I am going to offer Sam's reflections in a slightly different way than the other conversations in this book. Once Sam agreed to sit for an interview, as I did with others, I submitted my questions well in advance of our visit.

Sam and Lynn invited my wife Laura and me to stay with them in their home, so we had a good, long time having this important conversation. But shortly after we arrived, Sam said that my questions prompted him to write what he hoped our conversation would convey to the readers. So, what follows, is, in fact, that "statement of belief," if you will. I will end with some of the questions and answers we discussed as well. Let us begin with Sam's own reflection.

Sam's Reflections...

My father was a teacher. I was with him in the hospital the night before he died. He had been shaking, and I was holding him. Out of what I had thought was delirium, he all at once whispered perfectly clearly, "The young people must not be given the wrong idea." It was the last thing I heard him say, so, of course, it carries a lot of weight.

I'm grateful to you for inviting me to put what I believe into words. At the same time, I don't want to give anyone the wrong idea. Better to say nothing. But I'm 84. It's about time I left some account for my children, grandchildren, and anyone else who may be interested. Don't hide your light under a bushel![5]

It's been a great benefit to me, putting things that have been rattling around in a jumble in my head for a long time into words, sentences, and paragraphs. Also, hard!

I'm far from done. This is a snapshot of a moment in time, not in any sense a last word. Faith hasn't landed me in a place where everything is happy and simple and clear. By no means, and it didn't make me a wonderful person either, worse luck. I don't at all feel that belief makes me better than someone who doesn't. I know it doesn't.

I'm very excited to see where our conversation leads. Then we can decide together whether anyone else should be subjected to it.

People are saying all kinds of things about Christianity these days and using it for all kinds of things. Along with the fact that you asked me (!), it feels like now's a good time to give an account of faith from personal experience, separate from what we've been hearing in the "public square."

Unfortunate as it is that it even needs saying, with all the talk about what belief *has* to be to be considered legitimate, I believe it's worth reminding ourselves that belief is the original free choice. We have an obligation to the facts, but no one has a right to tell you what to believe.

In all of God's Creation, no one, not William James, not Bertrand Russell, not Samuel Beckett, Abraham Lincoln, your pastor, mine, not Karl Barth, Albert Camus, nor Albert Einstein, no teacher or student of physics, certainly not me, and not Richard Dawkins or whoever currently has the trendiest opinion about what's reasonable to think, no one has a right to tell anyone else what to believe (not that many haven't claimed it), or how to believe it.[6]

It's my deep belief that forced belief is not of God. I have it on good authority: even as He's revealing Himself, God does not make anyone believe in Him: "As Jesus spoke these things many believed in Him."[7] Notice it doesn't say "everyone." The alternative, "Believe in God or else," hides the Good News, the infinitely generous invitation to be loved. It buries the lede, as journalists would say.

A lot of smart people in my "coming of age" years thought it wasn't reasonable to believe God exists. Even going to church school, even raised going to church, even inclined by nature to believe, the current of rationalism that's been part of Western culture since way before the Enlightenment gave my faith a hard time. It didn't erase belief, didn't bother.

Instead, it pushed it around, aside, and down, quite a bit. Human unbelief and human certainty are the Scylla and Charybdis between which faith has to navigate.[8]

So, if there are others who, like me, found the "world's" unbelief, or disbelief, was the main obstacle for them, then answering what reason, as currently practiced, claims you MAY and MAY NOT reasonably think about belief could be of interest.

The modern triumph of reason dates back at least as far as the Enlightenment. Our Constitution and form of government are products of the Enlightenment. I'm speeding over the surface of history, but, when reason alone was found to be an unsatisfying and incomplete view of life, Romanticism was the response.

Reason came back to reclaim the field in the Scientific, Industrial, and Technological Revolutions, which, even as they empowered us and made life much easier, vastly increased our destructiveness, further shaking our faith, without, as you'd think they would have, generally shaking our faith in reason. Nothing can stand up to indoor toilets and air conditioning.

Fortunately, I bumped into other lines of thought. We value Shakespeare and Lincoln for their ability to eloquently say what they have seen, shine light on our experience and reveal what's real, to "hold, as 'twere, the mirror up to nature."[9] We value them, and others like them, because we know, from history, and from what they themselves said, wrote, and did, that they have "seen the elephant," felt the harsh bite of reality, looked into the abyss, both in their personal and public lives.

Wonderfully, I got to spend a lot of time studying both, while being paid for it! Their gifts and circumstances, and the size of their minds, had led them both to elevate paradox above logic—much as they admired logic, and were masters of reason—associative thinking over linear.

"There are more things in heaven and earth than are dreamt of in your philosophy," Hamlet says.[10]

Lincoln went from believing in "cold, calculating, unimpassioned"[11] reason alone in 1838, to saying in 1865, after living through four years of war:

> If we shall suppose that American slavery is one of those offenses which in the providence of God must needs come but which having continued through His appointed time He now wills to remove and that He gives to both North and South this terrible war as the woe due to those by whom the offense came shall we discern therein any departure from those divine attributes which the believers in a living God always ascribe to Him.[12]

That is almost a sermon in full.

If reason has ever been an impediment to faith for anyone beside me, Shakespeare and Lincoln are here to help. They changed my life and shaped my belief.

So, Russ, to the heart of your invitation—"What do I believe?" I believe God is, before all things; I believe God is Love; I believe in the principles "you shall love the Lord your God with all your heart and with all your soul and with all your mind and with all your strength." "You shall love your neighbor as yourself." "Do to others what you would have them do to you."[13]

Smart alecks like me have a tough time living with all that simplicity. "To be important, it must be more complicated than this," we think. "Reasonableness" has always had a field day with the likes of me.

I believe that to believe in God is to admit the truth. I believe the whole shebang, all that is, is here by intention, not accident. We and the "world" are the many and God is the name we give to the One that was before the many. Naming is a thing humans do, and it separates us by human steps from what we are trying to name—one of many difficulties you run into when the creatures set about to describe their Maker.

When I say "my belief," I really should say "our belief," because my wife Lynn and I, for as long as we've been together, more than half a century, have shared it. I can talk, as this statement is showing and our kids will tell you, but very much thanks to Lynn's understanding of which way is up, our faith has been much more walk than talk.

"Be still and know that I am God," have been words to live by for me for a long time.[14] They turn up here a lot.

I believe freedom is the first expression of God's Love in Creation, and includes order, not the other way around. It's a different kind of chicken and egg question. Not "which came first?" but "which is which?"

When he said, "God does not play dice with the Universe," Einstein was speaking in defense of "classical physics" and in reaction against the uncertainties and randomness (i.e., freedom) in quantum mechanics.[15] He was defending the idea that the wondrous variety of nature, the infinite variety of life, the uniqueness of snow flakes, all that, is the result of an inner order, to be discovered in physics and expressed in math.

I'm completely impressed, even awed, by it intellectually, and I once played Oppenheimer, so I'm aware of the excitement in it, and the power.[16] But I'm a big fan of paradox. I believe I can see reality better through the lens of paradox than, for all its virtues, reason. Paradox, the name for something both true and seemingly impossible, is fundamental to many a parable of Christ.

So, my belief and my profession are rooted in it. "Christ is wholly human and wholly God" is a paradox. The motto of my Episcopal church school is a paradox, "Whom to serve is perfect freedom."[17] Near the end of the play, Hamlet says, "Let be."[18] It may be the shortest, pithiest poem in the English language. It is a paradox. In Elizabethan English "to be" means "to take action," so "let be" means "acquiesce, resist" a quintessential paradox. Shakespeare is full of them. So, to my eyes, is daily life.

I believe in grace. I think I'm one of the many people who have benefited from it often without noticing, thinking it was luck, or chance, or just having a great day.

Believing God is, for sure, a great source of personal comfort, and people are generally nicer when they feel loved, so my belief in a God who loves me without reservation may be some practical benefit to others, too. I hope so.

As soon as I write down, "I believe in God" and "I'm a Christian," all the ways those seven words can be taken and mis-taken rise up. Talk is cheap. What has worked for Lynn and me is trying it. There's no substitute for being there. We belong to a very small congregation. We've been together a long time. We know each other pretty well now, the way you do, just by osmosis, from being around each other over time. We understand and share beliefs as a community, but not in the way you might think; less by signing on to a contract (we do have a common creed, but that's just the beginning), than by what we do together.

When Christ started preaching, someone said, "Can anything good come out of Nazareth?!" The answer was, "Come and see."[19] My advice? Go where people are living faith out, even quietly, especially quietly, and see. "Be still and know that I am God."

I meditate; you need a practice. We go to church on Sunday. Pretty familiar stuff.

The fights down here between religions over which one has it rightest, what's the right way to do it, make no spiritual sense to me. When they aren't fighting, don't they just enrich each other? Protestants doing Catholics good. Buddhists helping Christians. Christians influencing Judaism. Hindus and Muslims teaching us how welcoming the stranger is done, *ad infinitum.* They've enriched me.

I came to meditation riding the tidal wave of Western interest in Eastern religion. I've experimented with other frameworks of faith, and it did me good. When I was a young man in New York, other churches and other ways were all around and the list was long. I've gone through stretches when I thought I was fine without any faith.

For a while, I thought so, while meditating at the same time! From need and by grace, I'm back where I started. I'm glad I lived long enough to come back home, but even with some of the detours being dead ends, I'm much better for the trip. We're all pilgrims.

I'm immediately suspicious of anyone's claim they have God in their pocket, though. Who belongs to whom? There's a well-known story told of a man who asked Lincoln if he thought God was "on our side." Lincoln said, "Sir, my concern is not whether God is on our side; my greatest concern is to be on God's side."

When anyone says they have God on their side, I look for the earth-bound goal involving power and control attached. We're back to "Be still and know that I am God."

I read some years ago that CBS Anchor Dan Rather once asked Mother Teresa what she said during her prayers. She answered that her prayers weren't really the kind where you ask for things. Instead, she said, "I listen to God." Dan Rather asked, "Well then, what does God say?" And she said, "Oh, He listens, too."

Ever since, that's defined for me both meditation and where it leads. "Be still and know that I am God." That's about it.

Compassion, love, trying to live an honest life, thrive in people without belief and with other beliefs. My belief isn't a medal or a special category, it's a benefit; I don't so much feel proud—it's a gift—as lucky. It makes sense to me [that] choice is involved, and grace, that belief is not a fated and foregone conclusion and takes an active step of faith. That's freedom. As should be clear now, I believe freedom is the path to faith.

And on that path, my faith allows me to believe... the words of that great hymn, "The Great Creator of the Worlds" by F. Bland Tucker:

> The great Creator of the worlds,
> the sovereign God of heaven,
> His holy and immortal truth
> to all on earth, hath He given.
>
> He sent no angel of his host
> to bear this mighty word,
> but him through whom the worlds were made,
> the everlasting Lord.
>
> He sent him not in wrath and power,
> but grace and peace to bring;
> in kindness, as a king might send
> his Son, himself a king.
>
> He sent him down as sending God;
> in flesh to us he came;
> as one with us he dwelt with us,
> and bore a human name.
>
> He came as Savior to his own,
> the way of love he trod;
> he came to win us by good will,
> for force is not of God.
>
> Not to oppress, but summon all
> their truest life to find,
> in love God sent his Son to save,
> not to condemn mankind.[20]

Let's now turn to some of the questions that Sam and I discussed, and then I will close with a bit more from Sam's own writings on these matters. Let's talk a bit about your experiences. Did you ever have an "epiphany" or "ah ha" moment in your faith journey?

No, not in the way a lot of people talk about that. I have my parents to thank. I was baptized as a baby, they took me to church, and at the boarding school I went to, chapel was held every day, and if you felt like it, you could go twice. I was certainly shaped by those experiences.

There have been times when I longed to experience one of those "clouds opening in the sky" moments. People of all faiths and none sometimes are flooded with wonder at being alive at all. I've had those moments, but I don't know if they count as epiphanies.

Perhaps I had an epiphany without realizing it because it came in the context of day-to-day life that already had faith and practice in it. It's almost inevitable that a young person experiencing their independence will question all they learned in their upbringing. I did.

You have said that there was a season where you explored a kind of existentialism and how much it meant to your faith journey to move through that and then come back to faith. Do I have that right?

Right. When I was in college and after, it was cool to think of existentialism and determinism as pure courage, as looking straight into the void presented by a godless universe. We were kids, and we felt like brave realists throwing away the crutches of faith. We gave religion a lot of grief for being empty forms. But forms of faith, like any other forms, are by definition empty, when the content is removed, as we had done.

As time passed, that view began to look superficial. For me, in the end, none of this smart stuff can hold a candle to faith. But, to lots of people, it's the only reasonable view. I went to a church school.[21] The campus is built around a circle. The Schoolhouse is on one side of the circle, the chapel is on the other.

We had a physics teacher whose name was, appropriately, Mr. Zink. Anyway, we had a kid in class, a brilliant guy, who became a physics professor at Princeton, named Stephen Fels. Stephen questioned everything. One day, he started asking Mr. Zink questions about the connections between religion and what was being taught in physics. The question kind of irritated Mr. Zink, who said, "The Schoolhouse is on this side of the circle. The science lab is attached to the Schoolhouse. The chapel is on the other side of the circle. The things they teach over there, we don't study over here."

That kind of sums up the worldview I grew up in. The proposition that religion and science are separate domains is still with us, but I think they are connected—really, one.

Where do you experience God most in your day-to-day life?

I do believe that God is as near as your breath, as our priest Mary says. I told you about wanting a kind of "heavens-opening experience," but not having it. . . . I could be rationalizing my own experience, but maybe there is an advantage to being raised going to church and then confirmed while you're in high school following the regular pattern, because the subtext of that is: God has been here right along; here first, here all the time; that when I was a little shrimp, God was there, and when I was in college and I began to think that I didn't need to pay attention to religious questions at all, God was also there.

In your commencement address to the 2024 graduating class at Princeton, you referred to vocation, which of course is a calling. Would you say that God guided your relationship with Him?[22]

Am I an actor because that's what God intended or was it my choice? "Yes." I am not sure how it all operates. You know my theory about freedom being a first condition of creation. But Hamlet says, "There's a special providence in the fall of a sparrow."[23]

How do those two things go together? It's kind of more than I know. But it looks to me as if they do. Paradox!

Have there been times when God felt very distant to you? If so, how has your faith intervened in moments like that?

Yeah, I guess so. God does not feel very distant now so *(Sam laughs)*.

You know, you don't want to mess with anything when it's going well! But yes, there have been those times.

Greg Boyle is fond of saying, "I believe that God protects me from nothing but sustains me in everything."[24] That's another way of saying something I believe also—His presence is a condition of life.

I am not passing judgement here, but I am going to make a general observation and then a specific one with a question at the end! I think it is fair to say that a lot of people in your business end up on the ropes; ... many are plagued with scandals and trainwrecks. But not you. You have been married for a long time. There's no big "dark story" about Sam Waterston. What has kept you in the road?

I don't know—I mean obviously the kinds of things we have been talking about, like shared belief. Family. My beloved Lynn—you can't beat being lucky in love, Russ.

Also, luck and timing: strains not too heavy or too long for us; good parents, helping us; friends, near; my brother-in-law and his wife, near; busy hands, lots of jobs that needed us to be doing them.

I was born just at the front edge of the War Baby Generation, I still think of myself as an aging hippie, but I've led a fairly conservative life. I was born in New England and here I still am. We didn't settle in Los Angeles or New York. We've been lucky: the life we thought we wanted and tried to have turned out to be the life we did want and has been pretty much what we got. Also, good advice, at a time when you can hear it, is priceless. When I began to get ahead a little, my father wrote me he was glad to see it, and "I think success is like smoking; it probably won't do you much harm, provided you don't inhale."

When I was playing Nick Carraway in *The Great Gatsby*, I thought things just could not get any better. I was in my early thirties, and here I was in a movie with Robert Redford and Mia Farrow, stars everywhere, Scott Wilson, Bruce Dern, Karen Black, in Fitzgerald's most famous story, adapted by Francis Ford Coppola, directed by Jack Clayton.[25] And one day Redford comes over to me and says, "So, . . . what do you think of all this?" And I say, "This is incredible! I can't believe it! This is great." And he says, "Well, good. Enjoy it. Just don't be fooled into thinking that it's love. They're being nice to you because you have something they want."

Actors are looking for approval, obviously, and pleasing people is the job. Putting your feelings on the table is also the job. So, you can easily get approval and love mixed up. But what a wonderful job to have, though, and, like the song says, "There's no people like show people."[26] Paradox!

You have already shared how important Jesus's teaching on the greatest of the commandments, to love God and love your neighbor, has been. Do you have any other favorite verses?

The simple and direct ones. "O Mortal, what is good; and what does the Lord require of you but to do justice, and to love kindness, and to walk humbly with your God."[27]

Also, the many, many Old Testament stories where people are being wrong, mixed up, weak before temptation, a mixed bag of bad and good, with God present: the material and spiritual world as one.

A favorite parable?

The first thing I thought of was the prodigal son.[28] It reminds me of Greg Boyle's book *Forgive Everyone Everything*.[29]

I know you regularly meditate and pray. Can you tell me a bit more about how you practice those spiritual disciplines?

I don't really distinguish between them (thus speaks an amateur, right?). I meditate-and-pray twice a day, in the morning, before breakfast, and in the evening. There are some days I miss, but usually it is twice a day. I did it once a day for quite a while, but I didn't feel like I was getting anywhere, so I began to do it twice a day, and still do. Ned Beatty showed me how to meditate.[30] He taught me Transcendental Meditation. I learned Christian meditation from tapes made by a Benedictine monk, Father John Douglas Main.[31]

Where do you do this?

There's a sheltered spot behind our house where I like to meditate when the weather's warm. It's very nice and quiet. But I can meditate just about anywhere, even noisy places. I meditate on trains and subways, in the car (not while driving), in parks, different places in the house. I've gotten over being shy about doing it in public. No one minds. Ned's is the only training I've ever had, so maybe I'm doing it all wrong, but it feels like it works.

Do you have a mantra?

Yes, just the word, *Maranatha*. I learned it from Father Main's tapes. I recently found out it can be translated several ways, "Our Lord is come!"; "Come, O, Lord"; and "Make room for the Master!" I like that it can mean three complimentary/contradictory things at the same time. Words have their meanings, yes, but as I understand the mantra's *function*, it's to help you get out of your head; the meaning is secondary, or, in the function. In the morning, I usually repeat it over and over . . . "Maranatha."

Later on, I try to just sit in the silence and listen, the way Mother Teresa described doing when she was talking to Dan Rather.

I respond to Sam, "That may be the most important prayer of all!"
I know you like the writings of the sixteenth century essayist Michel de Montaigne.[32] *Let me get you to reflect on a few of his quotes:*
"On the highest throne in the world, we still sit on our bottoms. . . ."

Vintage Montaigne!

"My art and profession is to live."

Ditto! Among the cool things about Montaigne is that he always sounds exactly like himself!

Creation care and proper stewardship of the world's resources is deeply rooted in Christian theology. Montaigne wrote, "Let us give Nature a chance; she knows her business better than we do." Any thoughts on that as board chair for Oceana?

That's Oceana's elevator speech![33] At the core of its mission is the belief that if we give the ocean the protection it needs, it will restore *itself* and provide humankind with a billion healthy protein meals every day, for the rest of time.

It's been fantastic to me, and very discouraging, to watch politicians and interests twist such a plain, experience-tested fact all out of shape. You can fool people, but you can't fool nature.

In the commencement address you gave to the graduating class of 2024 at Princeton University, you said that upon retiring from Law and Order, *"an entire piece of myself I had been renting out was freed up, . . ."* and then you went on to say, that "Play and joy are what life is all about." Is this opened space, . . . this playfulness in some way connected to your own spiritual journey?*

Spiritual journey sounds very serious, but, if it implies lightness of heart, yes. Belief is ready help with the hard stuff, but by no means is it just about the hard stuff. And acting is play—they call it *playacting*. I'm one of the lucky ones for whom work has been play all along.

The whole point of theater is to show us what it's like to be us. I think that's why it's always connected to religion.

I found your film The Killing Fields *hard to watch, but it needed to be seen, and that story needed to be told. It was a reminder that there is evil in the world, and of course that story is also told in the decades that* Law and Order *has been on the air. Sam, what would you say about the problem of evil?*

Above my pay grade! But there is a down-to-earth answer to evil: Do not take it lying down. Do something. Whatever happens, you'll feel better.

Dr. Daniel Pauly is on Oceana's board and a big reason I'm on the board.[34] He's a fish expert known around the world. The story of his early life is a parade of obstacles that makes *Oliver Twist* sound like a walk in the park.

I called him an optimist once, and he said, "I am not an optimist. I'm not a pessimist, either. Those words don't mean much to me. When I was quite young, I learned, when I ran into an obstacle, if I did nothing about it, I felt worse; if I did something, I felt better. Ever since, that's what I do: I do something. That's all. And it works. I feel better."

The big challenge these days is how to answer rage without rage but doing nothing won't make you feel better.

So what would you say to those people out in the world [who] are looking at Sam and saying, "Look at all he's achieved, what he's gotten and attained—is that where the meaning of life is found?"

Well, Russ, do you think the material world and the spiritual world necessarily have to be in opposition to one another?

No, I don't.

Me neither. The materialist view of the world is that this is it, that it's all there is, that just, you know, the person who dies with the most stuff wins. Well, . . . I don't think that.

I like stuff as much as the next person, but, for me, stuff without love can't hold a candle to love without stuff. But it's not "Man can live without bread," it's "Man can't live by bread alone." Good and bad are acted out in the material world. It's what you do with the material world you're given that separates the sheep from the goats, and on that score it's a very good thing God is forgiving, because which of us doesn't abuse it?

Sam, . . . anything else?

After we got married, all kinds of things called and pushed us to pick up threads we'd dropped along the way, but "reasonableness" remained an issue for me, long after we were regular churchgoers again.

William James turned out to be a big help, starting with something he'd said I picked up [from] I don't know where that stuck with me. I've been misquoting it ever since as, "We are what we attend to." Those few words led me to the library and a book of his collected works, which included *The Varieties of Religious Experience*, in which he went to great lengths—five or six hundred pages of length—to review the record, concluding that the evidence of God's active presence in people's lives was about as solid as the evidence that there once was a person named Julius Caesar, which is to say, enough for a reasonable person to conclude that God may exist.[35]

May? Really? Pretty weak tea to faithful people, maybe, but a big help for my problem. Bertrand Russell, a mathematician and philosopher who had a way with words, said he'd be happy to believe in God if it weren't for the lack of evidence.

William James (the correct quote is, "My experience is what I agree to attend to") turned that inside out for me, showed to my satisfaction that belief is as much a part of the real world as pancakes and broke down the obstacle of "reasonableness."

So, now, I'm a pragmatist myself!

I'll stop. There's a lot to be said for shutting up: "Be still, and know that I am God."

For me, mystery remains at the heart of faith and not faith only, at the heart of things as they are. I remain full of curiosity, but I'm beyond fine with the mystery.

SAM WATERSTON

An Emmy, a Golden Globe, a SAG award, and Oscar and Tony Award nominations are just a few of Sam Waterston's many achievements in a long and prestigious career. He has been in some of the most memorable works of film, television, and stage.

Recently Sam starred in Emmy-winning limited series *The Dropout*, where he portrayed the polarizing figure George Shultz, opposite Amanda Seyfried. Additionally, he was a lead opposite Jane Fonda, Lily Tomlin, and Martin Sheen on the Emmy-nominated Netflix original series *Grace and Frankie*, which ran for seven seasons, making it the longest-running Netflix original series. Sam also costarred alongside Jeff Daniels and Emily Mortimer in the Aaron Sorkin HBO series *The Newsroom*. Sam is perhaps best known for his portrayal of Jack McCoy on the iconic *Law and Order* franchise.

Sam started his career on the New York stage, appearing in multiple revivals of Shakespeare. His theater credits include *Indians*, *The Trial of Cantonsville Nine*, *A Doll's House*, and *Hamlet*, and he received rave reviews for his portrayal of Abe Lincoln in Gerald Gutierrez's *Abe Lincoln in Illinois*, for which he received a Tony nomination.

On the big screen, Waterston played Nick Carraway opposite Robert Redford and Mia Farrow in *The Great Gatsby*. He also starred in Woody Allen's Academy Award-nominated *Interiors*, *Hanna and Her Sisters*, and *September*. Roland Joffe's biographical drama film about the Khmer Rouge, *The Killing Fields*, earned Waterston an Academy Award nomination for his role as Sydney Schanberg.

Sam has also served as Board Chair of Oceana, the world's largest ocean-focused NGO and on the Board of Refugees International.

Photo credit: © Courtesy of the author

"An awareness of God and His mercy is a powerful thing. If you can grab onto it and take it on board and make it a part of you. It changes everything...."

—Brit Hume

Brit Hume

The name Brit Hume is synonymous with the vocation of journalism. For over sixty years, since his graduation from the University of Virginia, Brit has worked in virtually every possible post known to the profession—beginning as a reporter for the *Hartford Times*, then working with famed investigative journalist Jack Anderson, onto ABC News in 1973—serving as their White House Correspondent from 1989 through 1996, and for the last seventeen years as chief political analyst for Fox News.[1]

He has been a columnist, a news reporter, an author, and a documentary film producer. Though openly conservative, Brit is respected by his peers along all sides of the political spectrum for his professionalism and commitment to clarity, truth, and a consistent ability to rise above the often overcrowded and noisy room of biased news reporting.

In my early adult years, I always knew when I was listening to or watching Brit Hume I was getting the story as it was. I had no idea that by a chance meeting in Washington, DC, a friendship would be forged and a story unveiled that only increased my admiration for Brit all the more.

It was a chilly morning, and Laura and I were standing near the entrance to the National Cathedral on December 5, 2018. The State Funeral for President George H. W. Bush had just concluded. As the priest and pastor to President Bush, I was asked to offer the final homily and co-officiate at the service. The service had concluded, and most of the crowd, the press, and onlookers had left the area. Laura and I were standing alone, waiting to be picked up by the Secret Service to be driven to Andrews Air Force Base to fly with the president's family and casket back to Houston for the Houston-based funeral and burial in College Station, Texas.[2]

Brit walked up and greeted the two of us, and much to our surprise began to say how touched he was that the State Funeral, which could have had the potential of being overshadowed by the president's political record, or even the political climate of the day, was to Brit thoroughly faithful to Bush's own faith as it was lived out in the Christian tradition. He said he hoped we could keep in touch, and that we did.

A few years later, the St. Martin's family was deeply touched when Brit openly shared his journey of faith and how Jesus strengthened him when he faced one of the darkest valleys any parent can tread. The next morning, Brit's wife, Kim, offered a similar story of her own faith to hundreds who had gathered to hear her in St. Martin's parish hall.

Since that time, I have stayed in touch with Brit and Kim and could not imagine sharing this collection of reflections without including his insights as well.

Please share a bit about your religious upbringing.

Well, I was born into a nominally Christian family. We were members of the Episcopal Church, going back generations. I was christened as a little baby, and then around the age of twelve, I was confirmed at the Episcopal Church we attended, St. Margaret's on Connecticut Avenue in Washington, DC.

For nine years, I went to St. Alban's School on the grounds of the National Cathedral. The students attended chapel every single day at 8:20 a.m., and we sang and prayed.

I cannot say that I was a model Christian in those days. If someone had asked me if I was a Christian, I would have said yes, and if somebody asked me if I believed in God, in Christ, I would have said yes to that as well.

But it was not central to my life. I would describe it as something that was "there." But I would also say, Russ, that looking back, my life "in the church," in those early days, planted a seed in me—which was always present. And then, years later, when life hit me right between the eyes, it was there for me.

So, when you say, "planted a seed," that being baptized, being in the church, saying the prayers, singing the hymns—was all of that "forming you" in a way that you found it more deeply at just the time you needed it?

Well, yes; and I would say the hymns. Think about going to chapel every morning for nine years—that's a lot of time in chapel, . . . a lot of hymns. We attend a little Methodist Church here, but even when we sing those hymns, or I hear the melody from hymns we sang in chapel all those years ago, it takes me back.

As an aside, I've been told quite explicitly by a person who sat in front of me at the service you did for President Bush, 41, at the National Cathedral, that I should sing "very softly." I had a rebuttal at the ready—"I'm supposed to make a joyful noise to the Lord," but that was not even enough to convince me that I should sing loud.

But I love the music, . . . I love the hymns, . . . and, well, I do sing quietly.

Do you have a favorite hymn?

Oh my goodness, . . . I don't even know where to start—so many! I like "Onward Christian Soldiers," "O God, Our Help in Ages Past," which we sang at my son's funeral, and so of course, it has always been meaningful to me.[3]

What drove you into journalism?

In some ways, I kind of fell into it. I graduated as an English major from the University of Virginia in 1965 and by fall of that year, I was unemployed. I was expecting a child, and I had to find a job. And I tried throughout that summer, after my graduation, to find various jobs.

Russ, I had no idea what I wanted to do. I just needed a job. And finally, through an employment agency, I got a job in the old *Hartford Times*, the afternoon paper in Hartford, Connecticut, and I signed up there.

And I'll never forget this. I went in that newsroom on basically the first day. And the newsroom in 1965, Russ, was not distinguishable, really, from the newsroom, of say, 1935—clattering typewriters, sort of an irreverent spirit in the place. And there was, there was a guy on the copy desk whose name was Bill Shea. . . . And if he hadn't been named Bill Shea, we would need to change his name to Bill Shea. This was the "Bill Shea" of all time. White haired, stogie in the mouth, ruddy cheeks, and a deep voice.

He would shout, "Copy!" across the room and the copy boy, which is what we called them back then, would come over and pick up a piece of copy and take it where it needed to go. And I thought to myself, "This is the coolest place I've ever been!"

Now I said a moment ago, I kind of fell into it, but when I look back, I realize what an incredible blessing it was. When I think about all the people in their twenties working for a decade, just trying to get their foot on the bottom rung of the right ladder, and there it was! I was an English major, which was useless for writing news, and I walked into that place and I realized "That's what I want to do!" And I have been a reporter ever since—that was sixty years ago!

Looking back, do you see God's hand in any of that?

Oh, do I ever! We were not in the best situation—I was young, married, a baby on the way, without a job. We weren't going to be hurting for something to eat or a place to live, because my wife's family helped—we were living with my mother-in-law. But I needed a job, and I landed one in the right spot for me.

So, yes. I absolutely see it as a blessing of God.

I think it might be fair to say you had a rather meteoric rise. I, like all of America, watched when you were on ABC with Peter Jennings. You were quickly thrust into of tens of millions of homes. Was that ever overwhelming?

Well, for a few years, I was not on the air, except for interviews. And, yes, then they asked me if I'd like to try it as a correspondent. I'll confess to you that at the time, my view was that television journalists were slightly comical figures that stood, put makeup on their face, lacquer on their hair, and then stand in front of an inanimate object and speak to it.

So, at first, when they asked me, I said, "No, . . . I don't think I want to do that." But I circled back to it, because I realized the reason I did not want to do it is that I thought I might fail.

I had just worked on a documentary for ABC, and I wanted to get back into the news and I think this ended up being a good opportunity.[4] So I agreed, and boy, I was bad the first time. I had my head tilted to one side. I didn't know I was doing it, and they couldn't use it.

The producer was Tom Capra, the son of the great Hollywood director Frank Capra. Tom was a very talented guy who had been in the business for a long time. He was friendly with me, but he was blunt. I had just done a piece straight to camera. I didn't fluff or tilt my head to the side. So, I thought I did fine.

I came out and I saw Capra walking down the hall and he said, "I just saw you on the air, you look like you were glued to the set!" *(Brit and I both laugh!)*

And I am sure that's exactly what I looked like.

But over time, I realized that the way we express ourselves on television is not a normal form of delivery. It's different. It needs to be. And when I finally faced up to that, I began to get better.

Remember, there were only three networks back then—ABC, NBC, and CBS—but for a long time, ABC was ranked as number three. Over time, some really good executives came, and we began to get a huge boost in the network's ratings and by that time, I wasn't nearly as bad as I had been at the start, so I was good enough so that I passed enough muster, and I got some opportunities. And eventually I covered Capitol Hill for eleven years, and then the White House for eight, and I have been here with Fox News for twenty-eight years.

You've met and know a lot of leaders from around the United States and the world. Of those you've gotten to know, who do you most admire and why?

That's a hard question, because I admire different leaders for different things. I will tell you this—the single most talented politician I ever covered, and the most charming man I ever met with, was Bill Clinton, hands down.

And probably the most decent and kind man, I mean, of the senior figures that I've covered, it would be awfully hard to top George H. W. Bush.

Those who know and admire your work, as I do, know you have a dogged commitment to the truth. In fact, your wife, Kim, likes to describe you as a "truth teller." What insights can you share about the importance of truth-telling as a journalist and now, as a commentator?

The first thing I learned when I got into this business as a young reporter was that there are at least two sides to every story. Now they're often not equal. As a reporter, you may make up your mind about a particular story, but your job is to give both sides equal play, and then let the audience or the reader make up their own minds.

That doesn't mean you give equal weight to everything, but it does mean you give a fair shake to everybody, and that you present the views, debates, commentary, whatever it is in a way that people who hold those views can recognize. I think your job is to present the stories in an honest and fair way.

When you change roles from a strict reporter to a commentator, the obligation to be fair should not go away. Yes, you are allowed to express your own opinions, but I think there is much more value to the audience if they're done in a way that makes the audience know that you recognize that there's another side to these stories—and I think that's appreciated.

There is, of course, a whole category of viewers and readers who have partisan interests and rooting interest, and if you say what they agree with, they're going to think you're a great journalist, and if you don't, they're going to think you're a bum.

I'm sorry, I cannot play it that way. I'm not trying to pander to an audience. As you know, I'm a conservative, and I think there's a lot of territory on the conservative side of the ledger that's not properly represented, but I still think it's necessary to be fair.

Being fair is the primary challenge in journalism. In the end, my view is, whether reporter or commentator, you need to be interesting and fair. The easiest way to jazz up a piece is by sticking in an opinion—try to give it some little edge, but as a reporter, you should not do that, and as a commentator, do it in a fair way.

At times, your truth-telling has gotten you into a little trouble. I suspect a lot of people might not know that there was a season when you and your family were surveilled by the Central Intelligence Agency! Can you say a bit more about that?

I was working for Jack Anderson, the syndicated columnist, at the time, and he had done a story based on a leak of papers that dealt with the India-Pakistan war during the Nixon years. And it had shown that the United States secretly had tilted toward Pakistan in that conflict, which was striking because India was then, as now, the largest democracy on the face of the earth.

And Pakistan was certainly not that. And the tilt toward Pakistan had strategic value, I'm sure, but it was a secret basis, and this exposed that. Jack would later get a Pulitzer Prize for that. But the CIA was alarmed about the leak, and yet, the CIA isn't supposed to investigate people in the continental United States. It's a foreign intelligence agency.

They started a surveillance operation. And we all had code names. I forget what Jack's was—I was called "Eggnog!" *(Brit laughs.)*

But, yes, they surveilled the house. They followed my wife and kids to school. I had absolutely nothing to hide—my life was an open book.

When I finally did find out about it, some people thought it must have been terrifying. It really did not feel that way.

But I will tell you about a time that was quite scary. This was even before I went to work with Jack, and I started working on a story about the United Mine Workers of America.[5] As I was doing my research, I ended up developing some sources.

I did a little story at the tail end of one of Jack's columns—it was not longer than your thumb, Russ. But I referenced something about papers being removed during an investigation. The result was a long running suit by a lawyer from the union—who sued under his own name. The purpose of the suit was clearly to get the name of my unnamed source, which as a reporter I was unwilling to do.

A judge ruled against us and said I had to disclose the name. We were allowed, eventually, to take it up on what's called an interlocutory appeal, where you appeal the issue before the case has been tried.

The whole thing dragged on for years and hung over me for a long time. I thought in the end, there was going to be a ruling against us—and I would then be faced with the possibility of a default judgment which would have been ruinous.

It all finally came down rather dramatically. Some years later my source came forward of her own volition and identified herself to the court. The case went to trial, but it had dragged on for four years. We won the case at trial.

I would love to tell you, Russ, at the time, that I was relying on my faith and the Lord to get through that, but the truth is, . . . I was . . . scared . . . to . . . death.

I had not really had to fall back on my faith yet, but that would certainly come later.

So let's turn to that moment that came later, when you had to live every parent's worst nightmare, the suicide of your beloved son, Sandy, in February 1998 at the age of twenty-eight. Can you talk a bit about that?

Sandy was such a good kid. He had been a good student, a good athlete. He'd been all-metropolitan lacrosse at Landon School, in Bethesda, just outside Washington. He was on the football team, and he had good grades. He graduated and went on to Middlebury College in Vermont and graduated with honors.

He followed me into journalism, and he was doing well, and he had just gotten a job [at] U.S. News & World Report.

He had some issues with drinking. He was not a constant drinker, but when he drank, he would get into trouble. He was a wild drunk. He had an incident with a doorman in New York. He was well up into his twenties now and after that happened, I told him, "Sandy, you are not doing anything that I didn't do when I was a young man, but you're older than I was when I was doing this stuff, and it's time for you to stop this stuff, it's got to stop."

But he went out one night with one of his friends. He had been drinking again and was speeding, and he got pulled over. He thought his life was going to be all over, . . . that he would lose his job—that it would be the end of everything.

It was a gross overestimation of the problem. And he killed himself.

So, I'm sitting in my office, not aware of any of this. And an Arlington County policeman came to see me, and he said, "Your son is dead."

It was absolutely devastating.

Amid going through that, something changed in your own faith journey. What happened?

I remember at the time, I had this feeling, this sense that this was so bad and so undeserved for Sandy and for all of us, and I kept thinking that God was there and that the phone was going to ring, or something like this was going to happen, and I would pick up the phone and a voice would say, "Brit, this is God, and this is what this is all about."

Of course, nothing like that happened, but some things did happen.

Look, in those days, I was at Fox News. Those were the early days, and Fox News was second only to being in the witness protection program for being invisible.

People look at me now and they think, "You are very well known." But I'm much more well known now than I was then.

But for some reason, the word of Sandy's suicide got around, and I started receiving sympathy notes and cards in the mail. And in the days after his death, I would come home to the mailbox in our place.

Our mailbox was one of those that fitted up against the wall. And I would come home and open it, and there would be so many letters, and notes and cards in there that I could hardly pull them all out. This went on for weeks, I was overwhelmed by the expressions of sympathy, and I felt loved, and I felt supported.

Fortunately, I didn't have a lot, I wasn't carrying a lot of guilt about a bad relationship, because Sandy and I had a really good relationship.

But I remember thinking, you know, "Brit, if you weren't a believer, you wouldn't be thinking this way. And I thought it's time to start to face up to what you now know you believe, because it had been there all along, I think I just neglected it. And so I began to try to live my life differently, and to try to be mindful of the love that God has bestowed on us all and the salvation that He has offered.

And I think what an extraordinary thing God's love is. It really is the greatest story ever told.

So, ever since then, I've been trying to live my life differently, in the knowledge of that love and what we believe in our faith.

Brit, before we move away from Sandy's death, what advice would you give to parents who have a child who takes their own life?

Well, the first thing I would say is that as painful and excruciating as it is—for it is like an amputation, really. You feel like something has been taken from you, a part of you that mattered deeply and it's never coming back—and that's the reality, . . . but, . . . it gets better. . . . God is good.

His love is real, and it's there for you, it's available to you, and just accept it, believe it. Pray, which helps bring an awareness of God. And you know, an awareness of God and His mercy is a powerful thing. If you can grab onto it and take it on board and make it a part of you, it changes everything.

All of that was many years ago. Now, my daughter has two daughters, so I have two granddaughters, both of whom are grown and out of college. And I love them so deeply. You are a grandfather, so you know it may be the most powerful force of the heart—an unbelievable thing.

And I feel doubly blessed. I really do. Kim and I have been married now going on thirty-two years, and she is such a wonderful wife. She's a believer—and let me tell you, she practices it, because I test her by being a pain in the butt all the time. She finds a way to absorb it all!

But what I am saying is, God is present. His love is real. Reach out and accept it, believe it, and you will find that there is life after tragedy.

As this turn in your faith journey happened, your friend, fellow broadcaster Fred Barnes, came alongside you and encouraged you in your faith. How important was that to you?[6]

I knew Fred Barnes back in high school, and he was the ultimate rationalist. If someone had told me back in those days, Russ, that he would end up being a committed Christian and a profound believer, I would have said, "I don't think so!"

In those days, if you could not prove something to him empirically right in front of him, he ain't buying it, because you could not get anything, I mean anything, by Fred Barnes! If you want to prove something, you had better have a good argument and the evidence to back it up, because he could be merciless!

But yes, he did turn to Jesus, which certainly interested me. But he would come alongside me in a very quiet and gentle way and tried to bring me along to the deeper place where he was. He gave me a copy of Malcolm Muggeridge's book *Jesus Rediscovered*.[7]

I read it and it was helpful. I didn't have any argument against it, but it just did not take hold of me the way it would later, when I made that decision to take my faith more seriously after Sandy's death. And so, yes, I am very grateful to him. He really encouraged me, and we began to attend Bible study with our wives and other friends.

Barnes also introduced you to Jerry Leachman, the former Alabama football player who had become a minister. How did that relationship help you?[8]

Well, after Sandy died, Jerry would come by my place in DC, I guess it was Friday mornings, and we would talk about the Lord. It was a great chance to tell him what I was thinking and what I was feeling, and he had a gift for listening. His relationship as a pastor, but also a friend, became very important to me, and remains so to this day. It is important to have those kinds of people in your life who can help you along the way, and Jerry sure did that for me.

Your wife, Kim, has a remarkable story of faith. She battled alcoholism for several years, and at one point, was so deep into despair that she asked God to kill her, ... but as she puts it, the message she heard back was no. And then she took her own deeper steps into her faith.

Well, she had reached a stage in her life where she was a very successful young producer, traveling around the world, but she had a drinking problem. And she realized if she did not stop, she was going to die. She was in her late twenties when she stopped. That was 1981, so she has not had a drink in forty-four years!

Her faith helped her through that—you just mentioned that prayer and yes, God was not going to take her! So she decided to give it up. She went to Alcoholics Anonymous meetings for years and years and all of that transformed her life.

She and I believe, as I'm sure you do, that AA is one of the greatest institutions in the world.

Can you say a bit more about how your marriage—as a couple committed to Christ—has impacted your faith?

I can't imagine going through my life without being married to a fellow believer. We married in 1993, over thirty years ago, but our faith strengthens us. Our faith is something we share, and it is a real bond between us. I think about it all the time and feel so blessed that she is the way she is. She's not just a Christian in name, she is a believer who is serious about her faith—but not in a priggish way.

When I think about all my failings, and I am filled with them(!), and yet her incredible tolerance and forgiveness, I realize how incredibly blessed I am.

As you know, we live on this little island in Florida, and we have attended a few churches here. We began in an Episcopal Church and now attend Lighthouse United Methodist Church. I will say, churches in this area are active. You know, with all the retired people here, it's kind of "God's waiting room"! People are trying to set things right with the Lord, because they think they are going to see him soon!

But that is a big part of our life. We love our pastor, and we love to worship together and sing the hymns. But so much would be missing if these were things, and beliefs, we did not share.

We have all heard the words, "the shot heard 'round the world." There was a moment when you made some comments in January of 2010, about Tiger Woods right after his rather public scandal. I am not hovering on Woods's past, as much has certainly improved in his life. But at that time he was sinking in a mire of personal and public scandals, and you were asked what advice you might have for him. Can you retell that story?

Back to Jerry Leachman, he had this great question to those who attended his Bible studies. "If someone accused you of being a Christian, would there be enough evidence to convict you?" And of course it would make me think, "Well, Hume, what have you done to prove you are a Christian?"

I could think of a few things to put on the scoreboard, but I had not really put it out there so to speak.

And of course, things have become much better for Tiger Woods, but back then, at the time, we had seen what a great golfer he was—what a determined man he could be, but he had fallen into this situation where it all blew up.

I remember thinking how devastating that must have been for him and for everyone around him and I thought what a wonderful thing if he could turn to Christ in all of that, and I said just that on *Fox News Sunday*. I knew once I said it it would really stir things up, and it certainly did. No one enjoys being criticized, but it goes with my business.

But, to this day, I am glad I said it and it was the right thing to say. Whoever you are, whatever you do, if your life is falling apart, I would tell you to turn to Christ. I did when everything was falling apart around me, and it got me through, and I would tell anyone to do the same. Like Jerry said, I think that tells others that I am a Christian and what I have found in Christ.

From the perspective of a journalist who is a Christian, what changes—if any—would you make in the face of what I will call the "climate" of news today?

When I started in this business, the line between news and opinion was pretty clearly drawn, and you just didn't get to editorialize. And the premium was really on becoming a smart, capable, hard-driving reporter whose stories were clear and easy to follow.

Your principal obligation was to inform your readers in a way that was interesting and fair and that was then up to them to be the ones that held people accountable.

But a lot of journalists have gotten into this business now of trying to influence the interpretation of the story, to influence not as a side effect but as the purpose of their reporting. And I think we need desperately to get away from that. And I think it's led our media into a lot of places where the trust level is now just collapsed, and you see the evidence everywhere.

I mean, newspapers are folding right and left now. Some of that [is] simply because the media technology has moved on. It's not an obsolete form of journalism, it is still influential, but their problems are worsened by the fact that they can't get it right on being fair and balanced.

And that's the direction I always say we go. That's, to me, the way I look at it as a Christian and really, I think it is a godly mission.

Brit, can you share a bit about your prayer life?

Well, I need to tell you that I have a little issue with praying for things we want or need. Because we worship a God whom we believe knows us better than we know ourselves. He already knows what we need, . . . certainly better than we do! And he certainly knows what we want.

If a friend of mine is sick, God knows that, right? The God I worship knows better than either the friend or I know what that person needs to do. Do I really need to "tell" God about that?

For me, the question is, "Well, why do we pray to Jesus?" And you know, Jesus wanted us to pray. Paul talked about praying unceasingly.[9]

So, I think to myself—I don't quite do that, but I do pray. I don't need to pray, "Dear God, I don't need to tell you this, but so and so needs healing," because God already knows that. I actually don't believe the loving God we worship is not going to provide for us because we don't ask him, right? I mean, He loves us.

So, when I pray, I am opening myself up to be continually aware of God's presence, that He's looking out for me and so mostly, I offer prayers of gratitude for all He has done and is doing in my life and the lives of those I love.

Wasn't it Mother Teresa who was asked by Dan Rather, "When you pray, what do you say to God?" And she said, "I don't say anything, I listen." And Rather says back, "Okay, when God speaks to you, what does he say?" And she said back, "He listens . . . !" Great story!

Yes! Actually, Sam Waterston referenced that story in our time together! Well, let me ask if you have any other spiritual disciplines?

We are still in a prayer group—a Bible study. . . . I am always on the lookout for a good Bible study!

Do you have a favorite Bible verse?

Yes, . . . Matthew 25:40, "Truly I tell you, just as you did it to one of the least of these brothers and sisters of mine *[Brit tears up and his voice cracks a bit]*, . . . you did it to me."

That verse really moves me. I stumble through it, just as I am stumbling through it now.

And I think of it often. You may know that I have served on the board of the Youth For Tomorrow home for boys located in Bristow, Virginia. NFL Coach Joe Gibbes started it back in 1986 and that verse is one of the underlying principles of the work they do. Joe's still very involved and he keeps that verse on a plaque on his desk in front of him.

Before we wrap up, let me ask you, from your unique perspective of someone who has been in this work for sixty years, do you believe America has a moral role to play in helping to address those myriads of problems in our world today?

Yes. There are times when power is required to do the right thing, and America should play a role in that around the world. There is nothing ungodly about that.

Think of this situation in eastern Europe right now, where you have this completely unprovoked invasion by one country against another. We have been providing support, which I actually think may be insufficient. We need to think about the power of our example. What would the consequences be if the United States pulled the plug on Ukraine and left it to the tender mercies of Vladimir Putin?

So, I believe we do have a role to play in the world—a moral role—it is one of the reasons people are beating down the doors to get in our country every day.

Let me ask a question I have asked of others in this book. You have attained a lot of what the world values as success—fame, influence, power, success. What would you say to people who believe what you have is all you really need, and nothing more?

Well, I would say, that really does not work. I mean, it's a lot better to have those things [than] not have them. I'm not making any argument about that.

But I would say that in the end, the things that matter most are the people in your life and the love you share.

You are invested in them and they in you. Deep down, I think everyone has that sense of doing worthy work and making some contribution to your fellow man.

And if you don't have any of that—the love, the relationships, the purposeful work, you can pile the gold up as high as it goes, and still not be fulfilled.

No, what is the most important thing is loving others and making the world a better place, and as we have been talking about here, my faith inspires me to do that.

How would you like to be remembered?

I'd like to be remembered as a guy who did his best to do an honest job, . . . and . . . who loved the Lord.

BRIT HUME

Brit Hume currently serves as a chief political analyst for Fox News Channel (FNC). He acts as a regular panelist on Fox's weekly public affairs program, *Fox News Sunday*, and contributes to all major political coverage. He joined the network in 1996.

Hume has provided analyses of every major political event since joining the network. On Inauguration Day 2025, Hume contributed to the extensive coverage live from Washington, DC, commentating on President-elect Donald Trump and Vice President-elect JD Vance being sworn into office. He contributed to the network's 2024 election coverage, as well as FNC's 2022 midterm election coverage, and previously provided coverage during the 2020 presidential and vice presidential debates, and the Democratic and Republican National Conventions. Most recently, Hume contributed to the extensive coverage of the 2024 Republican National Convention and President Biden's withdrawal from his candidacy in the 2024 election.

Previously, from September 2016 until the 2016 presidential election, Hume stepped in as interim host of *On the Record*. He also previously anchored *Special Report* and led the program for more than ten years, stepping down in December 2008. Under his leadership, *Special Report* was the highest rated political program on cable television. In this capacity, Hume also served as the Washington managing editor and was responsible for overseeing news content for Fox News's Washington bureau. He also anchored all of the network's coverage for every presidential election from 1996-2008.

Before joining Fox News in 1996, Hume was with ABC News for twenty-three years, serving as chief White House correspondent from 1989 through 1996. During his tenure, he contributed to *World News Tonight with Peter Jennings*, *Nightline* and *This Week*, as well as various specials for the news division.

Earlier, Hume reported for United Press International, beginning his career as a newspaper reporter with *The Hartford Times* and *The Baltimore Evening Sun*.

He has received numerous honors and awards, including the 2003 Sol Taishoff Award for Excellence in Broadcast Journalism from the National Press Foundation and a 1991 Emmy Award for his coverage of the Gulf War. The author of two books, *Inside Story* and *Death and the Mines*, Hume was named "the best in the business" by the *American Journalism Review* for his extensive news coverage of the White House.

A graduate of the University of Virginia, Hume resides in Florida with his wife Kim Schiller Hume.

Photo credit: © Katherine Holland

"Did God exist? Of course. God was as real to me as the wind that rustled through our garden... my faith gives me an inner peace that gives meaning to my life..."

—Dr. Jane Goodall

Dr. Jane Goodall

I have known Jane Goodall's name since my days in elementary school. Growing up in the late 1960s, a shift toward what you and I know as environmentalism was beginning to sweep the globe. The first "Earth Day" was actually held on April 22, 1970, which heralded the clarion call to care for the planet we inhabit, and tend and care for it, as it has cared for humanity since we began to walk upon its face. Dr. Jane Goodall was and continues to be at the very heart of this movement.

Few, if any, have done more for the cause of caring for creation than Dr. Jane Goodall, and yet, I had no idea that she would be included in this collection of conversations until just shortly before I began to pull this book together.

Yes, I knew of Dr. Goodall's work in Africa, particularly among the chimpanzees in Africa, but I think in all fairness, what I knew stopped there. Until my wife introduced me to some of her writings. As I read, and as we listened to Dr. Goodall's books, frankly I became mesmerized and enthralled as the extraordinary story of this naturalist who has, since first stepping onto the continent of Africa over 65 years ago, literally changed the world.

If one were to number all the people to whom she has spoken over the years about her mission (and it is precisely that) to call others to not only give thanks for what we receive in Creation, but also to care for it—well, it would outnumber perhaps all of the clergy who have ever preached sermons in the same amount of time.

I am indebted to my mentor and friend, Secretary James Baker III, who has a very special friendship with Dr. Goodall. During his years as Secretary of State, Secretary Baker, who, as you have read here, also loves God's gift of creation—and often experiences God in nature—paved the way for Dr. Goodall to broaden her work beyond the confines of Gombe, Tanzania to untold numbers of countries around the globe. Their special friendship, is, in fact, just that. So much so that Dr. Goodall named one of her famous chimps "James" (and that chimp is still around today!).

Jim and Susan Baker connected us with a wonderful member of Dr. Goodall's staff—Susana Name. And, after a vigorous appeal on my part, Dr. Jane Goodall agreed to spend some time in conversation.

At the time, Dr. Goodall had just settled into a modest cabin in Nebraska—a trek she made annually, as her busy schedule would allow—to witness a crane migration. Over 90 years of age, Dr. Goodall still travels the world (roughly 300 days a year), on her mission to help not only protect, but to save our bruised and ailing planet.

I confess that I had no idea that Dr. Goodall was a believer until I began to read her works and listen to her lectures. If there ever was an evangelist to state the case for creation care, her name is Dr. Jane Goodall. But her witness does not end there. In her own words now, let me introduce you to a new friend, "Dr. Jane," who knows the Great Spiritual Power of the Universe, and the gift that power offers in what she calls "The Next Great Adventure."

Before the opening lines of "Jungle Book," Rudyard Kipling quotes a bit of verse from his own poem, "Night-song in the Jungle," ... "Oh hear the call!"[1] *You "heard the call" to the jungle at a very young age, can you say just a bit more about that?*

As long as I can recall, I loved animals. I was fascinated with them. Let me give you an example. When I was 18 months old, I brought a group of worms from the outside into my bedroom!

When my mum found out, instead of being angry and throwing them out, she noticed that I was watching them so intently. She told me she thought that I must have been wondering how they could move without legs. Gently, she told me how they needed to be in the earth, or they would die, and so we took them back out into the garden.

One time, when I was four years old, Mum took me for a holiday on a farm. It was a proper farm with animals in the fields, hens in the farmyard sleeping at night in little hen houses to keep them safe from foxes—and there were nest boxes around for hens to lay their eggs, and I helped collect eggs.

Once again, very curious, I began to ask my mum about where the hole was for the egg to come out! So one, day, I saw a hen go into the hen house and thought she was getting ready to lay an egg—so I followed her! What a mistake! She flew out with squawks of fear. In my little mind I must have thought that no hen would lay in that scary place. So I went into an empty hen house and waited. I sat quietly for four hours! Of course, my mum wondered where I was and was just about to call the police—when she saw me rushing to the house.

Instead of scolding me, she listened to my wonderful story of how a hen lays an egg!

What my mum was doing with her gentle way was the making of little scientist—curiosity, asking questions, not getting answers, deciding to find out myself, making a mistake, not giving up, learning patience.

I suppose different mothers might have said, "How dare you go off like that without telling us! Don't you dare to that again!" And in doing that, one might be crushing scientific curiosity. If that had happened to me, I might not have done what I chose to do!

It is of extreme value to have supportive parents. (I would add it is the same with chimp mothers!)

You know, our world was pretty simple back then. We had no television of course; it was not even invented yet. So, I learned from nature, from books. . . . Oh, I loved books!

I spent most of my Saturday afternoons in secondhand bookshops.

The first book I really loved was *Dr. Doolittle*.[2] Then, at age ten, I found a little cheap edition of *Tarzan of the Apes*.[3] And I fell in love with the lord of jungle. Of course, it still bothers me that he married the wrong Jane!

But that's when my dream began—to go to Africa and live with wild animals and write books about them.

Back then, I was not really thinking of being a scientist, because girls just did not do that back then!

Your grandmother's (Danny's) favorite Bible verse, and yours as well, is from Deuteronomy 33:25, ". . . as thy days, so shall thy strength be . . . ,"[4] Why does that verse speak to you?

Well, it just means there will be no task that I won't be able to do. It just means, you know, "Just believe," that if a task has been given to you, you will be able to live up to it. You will be given the strength to get it done!

Can you say a bit more about your religious upbringing? How did you practice your faith in your home?

My grandfather was a Congregational Minister. He was amazing—I never met him, but I wish I had. He died before I was born. Danny married a much older man. When the war broke out, Mum, Judy and I came to Bournemouth to live in the Birches with Danny, and her other two daughters.[5]

We were not especially religious, but we went to church quite often. We worshipped at Richmond Hill Congregational Church, which was the last church my grandfather served before he got cancer.[6]

We attended a Church of England School. We said grace before every meal. My Mum's older sister, Olly, sang in the choir.

I had a picture (still have it) of Jesus on the mountainside reaching down to rescue a lamb. Mum told me that I was a Christian and believed in *God* because I was born into a Christian family, and so I grew up in a Christian family that held Christian beliefs.

But I suppose if I'd been born in Egypt, I'd be a Muslim and believe in Allah and so on. But that the name God, Allah, Jehovah—must of course be speaking of the same—God.

Can you share a bit about the "Bible Box," and what role it played in your childhood home? Do you still have that box?

When I was about 14, I made Danny a "Bible Box." She had one with rolled up strips of paper containing texts from the Bible. All very soothing and reassuring. But I knew the Bible was not like that. I read EVERY chapter of the

Bible and wrote out the texts on tiny strips of paper—the height of the tray of the original match boxes—and I put the book, chapter and verse on the back.

I glued six match boxes together, three high and put little handles on them using paper clips. I covered it all with blue paper and gave it to Danny as a Christmas present. It took about three months to make.

Sometimes when I am having to pack and get on the road again, these days, my sister, Judy, says I should go and pull out a text!

There are about twenty texts in each drawer, and we put them back in different places. Three different times I have pulled out "He who has once set his hand to the plough share, and looketh back, is not fit for the Kingdom of Heaven!"[7]

Judy says with a grin when I have pulled that out—"Off you go and stop complaining!" Amazing.

And yes, so, I still have box! Though some texts got lost over the years.

At the age of sixteen, it seems your faith really blossomed, perhaps in part due to the preaching of your vicar, the Reverend Trevor Davies. You have written of that season of life, "I felt very close to Jesus, and I prayed to him a good deal."[8] Can you share a bit more about that time in your life?

Indeed, Trevor was Welsh, had a wonderful voice, and preached wonderful sermons. I was platonically in love. We were very young at that time, compared with 16-year-olds in those days—probably more like a 13-year-old today! We were very innocent.

I went to church to hear him. He preached incredible sermons, and I would do what I could to run into him from time to time!

When I left home and first went to London to do secretarial training and then got a job in Oxford, Jesus was as real as the people in my life.

When I got a job in London a year later this phase gradually faded. As I grew older and began to read about the horrors of the wars fought in the name of religion—the horrors of the Inquisition and so on, I began to see that religion could lead to fanaticism and persecution.

So, while my faith in the Great Spiritual Force remained, it became different from religion per se.

People often remark on your countenance. . . . In secretarial school, someone once said to you, "You so often have a little smile on your face . . . as if you have a wonderful secret." And you have written of that, "I did—I felt as though I had a personal relationship with Jesus."[9] In some ways, you want to keep that a secret, because your faith is a very personal thing, but you still have that smile—as we visit today, you have that smile even now! And you still apparently have that "secret." How does that manifest itself in your day-to-day life now?

Today, at this point in my life, I have a very strong belief in a Great Spiritual Power "in which I live and move and have my being."[10] How else could I cope with the crazy schedule I have now!

Sometimes, I feel too tired to give a lecture, I feel like curling up and hiding. Yet I get out on the stage and give one of my very best lectures. People with me notice it. I do not take it for granted—I am grateful. Then there have been a number of times when I should have died, or at least been very badly hurt, and for some reason, I have been spared. *Something* saves me. That *Something* is that Great Spiritual Power, it is God. But my understanding and experience of God has changed over the years.

You have read some of what I have written, and when asked, "Did God exist?" My answer is, of course! God is as real to me as the wind that rustles through our garden . . . my faith gives me an inner peace that gives meaning to my life . . .

Did I tell you about the dream I had?

I don't think so?

It was one of the most vivid dreams I have ever, ever had. It was not too long after that time in my life, of course, many years ago. In the dream, I found myself in Jerusalem, and there was a great throng of noisy people shouting. I could smell the sweat, and I was right in the middle of them. And I saw this cross up ahead, with this man penned to it, and I pushed through all these people, and I got right to the foot of that cross. And I looked up at Jesus. And it was a terrible moment when I could feel his suffering, and then it ended, and I awoke. It was amazingly powerful, and I can still remember it clearly now—decades later.

In March 1957, a life-changing moment occurred when you met Dr. Louis Leakey. You have spoken and written not only in your belief that many moments like this are not "random," and, allow me to borrow your words, "I do believe somehow that I was put here for a reason . . . when I look back over my life I can't help thinking there was some kind of path mapped out for me—I was given opportunities and I had to just make the right choices."[11] Dr. Goodall, do you believe that path was placed before you by, as you sometimes say, quoting the Apostle Paul (who was quoting the ancient poets of Athens) "the one in whom we live and move and have our being"?[12]

I do definitely believe in free will, and I did not have to make the choices I made, but I cannot help but feel I have been put into this world with a mission that I am trying my best to fulfill.

Perhaps aside from Almighty, no one was a bigger cheerleader for Jane Goodall than Dr. Leakey, . . . who else?

Oh, my family, especially my mother!

I love how, when you faced moments of doubt about whether you were the right person to continue expanding the research Dr. Leakey had begun, that he would write you, "I KNOW you can!" How important is it to have those kinds of people in our lives? How important is it for us to offer that kind of encouragement to others?[13]

It was somewhat frustrating at the time, because I was doubting myself so much. I felt like I could not do it, but then he would write that! I "know" you can!

I think that it is desperately necessary to have people who can give support, reach out a helping hand when needed, boost your morale when you are down, praise you when you do a good job. And we should definitely help others in the same way. People have told me that I do that for them, which I am honored to do.

What might you say to young people today—or perhaps people of any age, who are looking for such a path?

I tell them that I think everyone has a role to play. Many people never find out what that is. I tell them to wait and hopefully they will suddenly say "Ah, that is what I want to do." And then roll up their sleeves and work at it. But if, say, halfway through a degree they find that after all it is not what they want to do, they should not be afraid of admitting this and changing course. But we need those encouragers, . . . and we need to encourage others!

So on July 16, 1960, you began your first journey to Gombe, Tanzania, which from that point forward would be another "home" in many ways. I think most of us cannot imagine the kinds of thoughts that filled your heart and mind at the beginning of that great adventure, but can you tell our readers about another particularly moving experience you had while alone in the jungle?[14]

Let me share one moment that occurred with one of the chimps I named, Flo.[15] For four months the chimpanzees ran from me. I can never forget the first time they let me sit near them without running off. I can never forget when old Flo allowed her precious infant to totter up to me (keeping a protective hand under his tummy), looking up with those big wide eyes, and he reached out and touched my nose.

But beyond those kinds of moments, there have been these incredible experiences. It only happens when I am alone in the forest, and it has only happened four of five times—I become one with the natural world. When with another, even someone you love, you are two humans "in" nature. Alone the I is not there; it is that I am just part of nature. It is hard to explain, but I am, in some way, one with nature.

You have said that one of the myriads of lessons you learned from the chimpanzees is that child-rearing should be fun, something you tried to mimic once your son Grub came along. Again, in your own words, "We all need, as adults, some experience to make us look at the world again through the eyes of a child."[16] *Jesus taught that we all should receive the gift of God's kingdom like a child—which puts you in good company!*[17] *Why do you, and Jesus, think children have so much to teach us?*

They are so innocent. They are full of wonder. They are full of fun. Every new experience adds to their growing knowledge. Sadly, all too soon, they learn that the world is not all fun. Sadly, today, millions of children are born into war. Into hunger and suffering. And learning not all people are nice and loving.

In the spring of 1974, on the heels of several deep challenges in your life, you visited Notre Dame Cathedral and had a remarkable experience. Can you share about that . . . ?

I had gone to Paris for a UNESCO conference on aggression.[18] I had always been fascinated by the Cathedral and wanted to go inside ever since I read Victor Hugo's *The Hunchback of Notre Dame*.[19] I made my way into the Cathedral—there were not many people around, and it was quiet and still inside. I gazed in silent awe at the great Rose Window, glowing in the morning sun. And all at once the Cathedral was filled with this huge volume of sound. There was an organ playing Bach's *Toccata and Fugue in D Minor* for a wedding taking place in a distant corner of the Cathedral. I always loved the opening of that piece, but in that space, filling its vastness, it seemed to literally enter and possess my whole self. It was as though the music was in some way alive.

In that moment, I suddenly captured a moment of eternity. It was perhaps the closest I ever came to experiencing ecstasy—mystical ecstasy. The whole experience completely revived my old preoccupation with philosophy and the meaning of life. I began to ask myself, "Was there a guiding force in the universe? A Creator of matter and thus of life itself? Was there a purpose to life on planet earth? And if so, what role are we to play in the world? And yes, what role should "I" play?

I wrote about this in my book *Reason for Hope*, but there really are only two ways that we can think about our existence here on earth. Either we agree with Macbeth that life is nothing more than a "tale told by an idiot," a purposeless emergence of life-forms, including the clever, greedy, selfish and unfortunately destructive species that we call *Homo sapiens*—an "evolutionary goof."[20] That's one way to see things, . . . or as Pierre Teilhard de Chardin suggested, there is something going on in the universe that looks very much like conception, . . . like birth.[21]

The more I thought about all of this, these ultimate questions, during the trying time of my divorce, I came to realize that my time in the forest and my understanding of the chimpanzees had given me a new perspective. I became utterly convinced that there was a great spiritual power that we call God.[22]

Also, you have called the outcome of that experience as a call to action. I think we all know, but do you mind sharing what, specifically, that call has become?

It was a kind of call to action, in a way that was suitable to my mortal ears—the voice of God if you will, but at the time, I did not think like that. I did not "hear" words, only the sound. Words or not, that experience was powerful, and it jolted me back into the world, the twentieth century with all of its myriad of problems. And it helped me realize that the spiritual power that I felt so strongly out in the wild and beautiful world of the forest was one and the same with that which I had known in my childhood, in those days of Trevor, in the days when I used to spend long hours in ancient cathedrals. It was a milestone in my spiritual journey.

But there was another moment, a more significant one. In October of 1986, my life changed forever. It was actually an indirect outcome of the publication of my book *The Chimpanzees of Gombe*.[23] To celebrate the publication of the book, the director of the Chicago Academy of Sciences at that time, suggested we hold a conference on "Understanding Chimpanzees." It was an amazing gathering that lasted over four days, and it brought about a cataclysmic change in me. I call it my "Damascus Road" experience, much like the experience the Apostle Paul had.[24]

When I arrived at that conference, I was a research scientist. When I left, I was a changed woman utterly committed to conservation. I think everyone there was shocked to learn the rate that chimpanzees across Africa were vanishing. The growing human population was wreaking havoc on the habitats of chimpanzees as trees were being razed for homes, firewood, charcoal.[25]

I came in a scientist; I left an activist. It has been gradual, as one thing has led to another. Working to alleviate poverty—our TACARE program that helps people find a way of making a living without destroying their environment, based now around Gombe's 105 villages and five other African countries where the Jane Goodall Institute continues to study and conserve chimpanzees and their habitat.[26]

We are working for better conditions for animals in zoos, banning circuses, sports hunting, etc.

We implore people to follow a plant based diet for four reasons: First, the way food animals are kept is often intensely, unbelievably cruel; second, vast areas of habitat are destroyed to grow the grain to feed the billions of cows, pigs, etc.; third, it takes a lot of water to transform plant to animal protein; and fourth, it is much more healthy for us.

And I created Roots & Shoots, a program for students and educators to learn more about the importance of conservation and how to make a positive impact on the world around us.[27]

And I give lectures that raise awareness about the dangers and realities of climate change, and the importance of conserving the environment.

All of this is the result of that seismic change I experienced at that 1986 conference.

To me at least, one of the fascinating aspects of your spiritual journey is your willingness to wrestle with very hard questions—and specifically theodicy—how there can be such suffering in the world if we have a loving God. You have reflected on the horrors of the Holocaust, eras of time when religious extremism led to torture and violence, the kidnapping of four of your research assistants, the feelings of despair after your first marriage to Hugo van Lawick ended in divorce in 1974, the pain your second husband Derek Bryceson endured in his final days of battling cancer until his death, and your own ensuing grief. There is much there. You have truly allowed yourself to walk through those "valleys of the shadow of death."[28] There have been times when you were stuck in those valleys of doubt, and at times, even rejection, but then you emerge with this incredible resilience, for you continue to return to your faith, writing with clarity, "my faith gives me an inner peace that gives meaning to my life..."[29] Many people get stuck in those valleys, but how has your faith seen you to the other side?

I will start by saying, I think it is something I was born with. Faith and hope are somehow related. And I sometimes think that we are here to be tested.

In our present age, it seems to me that things are getting harder and harder. There are parts of the world where genocide is occurring today, just like what we experienced in World War II under Hitler. I will be honest and tell you even now, I am having trouble sleeping thinking of the horror being experienced by innocent Palestinians in Gaza, displaced without access to food, water, health care. What is going on in the Ukraine and yes, the Russians who also suffer by watching their sons go off to war. We continue to see discrimination and oppression.

As you know, I lived through World War II and believe all of Europe is in mind that unless we push back against dictators, against nationalistic aggression, we may see a return to that kind of horror. It is a real possibility!

But there is just something in my nature that will not let me give up. This is one of the reasons I give lectures on hope. I think it is important to promote hope, for without hope people so often become apathetic, do nothing. Why bother? Apathy is a great danger! If we all become apathetic, we are doomed. In fact, the worse the situation—whatever it is—then we must work harder than ever, which is much easier if you have hope that your actions are or will make a difference.

For me, I am obstinate! I will NOT give in but fight even harder.

One of the persons who has inspired you to see through the suffering is Holocaust survivor Henri Landwirth, who moved to America and began Give Kids the World, a nonprofit organization that provides terminally ill children the opportunity to visit and experience Walt Disney World. His words have been a beacon to you, "Where does a heart truly broken, a spirit hopelessly abandoned, find hope? What exists within a human being that allows for survival amidst such devastation? It must be God....Who else could it be?"[30] Any thoughts?

Well, it is surely God—which is the only name I have for the Great Spiritual Power. It must be That which gives us the inner strength, the courage, the determination to not give in.

Allow me to ask you just a bit more about your views of evil. You believe in evil and even say that your world was somewhat shattered when the chimpanzees you believed to be better than humans in fact exhibited evil themselves. As I understand it, in your research, you began to unveil a precursor to the human condition of pseudo-speciation or as you prefer to call it, cultural speciation. Can you explain for our reader what that looks like in the world of chimpanzees, but then even more in the world of humans?

Actually, I think only humans can be truly evil. Chimpanzees can be—and often are—brutal. But only humans can sit and deliberately plan a regime of torture, of discrimination and so on. Chimps respond to emotions of the moment. Chimpanzees live in communities with carefully patrolled territories. If they see an individual of a neighboring community, they will chase and brutally attack—including older females.

Only young females who have not yet given birth are safe—the males may try to lead them back into their community—which prevents inbreeding of course. The worst was when the main study group divided and, after four years, what I can only describe as civil war broke out. Males were attacking brutally individuals they had played with, groomed, fed with, and so on.

But now they treated them as if they were strangers. Although they knew them as individuals, they were treated as part of another community, or we could say a new culture. It is something that was terrible to watch. It looked like hate—appeared to be hate, but it is a reaction—in the moment, . . . not planned.

Humans, on the other hand, have the capacity to plan and carry out evil. Humans think through and devise ways of treating others cruelly—carry out premeditated crime, torture our fellow humans, plan and start invasions of neighboring countries, wars. We are seeing this take place today on massive scales around the world.

Your mentor Dr. Leaky believed bigotry to be the worst of sins, and you believe cruelty to be. It is fair to say they are both uniquely human behaviors that spring from evil. I think I am correct when I say that you have suggested that our worst behaviors are deeply imbedded in our primitive heritage.[31] *Those in my vocation might call that "original sin," that we are tainted in some way from the get-go. Would you agree with that?*

I would not say we are tainted. I say that we have inherited from a common ancestor with chimpanzees, about six million years ago, certain characteristics. Violence and brutality on the one hand. Love and compassion and altruism on the other. Chimps show both. Also, we share similar characteristics with them in other ways: lust for power (the males fight for dominance), and greed. But just as only we can be truly evil (in my view!), so only we are capable of true altruism—acting KNOWING that it might cost us our lives to save another individual—including an animal. Again, chimps just act on the spur of the moment. Though we are learning so much more about animals, I could be wrong!

But you have also found that as chimpanzees are actually capable of dark behavior, they are also capable of altruistic behavior! How does that bring you a sense of hope about what you have called the struggle between "saint and sinner" that lives within each of us?

Yes, this is where we can use our superior intellect to consciously plan our behavior. Once we understand that there are alternative ways to act in a given situation, we are very often able to control aggressive responses. Most of the time we do. We may feel like hurting someone who has crossed us, but mostly we do not. This is a great hope for we humans—we have the capacity to change things for the better. As we can plan to treat others cruelly, we can also plan to treat others with care; as we could oppress, we can choose to work for justice; as we can devise war, we can also seek to wage peace and so on. The choice is up to us.

What is "eco-grief"? And how do you experience it?

I think eco-grief is when we look at what humans have done and continue to do to nature and feel powerless to do anything about it. When we look at the whole picture, rather than concentrate on doing what we can in our own corner of the planet. I think the only way to counteract eco-grief is through action. Tackle what you CAN do and then realize others are working in other places making a difference in their own communities around the world—remembering we are not alone.

Your mentor Dr. Leakey and you, and your interviewer here by the way, believe that it is absolutely possible to couple the worlds of science and religion. This book began with an interview with the physician and scientist Dr. Francis Collins, who believes it is absolutely possible to believe in creation and some form of evolution—that the two do not stand diametrically opposed to one another, which I think is your belief. Do I have that right?

Absolutely! I see no conflict between the two. More and more scientists are beginning to be believe in an intelligence that rests behind the beginning of the universe. You and I call that intelligence "God."

Some will still hold to a theory of a "Big Bang," and I do not dismiss that, but what was before the "Big Bang"? I believe, as do growing numbers of people in the sphere of science, that creation by God is not only sensible, but logical!

You tell a wonderful story about having a long encounter with a bellhop at a hotel in Dallas, Texas, with whom you began a discussion about these matters and then you share the more important point with him, that what matters most is not how we humans got to be the way we are, but instead are ". . . we going to go on destroying God's creation, fighting each other, hurting the creatures of His planet? Or were we going to find ways to live in greater harmony with each other and the natural world?"[32]

Yes, to me it is as though we have evolved the most intellectual brain of any other creature, yet lost wisdom. I say "intellectual" rather than intelligent. If we were intelligent, we would not be destroying our planet!

You have what I think is a remarkable commentary on Genesis, a subject you preached on some years back at Grace Episcopal Cathedral in San Francisco.

You focused on 1:26, "And God said, let us make man in our own image, after our likeness: and let them have dominion over the fish . . . fowl . . . cattle . . . and every creeping thing." (KJV) You make a very important distinction about that word "dominion." Can you share a bit more about that?

It appears that many have interpreted the word *dominion* in a different way than the original Hebrew word implies. Dominion is not intended to mean the right to exploit the world around us, but instead that we were given the world and are called to be good stewards of the gift. That makes a huge difference.

And, well, we have been terrible stewards. In many places around the world, humans continue to exploit the natural world. If we carry on with business as usual, we are doomed. We shall reach a tipping point when the planet heats up so much that life will be intolerable.

Natural resources are not infinite. In some places we are using them up faster than nature can replenish. Water is getting very scarce in some places. There are already climate refugees. Humans are not exempt from extinction.

That is why I put a lot of hope in young people, particularly those in my Roots & Shoots, which I began in 1991. This program for young people from kindergarten through university is now in seventy-five countries, and participants are working on projects to help people, animals, and the environment. Along the way practicing qualities of respect and compassion—for each other and animals and nature.

Already some have come into decision-making positions, and they seem to retain those qualities. Hundreds of people have told me it changed their lives, made them better people.

One of the things we try and do is bring people together from different countries, cultures, and religions. When we do that, it is no surprise that they come to realize that more important than color of skin or culture is the fact we are all human. We all laugh and cry, feel sad and happy, and we all love. Unfortunately we can all hate—but can also love; there is evil and good, and we hope that the good side will win out!

I know you are, as any thinking person is, deeply troubled by the threats not just to our environment, but to our planet. It is not hyperbolic to say, if we do not turn the tide, we are committing a kind of environmental homicide that will, in the end, mean our own demise. Tell your reader here, Dr. Goodall, what concrete steps can the person on the street take to begin to push back the tide of climate change and all that goes with it?

Yes, well we have already talked about this threat to some degree. But yes, to push the point, everyone makes a difference every day just by being alive. We can all do little things—turn off the tap, pick up trash, conserve water, care for a sick person or animal, protest the destruction of habitat for yet another animal, start a "Roots & Shoots" group.

And, of course, children can influence their parents and grandparents. Many parents tell me they started recycling, or buying products made in a sustainable way, because their children brought it up and encouraged them.

Consumer pressure is beginning to work. People ask how a product was made: did it harm the environment? Was it cruel to animals (factory farms, fur farms and so on)? Is it cheap because of unfair wages? Products made ethically, at least initially, are likely to cost a bit more. Then we will *value* them more and *waste* less. Human waste is a huge problem.

There are so many things we can do, and it does not have to be a big thing, . . . little things can add up to big things! Do what you can, where you are. . . . Every step in the right direction helps.

And if it is, in fact, God's creation, and God's gift to us, is it not the godly thing to do to care for, protect, and preserve that creation for the generations yet to come?

Indeed, yes. And add to that, if we don't protect, if we go on relentlessly destroying, we are, as I said a moment ago, doomed. I feel desperate when I see small children so sweet and innocent and full of joy and then I think of the world into which they are being born.

This is why I have to go on fighting for the planet, 300 days on the road at 90, but by the time your book comes out, I will be 91!

People tell me I should slow down—but the closer I get to the end of my life, the harder I must work because there is less and less time to do what I was put on the planet to do. Whatever years I have left, God gives me, I will continue to do this work until the end.

You have written that "the hallmark of wisdom is asking 'What effects will the decisions I make today have on future generations?'"[33] How does that apply to our call to help "save" God's gift of creation to us?

That is the wisdom of the Indigenous people. What concerns me about the time in which we live is that people, many world leaders in the West as well as other parts of the world, seem only concerned with the here, and the now; with wealth and power and how it benefits our time, and not the future.

We need to change that way of thinking. We need to ask about every major decision we make as a people, as a nation, "How will what we do today affect our people seven generations ahead?"

If we think like that, we will work to protect the natural world of which we are a part, and *on which we depend*. For food, water—well, everything.

It would be easy to collapse into despair, but you are a person of unfathomable hope. You have uttered some wonderfully wise words about the power of hope. You do not believe it is a kind of blind and impotent and passive optimism, writing that "hope does not deny evil, it is a response to it!"[34] How does hope drive you to respond to the evil of the world?

I would put it the other way round. I am driven to do what I can to tackle evil (lectures, Roots & Shoots, activism) because of my hatred of what we are doing to harm the future for our children and their children, of what we are doing to harm innocent animals. I go on working for this because I know that I am making a difference—because many hundreds of people tell me it is so! Knowing this gives me hope that together we can change the world. But we must act now, before it is too late. Yes, we can—we have the knowledge and the tools. But do we have the will?

We are living in a moment in history when the dividing lines seem to be written not in sand, but concrete. Thoughtful dialogue and debate have given way to anger and divisiveness. Many people have come to believe the way to convince others is fury. But you have written quite clearly, "the aggressive approach simply does not work . . . ," but gentleness does.[35] Can you unpack that for me just a bit?

Well, when I am talking with someone who believes in different values, ethics, morals—I have found that arguing, being aggressive, does not work.

I listen. My mum taught me the value of listening to opposing views and then trying to reach not the head—but the heart. I do that with a carefully selected story. You may not know at the time that you reached the heart, but maybe you did. And I truly believe that only when head and heart work in harmony can we achieve our true human potential.

Describe your belief that we humans really need to develop a "universal code" of human behavior.

Does that not simply mean that you must learn to be respectful, compassionate and understand and control aggressive impulses? And use our amazing intellect for the good of people, animals, the environment—the world around us.

What is the difference between "moral" and "spiritual" evolution?

Well, this is only my own view. Moral evolution is when we move towards a life where we understand what is good, what is bad, and try desperately to live a "good" life—being kind and respectful to each other and to other living beings—and by the way, this includes trees! We now know that they can communicate with one another in various ways!

But spiritual evolution is when we believe that we "live and move and have our being" in the Great Spiritual Power that we call God by whatever name we call God, depending on the culture into which we are born.

You had a remarkable experience shortly after the death of your beloved Derek. Can you share some about that and how it helped you perhaps reframe death as we understand it?

It was about a month after he died. I woke up in the night—I was on my own in my Gombe house. Derek was there. He was telling me wonderful things. That all was well. He vanished. I wanted to remember what he said, and as I tried it felt like fainting, a roaring in my ears.

When he went away, I began desperately to try to remember what he said—the roaring began again. And after that I could not remember anything.

Well, speaking of death, our journey to the end of this interview, and the end of this book is drawing nigh, so now I want to turn to what we preachers and priests call questions of "the end." You have come close to death on more than one occasion. You survived a plane crash, a steep fall from a rock climb, almost being crushed by a rock, not to mention simply the dangers of living in the jungle. And yet, you say you have never been afraid of death. Many do fear death, why do you not?

I think we are all afraid of the dying process—that we may have to endure the pain of a terrible cancer, that we may have to live for a time totally dependent on others, and I understand that.

But I have never been afraid of death itself. Why? Because I do not believe death is the end. It is, perhaps, more like the beginning. After the injustices and pain of this life that many must endure—then there will be peace.

Now Dr. Goodall, . . .

(Dr. Goodall begins to laugh, not the first time during our interview, I should add, and says, "Now, let's say 'Jane,' but no 'Dr. Goodall.' . . ." She smiles and says, "Some of my students call me 'Dr. Jane,' . . . but 'Jane' or 'Dr. Jane' is fine, but no 'Dr. Goodall.'")

I continue, "Well, I think I am a 'student' of the wise Dr. Goodall, so I will go with 'Dr. Jane'! So, Dr. Jane, I ask a question which you have grown fond of answering. You have had so many great adventures . . . what do you think is your next great adventure, and why?"

Well, you know perfectly well how I will answer that! *(Jane laughs again!)* Because I think it is the reason you decided to interview me, I gather!

Well, when you die, there is either nothing, or there is something. And if you believe there is something, as I do, then I can't think of a greater adventure than finding out what that something is!

When I share that with others, so many people have told me how they think about death differently now. My next great adventure is dying, and finding out what that is will be the most exciting adventure ever!

My last two questions. You have loved nature your whole life through; how has nature loved you?

Nature loves me because when I am alone in nature, or even with people in nature, I get this calming feeling. Let me say, I am not the kind of person who easily gets stressed, fortunately. I think it is because I live very much in the moment and do what I can do and leave it at that.

But when I am in nature, it is just very calming. . . . It's like being hugged!

Because when I am in nature, even sitting under a tree in a city park, I am filled with peace. And because my time in the forest has been so meaningful, I take the peace of the forest within me.

What might we do, to love her, in return?

Protect her. Protect her! Respect her. Help when we can. Join movements that protect habitats, animal species. Share the importance of maintaining healthy ecosystems with those around us. Writers can write, painters can paint, photographers can take photos to share the beauty, wonder, and joy that we find in nature with those who cannot experience this for themselves. Everyone can do something, so . . . do something to protect her and love her in return as she has loved us!

DR. JANE GOODALL

Dr. Jane Goodall, DBE, founder of the Jane Goodall Institute and UN Messenger of Peace, is a world-renowned ethologist and conservationist. Jane is known for her groundbreaking research into the lives of wild chimpanzee communities. At twenty-six, Jane followed her passion for wildlife and Africa to Gombe, Tanzania, and under the mentorship of paleoanthropologist Dr. Louis Leakey, began her landmark study of wild chimpanzees. Her revelatory observation that chimpanzees make and use tools rocked the scientific world and forever redefined our understanding of the relationship between humans and other animals, and nearly sixty-five years later this work continues.

Jane founded the first Jane Goodall Institute (JGI) in 1977 and today twenty-four institutes work to support her holistic approach to conservation. JGI's work, includes TACARE, a community-led conservation program, two sanctuaries for orphan chimpanzees, the ongoing research at Gombe, and Jane Goodall's Roots & Shoots. Roots & Shoots empowers young people of all ages in seventy countries to undertake hands-on projects of their choosing to benefit the community, animals (including domestic animals), and the environment.

Jane travels globally around 300 days each year, inspiring audiences through speaking tours, media engagements, written publications, and a wide array of film, television, and podcast projects. She has authored many books for adults and children. Her latest publication, *The Book of Hope: A Survival Guide for Trying Times*, has been translated into more than twenty languages. Jane is a global icon spreading hope and reminding us all that our daily actions make a difference and it's up to us the kind of difference we make.

CLOSING THOUGHTS

Come to me, all you ...

—Matthew 11:28

What to do with an invitation?

I began this work by reflecting on Jesus's invitation to his first disciples, "Follow me...." And I also suggested some followed, some did not, perhaps others waited before making any decision.

What I have tried to do with this volume is introduce you to twelve people who made that decision to follow.

My great-grandmother was named Rose. She was born at the tail end of the 1800s. She married, gave birth to my grandmother, divorced, remarried, and had almost a dozen more children.

My siblings and I spent a number of our free weekends and summers in her small, very modest home in central Alabama. She had stepped into the twentieth century, but not with both feet. She washed many of her clothes by hand, churned her own butter, and occasionally, to save money, would burn kerosene lamps at night by which to read, or visit, or prepare for bed.

She was also a host for quilt parties. If you have never been to one, or know not what one is, let me explain. Until the day of her death in 1988 at the age of ninety-nine, she had a "quilting frame" in the ceiling of her kitchen. It was a large, square of wooden beams which would be lowered into the center of her kitchen. Family and friends would be invited over to bring their own small squares of cloth, and then working together over meals, and laughter, parables, and stories, they would weave a variety of fabrics into one large quilt.

Rose provided the framework, and those who brought their own pieces allowed the finished quilt to be crafted—to be wrapped around for comfort; placed upon a bed for warmth; laid upon the ground for a picnic, games with children, embraces with a loved one. To this day, I have several of those quilts in my home, and they remind me of my great-grandmother's small "corporate" endeavor to gather others to allow them to bring their smaller pieces to become part of a larger piece.

What I have attempted to do here is provide a frame, and I am so grateful for the twelve disciples, pilgrims if you will, who brought their own piece to a larger tapestry that—well, holds together. Their stories are intrinsically linked to the birth of a babe in a manger some 2,000 years ago, to the life of a shepherd turned king some 2,000 years before that, to the dawn of creation when, as Francis Collins and Jane Goodall have so wonderfully described, God decided to bring into creation from creation the first Mother Eve and Father Adam.

Their stories are remarkable, are they not? I left each conversation as a changed person. What these wonderful followers shared challenged me, deepened me, inspired me, and in many ways, reminded me why I decided to follow decades ago.

As I promised you at the beginning of this book, these are not followers who are cut and pasted from the same mold. They see God in different ways, but they are still followers. They confess to still growing and still learning—to still being on their own unique pilgrimages.

They have no need that others share the way they have come to know God and follow Jesus, but they do share a hope that everyone might come to know the love the Trinitarian Almighty has for each human who walks, or has ever walked, the earth.

And though different, in many ways, did you notice the similarities?

Humility—how many said to me, "I am so honored to be included with a list of such incredible people." Each could have dismissed this would-be author peppering them with questions, but they welcomed the opportunity to reflect on their faith journeys. Each was careful to say in one way or another "my way is not the only way," which is the first stepping stone to authentic humility.

Joy—in every conversation, there was laughter and smiles. Dr. Jane Goodall's smile that contained a "little secret," was something that was written on the face of each pilgrim here.

Sincerity—I did not pray "for" each person, but "with" each person—and suddenly, whether in the same room, or virtually connected though hundreds of miles apart, we were no longer strangers, but friends submitting to the presence of God and God's purposes for this work.

Devotion—not just to God, but to friends, and family. Each of these pilgrims felt that the essence of who they were came through the relationships given (parents, siblings) and the ones they chose (spouses, friends, mentors). The sum of their being was the fruit of being blessed by the love and friendship of others.

Generosity—an authentic embrace that all gifts in this world and the next come from the hands of a generous God, and if God has been generous, then each has chosen to be generous in return—by caring for creation, the homeless, the needy, the poor, the outcast, the sick, the wounded. Each person you have come to know here is engaged in investing in the lives of others to make this world a better place—not for greater earthly adulation, but because they have been called by their Lord to love others, as they have been loved.[1]

Perhaps above all these qualities, I would add *wisdom*. Solomon so accurately describes the value of this godly trait:

Happy are those who find wisdom,
and those who get understanding,
for her income is better than silver,
and her revenue better than gold.
  She is more precious than jewels,
and nothing you desire can compare with her.
  Long life is in her right hand;

in her left hand are riches and honor.
Her ways are ways of pleasantness,
and all her paths are peace.
She is a tree of life to those who lay hold of her;
those who hold her fast are called happy.[2]

Wisdom is no small thing in a world that pummels us constantly with its own messages, noises, and voices. But the "word" of these twelve pilgrims points us beyond this world, to one that is eternal.

This wisdom comes from experience and is shared with extraordinary honesty. All twelve pilgrims have been open about their own frailties and sins. They have been brazenly transparent about their seasons of doubt and despair—walking through the valleys of life—abuse, betrayal, broken relationships, discrimination, grief, rejection. You have met a pilgrim who suffered the assault of his daughter, another who lovingly cared for a son as he battled cancer to the end of this life, and the crushing blow of another whose son took his own life.

But each, again, in their own way and time, found a path to what Nikki Haley described as her spiritual discipline—to hold on tighter to the Hands that are already holding onto you. Each has emerged as a person of faith and hope.

They have, by the world's standards, achieved much—these are influential, famous, successful pilgrims—but not one of them believes any of those material blessings are the Source from which true meaning, purpose, and life flows. For that, they turn to, hold on to, and follow the One who is the Author of the qualities that make life worth living, and in fact, carry us from this life to the next—peace, tranquility, love.

Now, what about you?

So, now, I come back to you. The author of the ancient text Ecclesiastes wisely wrote, "For everything there is a season, and a time for every matter under heaven."[3] I suppose two of the blessings of Jesus's invitation is that it comes not as a demand, and there is no expiration date.

As you read through these conversations, you learned that some of our pilgrims here heard or felt that invitation to go deeper but waited: "I was not ready," Denzel Washington shared with us.

I suspect such was the case for almost everyone who followed. I have sometimes wondered about the Gospel writer Mark's description of Jesus's call to follow. He writes upon Jesus's invitation, "they immediately left their nets and followed him."[4] But a characteristic of Mark's Gospel is the sense of urgency. Mark, alone among the Gospel writers, uses the word *immediately* no less than forty-one times in his Gospel account.[5]

Matthew, whom scholars believe used Mark as a resource, also uses the word *immediately*, but Luke does not. John's Gospel tells the calling of the first to follow in a completely different way, as they were not as quick to follow a wandering Nazarene carpenter as the other Gospels imply![6]

All of this has made me wonder if there is a particular moment where one moves from belief to actually following—from concept to commitment, from assent through belief to acceptance. I once heard a theologian describe the process much like when one agrees to be treated with medication. It is one thing to assent to the truth that an antibiotic will bring me healing to an infection I may have in my body. It is yet another to actually believe that if the doctor prescribes the medication, and I go to the pharmacist and purchase it, and prepare to swallow it down with a glass of water, it will bring me the healing I need. But in the end, in order to have the infection dealt with, I have to take it within myself.

Not everyone follows this path in the same way, but I do think it is fair to agree with my pilgrims here, that if one does not receive the love and presence of Jesus into their lives, they will, in fact, always feel as if something is missing.

One of the most famous of Augustine's confessions to God was "My heart is restless until it rests in Thee."[7] But it is said, as he pondered his own step of faith and what a life of service to Christ might require of him, that he once prayed, "Oh, Master, make me chaste and celibate—but not yet!"[8]

It is not, as was put to me in a few of these conversations, that the material world and the spiritual world are at odds with one another. But while the material may very well be put in its proper place by the spiritual, the opposite is not the case. I love the old joke often told by preachers about a spiritual seeker who interrupted his busy, wealthy lifestyle to spend a few days in a monastery. "I hope your stay is a blessed one," says the monk who shows him to his simple cell. Then he smiles and says, "If you need anything, let us know, and we'll teach you how to live without it."

If I am completely honest, there are a lot of things about this world I do not want to give up, but I also know they cannot give me what only God can, or to borrow the words of the seventeenth-century author, philosopher, and Christian Blaise Pascal, "The infinite abyss can only be filled by an infinite and immutable object, that is to say, only by God Himself."[9]

C. S. Lewis says this with even greater clarity,

> God made us: invented us as a man invents an engine. A car is made to run on petrol, and it would not run properly on anything else. Now God designed the human machine to run on Himself. He Himself is the fuel our spirits were designed to burn, or the food our spirits were designed to feed on. There is no other. That is why it is just no good asking God to make us happy in our own way without bothering about religion. God cannot give us a happiness and peace apart from Himself, because it is not there.[10]

One of the things we saw in my conversation with Dr. Francis Collins was his own wrestling with a journey into belief, which really began in a substantive way with the question of one of his patients, "What do you believe?"

As C. S. Lewis puts it,

> Creatures are not born with desires unless satisfaction for those desires exists. A baby feels hunger: well, there is such a thing as food. A duckling wants to swim: well, there is such a thing as water. Men feel sexual desire: well, there is such a thing as sex. If I find in myself a desire which no experience in this world can satisfy, the most probably explanation is that I was made for another world.[11]

My hope, and I mean this quite literally, is that as you consider all the signposts that you find in this closing chapter, coupled with the personal experiences of our twelve pilgrims here, you will be led to that place Dr. Collins found himself, "Finally, seeing no escape, I leapt."[12]

"Why a decision?"

One of the most profound of Christian thinkers and apologists of the last generation is Dr. Alister McGrath. In his book *The Unknown God*, he answers the question some of you may be asking—"Why a decision?" Dr. McGrath writes, "While many people are troubled by the thought of dying, others are disturbed by a much more profound anxiety—that we might die without having really begun to live."[13]

Allow me to track back to the preface. I referenced Paul's wonderful word to his protégé Timothy, to "take hold of the life that really is life." But let me include, here, the full passage,

> As for those who in the present age are rich, command them not to be haughty, or to set their hopes on the uncertainty of riches, but rather on God who richly provides us with everything for our enjoyment. They are to do good, to be rich in good works, generous, and ready to share, thus storing up for themselves the treasure of a good foundation for the future, so that they may take hold of the life that really is life.[14]

In all fairness, is that not what our pilgrims have shown us? All twelve are what you and I might call "rich" in this present age—but none exhibit pride in their achievements, but instead gratitude; and none of them have set their ultimate hope on the "uncertainty of riches," but rather on God; and all of them have proven to be "rich in good works, ... generous, ... ready to share, ... storing up for themselves the treasure of a good foundation for the future. ..." Why? That in doing so, to press the point, "they may take hold of the life that really is life."

This, then, is the antidote to Dr. McGrath's assertion that many live with anxiety that life will come to its end without having ever been fully lived whatsoever. This is precisely what Dr. Goodall said her relationship with God offered her: "My faith gives me an inner peace that gives meaning to my life."

So, then, where do we go from here?

If you have made it to the end of this book, you and I have spent a lot of time together! Our pilgrims and I, working together here, have put a lot before you. You may already be a believer, and if so, I hope this work has broadened your understanding of the meaning and purposes of a relationship with God. And if your belief also includes a relationship with Jesus, then my hope remains. Maybe these words have stirred you to make a deeper commitment to your faith, or a re-commitment—here, here!

If you have begun a journey of faith, but you still have doubts and reservations about going all in, so to speak—fair enough. You are on the path, you have begun to follow, and my counsel as a quilt-maker here is to keep at it.... Ask for God's hand to guide you, and He will. I assure you, He will not let you go.

And if you have no belief at all, and you have taken the time to read from beginning to end, then my plea to you is to consider the conversations you have read here. If, even in your unbelief, you have a hunger for meaning and purpose—stop for a bit. Take a deep breath. Utter a prayer—even if you believe it will fall on deaf ears, or no ears at all.

Many of our pilgrims here have shared with me the value of that one little verse that has given great meaning to Sam Waterston, "Be still, and know that I am God."[15] And then, maybe, borrow Sam's prayer, "*Maranatha, . . .* Come, Lord . . ."

Paths to a Deeper Relationship?

A thermometer, as you know, measures the temperature of a room. It has no control over that temperature—it only reports. In my nearly four decades of ministry, I have often had people describe their belief system as frozen, immovable. A thermostat, unlike the thermometer, actually changes the temperature in its environment—up and down. There are things we can do to adjust the temperature of our faith—being still, meditation, prayer, service to others, worship. All of these spiritual disciplines are practiced by our twelve pilgrims, and it does, in fact, produce a difference in their day-to-day lives in a way that fame, money, success and other material blessings cannot, and in fact, do not.

The spiritual disciplines can raise the temperature of your faith—regardless of where it has landed.

Let me suggest another very practical step you can take—find a way to serve others. On pages 232–233 of this book, you will find a list of various organizations to which our pilgrims have pledged their time and their financial support. They believe in each of these organizations which touch and, literally, change the lives of millions of people.

One of Jesus's most well-known quotes that calls others to service is simply, "I tell you, just as you did it to one of the least of these who are members of my family, you did it to me."[16] There are literally hundreds of verses through the whole of the Bible that call God's followers to serve their fellow humans.

And if you do not know where to start, perhaps borrow from our pilgrims. Secretary Rice who prays as her morning begins, "Lord, help me get through this," or "Give me wisdom," or "Help me to be someone who helps."

Though not in our conversation for this book, Gary Sinise once shared with me that he and his wife Moira often pray, "Lord, take me where you want me to go. Let me meet who you want me to meet. Tell me what you want me to say. And keep me out of your way...."

Serving others, for Christ's sake, is not for the applause of others, or even for the attaboy from God. Serving others brings us into a place that allows us to experience God more deeply, for when we serve others, we are, in fact, serving God—having a one-on-one encounter with the Almighty. Which brings me to one other ingredient that will help raise the temperature of your spiritual journey—love.

Jesus's disciple, John, had a lot to say on this topic and wrote:

> Beloved, let us love one another, because love is from God; everyone who loves is born of God and knows God. Whoever does not love does not know God, for God is love. God's love was revealed among us in this way: God sent his only Son into the world so that we might live through him. In this is love, not that we loved God but that he loved us and sent his Son to be the atoning sacrifice for our sins. Beloved, since God loved us so much, we also ought to love one another. No one has ever seen God; if we love one another, God lives in us, and his love is perfected in us.[17]

In a very real sense, what John is suggesting is whether someone knows it or not, when they experience love as a gift given or a gift offered, they have already stepped into the divine circle of God's presence.

Jesus Christ calls his followers to take that a step further—to make a conscious decision to invite that love to live within a person's life. When one does that, to press the point, the temperature changes.

The spiritual disciplines, serving others, loving others—these invite the presence of God into our daily lives. Time and time again, in the stories you have here, you have read about this. The experience of life itself, fully lived and fully considered, was the very inspiration for the faith of our pilgrims. As Secretary Baker said, "I look at my life and consider all that God has given me, . . . and how could I not believe? How could I not have faith?"

But I began this section with a question, "Where do we go from here?" We are offered that ancient choice with those first words of Jesus, *"Follow me . . ."* Where might you go from here? Follow more deeply? Follow more fully? Follow for the first time? Jesus has left that up to you.

One More Witness to Belief...

My attempt in sharing these conversations has been offered to help you in your decision about how to respond to that invitation. I hope the time you have given to reading this has helped adjust your spiritual thermostat some, by introducing you for the first time, or the hundredth, to God as He has made Himself known in the lives of others.

Award-winning author Annie Dillard once wrote, "I had been my whole life a bell, and never knew it until at that moment I was lifted and struck."[18] Forgive the pun, but sometimes we just need to be lifted up and have our bell rung! I have heard people describe their own spiritual epiphanies in that way. They also use metaphors like "conversion" or "born again" or "coming to faith." Some do so once, others many times, some simply grow up with a knowledge of God and God's love, others may take years, some a lifetime, still others in a moment.

I have shared twelve stories here. As you consider my question "Where do we go from here?" let me close our time together by sharing a particular moment when I had my own spiritual bell rung. With a measure of humility and trepidation, allow me to take the witness stand to offer my own testimony of belief.

I was baptized and reared in the Church. My parents divorced when I was young, and my father had sole custody of my two sisters and myself for several years. Of the many ways he cared for us, making sure we attended church and Sunday school was important. He was a busy businessman, often working six days a week, sometimes twelve or more hours a day, but he believed that having some framework of belief was important not only for his children, but for himself. So, for a number of years, we did all the churchy things. I eventually got confirmed, was somewhat active in the youth group, and so on.

But, like many teenagers, I had a number of questions. I grew up in the late 1960s and early 1970s when the Jesus movement was making its way across the globe, throughout Australia, New Zealand, Europe, and the United States. For a variety of reasons, teenagers and young adults were stepping away from historic church worship and flocking to prayer meetings, Bible studies, and worship that was characterized more by contemporary music styles than traditional.[19]

What I noticed about my friends who were being drawn to this movement, whether through organized parachurch groups, or just small Bible study and prayer groups, is that they talked about a relationship with God in a way that had not occurred to me, nor in a way that I had experienced. They spoke of having a personal relationship with God, and for these friends at least, it was a personal relationship with Jesus.

I was struck by something many of them said they were experiencing—a "closeness" to Jesus, . . . a friendship with Jesus, much like our pilgrim Dr. Jane Goodall described.

And while I had grown accustomed to church and all that it offered, it did not seem to offer me the satisfaction for that longing that Dr. McGrath, Dr. Lewis, and others described in their writings.

I sought out several clergy whom I had come to know and asked to meet with them, often armed with a myriad of questions. Then one day, I connected with a friend named, of all things, "Pastor Carpenter" (that is not a preacher's joke). He worked mostly with college and university students, so he was used to the cross-examination they often brought to his bench. After perhaps an hour of questions or so, my friend finally said to me, "Russell, we can discuss these kinds of questions all day long, . . . but the real question is, "Have you chosen to follow Jesus's invitation?"

I remember kind of stumbling through my answer. "Well, yes, . . . I think so, . . . I mean I was baptized as a baby, . . . confirmed, . . . I go to church, etc., etc." I blabbed on for a while and he listened patiently.

"But what I am asking, Russell, is have you given your life to Jesus? Are you in a relationship with Jesus?"

I had to be honest, "I am not sure . . ."

"Well, why don't you think on that and then we can come back to the questions."

Fair enough, . . . gentle enough, . . . offered with a smile, . . . no condemnation, . . . no formula, just a legit question, "Have you chosen to follow?"

I thought about that conversation all afternoon, and into the evening. I prepared for bed and that evening before slipping beneath the sheets, I knelt down and prayed. I am not completely sure of what I said as I offer you these words. I said something along the lines of "I want what my friends seem to have. . . . I want a personal relationship with you. . . . I want to be converted, . . . or born again, . . . or whatever it is, but this I know, I want to be in a relationship with you."

I said my "Amen," and then I waited. I waited for what seemed like a long time. I thought maybe there would be a light, or swelling music, or a mystical feeling, or that an angel would tap me on the shoulder. Nothing. And I mean nothing. Oh well, I went into bed.

The next morning, I woke, and while there still was no spiritual light about me, no angel at the foot of my bed—there was something that I experienced, and it was as real to be as this book you hold in your hand. Never, not once in the last four and a half decades of life, since that evening, . . . not once have I not known the presence of Jesus Christ in my life.

Let me be clear. I was a young man at this time, well, barely a man. I had a lot of life yet to live. This was just before college and all that often comes with those years. All the worst things I have done in my life happened after that evening. I have not lived a perfect life, but since that moment, it has also not been a life void of the presence of the living God.

There have been times when I have been angry with God. Times when I doubted and even wanted to give up believing. There have been times when my belief system was challenged and times when it has changed. Some of the things I believed about Christianity have been jettisoned, others have been confirmed. There are times when God, the Great Spiritual Being, as Dr. Goodall refers to God, has seemed as far away as the next galaxy, and there have also been times when God has seemed, again borrowing Dr. Goodall's words, like the wind on my face, or perhaps the person in the pew next to me, or most certainly in a small piece of bread and a small sip of wine.

I am, most days, earnest to shout with all I am, like each of our pilgrims—"I believe in God, because I experience God in my daily life." I am a believer, because I decided to follow—not a particular church, or denomination, or theological perspective, but a relationship with the One Who desires to have a relationship with each of one of us—not for this life alone, but for all eternity. Before I close, allow me to hover over the gift not just of life, but life eternal.

More to Come.... "The Last Great Adventure...!"

I purposely chose to end the twelve conversations here with Dr. Jane Goodall, or "Dr. Jane," as she invited me to call her. The question about her "next great adventure" is one that has been put to her a few times in a few ways over the last few years. The first time I "heard" her talk about it was when my wife Laura and I were listening to an audio version of her book *The Book of Hope: A Survival Guide for Trying Times*. Dr. Jane comes to a point in the book where she shares that her next great adventure would be death, and it was a bit unnerving. But then as she unpacked it, Laura and I were literally moved to tears. For is not life eternal the ultimate gift of God to His children?

Jesus put the promise of life eternal beautifully. "My sheep hear my voice. I know them, and they follow me. I give them eternal life, and they will never perish. No one will snatch them out of my hand...."[20]

Dr. Jane's wisdom on the matter of life after death is profound, and it is godly. If God seeks to be in relationship with His children, why would He limit it to a tiny pinprick of time in the whole of eternity? This leads your preacher/author to ask, "Can I have an 'Amen'!?"

Since first hearing Dr. Jane speak these words through her book, and then again, personally in our conversation, it has not only given me a new insight about dying, death, and what rests beyond death's door, but it has also helped me, many years now into ordained ministry, invite others to embrace what, at the end, God wants to give to each of us—a new beginning.

Over the years, I have had so many people ask me—in my office, in church, in the hospital or nursing home, or on their deathbed—questions about life after death: "How old will I be?" "Will we get to eat?" "Who will I meet?" I have no answer. When the questions are more general, "What will heaven be like?" I am still a bit of a loss for words, but I do believe there are hints of heaven all around us in everyday life. This is what Dr. Collins spoke of when he experienced the numinous feeling brought about by music; or Gary Sinise when he experienced God's comfort in the depths of grief; or William McRaven when he felt rescued by the hand of God; or Jim Nantz when he prays in the bosom of his family; or Amy Grant when she sings the Scriptures; or Denzel Washington when he chose to step through a crack in the door of his mother's church, which led to a decision to be baptized; or Secretary Rice at a funeral in Rome; or Secretary Baker when he prays with his wife Susan; or, yes, Dr. Jane, when she feels at one with the Almighty in the bosom of nature's embrace. On and on the stories have gone, and each are whispers. They each are what the Celtic Christians called "thin places"—those places where the distance between heaven and earth are so close, it is hard to determine one from the other.

But in those moments—these thin places—what God is offering is, in fact, a glimpse of what we can now only imagine.

What is beyond the gate of death? The realized promise and hope that what has begun in the here and now will go on forever. In the end all that we have been sharing in these pages together invites us to agree with our Lord, and Dr. Jane, that the next great adventure is death, and the splendor that awaits us.

A Closing Invitation...

Let me offer my closing invitation—consider Jesus's invitation. It comes not with a pointing finger, or a gavel, or the harsh word of judgement. Perhaps the most quoted verse in all of Scripture is John 3:16, "For God so loved the world that he gave his only Son, so that everyone who believes in him may not perish but may have eternal life." It is a beautiful verse, if taken at face value, but I have seen it used as a baseball bat. It has been used, too, to pigeonhole people with the suggestion that everyone is to specifically "believe in him," in a particular way, through a particular denomination or religious tradition, with specific words.

A full reading of the passage should always include the following verse, "Indeed, God did not send the Son into the world to condemn the world, but in order that the world might be saved through him."[21]

As complex as religionists, including your author here, have often made the journey to a relationship with God, as I sit at the end of this time with you, I believe such a journey is far simpler than it is often made out to be. How simple? "God created.... God loved.... God sent,... not to condemn, but to save."

Thank you, reader, for taking this book in hand. As I have offered at the beginning and offer now at the close, my hope is that the stories you find here will bring you into that blessed walk with the One Who created us.

My closing invitation? Listen to Jesus. His invitation is simple: Follow me. Your decision can be a simple yes.

Then, may your prayer be, day after day, simple,... perhaps just a few words: "*Maranatha*,... Come, Lord..."

And the Lord will come.... The Lord will come as the Lord chooses to come, in his own way, in his own time.

I bid you to welcome that...

and be a witness to belief as well.

Bless you, in your journey.

WORDS OF GRATITUDE (ACKNOWLEDGMENTS)

Witness to Belief: Conversations on Faith and Meaning could only have happened because of the contributions and support of so many people, so allow me a bit of space to thank my circle of support.

Before I do that, whenever I have completed a book it behooves me to be grateful to anyone who takes the time to pick it up and read it. This was over a year in the making and the fruit of that labor that you hold in your hands now is not offered without a tremendous measure of appreciation of anyone who takes the time to read it. So, thank you reader!

First and foremost, I am in perpetual debt for the care and love of my wife of over forty years, Laura. Laura was the first person with whom I discussed this work, and from beginning to end, she has been my encourager—as she is in so many other areas of my life and our life together. My time preparing this work for you required untold hours away from her, and, now, God willing, I will step out of the study for a season and make some memories that do not require a keyboard!

Second, the "twelve pilgrims," who spent generous time with me not only in conversation, but in follow up visits for clarifications, securing photographs, permissions, and other paperwork associated with pulling *Witness to Belief* together. Thank you friends—Secretary James A. Baker III, Dr. Francis Collins, "Dr. Jane" Goodall, Amy Grant, Ambassador Nikki Haley, Brit

Hume, Admiral William McRaven, Jim Nantz, Secretary Condoleezza Rice, Sam Waterston, Denzel Washington, and Gary Sinise.

Third, there are a few people who have known about this project for quite some time as well, and from time to time, I have returned to them for their own insights and thoughts. To that small circle—the Reverend Dr. Barney Hawkins; the Very Reverend Dr. Ian Markham, from my alma mater, Virginia Theological Seminary; and Mr. Jake Reiss, founder and president of The Alabama Booksmith in Homewood, Alabama. And there are the people who so kindly endorsed this book—Presiding Bishop Michael Curry, founder of Homeboy Industries Greg Boyle, and author and speaker Jeanie Miley—all for whom I have the greatest admiration for their respective ministries and the witness of their own lives and faith.

Fourth, the Reverend Huey Gardiner, rector of St. Mary on the Highlands in Birmingham, Alabama, and members of the wonderful staff at the vibrant church—Melodie Elam, Cissy Hartz, Rhea Pelekis, and Matt Watson. While many of the conversations in this book took place in person, some took place virtually, and these hardworking members of the St. Mary's family helped me put that in place.

Next, the Church Publishing/Morehouse team, Airié Stuart, Anita Manbodh, and I think above all, Fiona Hallowell, my editor and daily cheerleader—who spent far more time with my words than I did and took my many words and made them clearer, more concise and, hopefully, shaped in a way that makes this work something you have enjoyed, or at the very least, found to be a companion along your own pilgrim's way.

Last, I am grateful to God—the Creator Who gave me life and with it a body to enjoy and use, a mind to think, a heart to love and be loved, and a soul to pray, and by Whose grace, made chiefly known to me in the life of His Son Jesus, I have received the life that is truly life, and after that, . . . "The Great Adventure!"

AUTHOR'S NOTE

I have committed to donating a portion of the proceeds from the sale of *Witness to Belief: Conversations on Faith and Meaning* to the causes of the wonderful people who agreed to have the conversations you have read in this book. These organizations, listed below, are all doing important work, and I urge you to learn more about them.

—Russell J. Levenson, Jr.

The Honorable James A. Baker III.
The Baker Institute for Public Policy
6100 Main Street
Baker Hall MS-40, Suite 120
Houston, Texas 77005
Telephone: (713) 348-4683

Dr. Francis Collins
Biologos
www.biologos.org
3940 Peninsular Drive SE, #200
Grand Rapids, MI 49546
Telephone: 1-800-405-5798

Dr. Jane Goodall
The Jane Goodall Institute "Roots & Shoots" Program
1120 20th St. NW #520s
Washington, DC 20036
Telephone: (703) 682-9220

Amy Grant
Compassion International Nurture Center
www.compassion.com
12290 Voyager Parkway
Colorado Springs, CO 80921
Telephone: 1-800-336-7676

The Honorable Nikki Haley
The Original Six Foundation
info@originalsixfoundation.org
P.O. Box 2246
Columbia, South Carolina 29202
Telephone (803) 422-6081

Brit Hume
Youth for Tomorrow Boys' and Girls' Home
www.youthfortomorrow.org
11835 Hazel Circle Dr, Bristow, VA 20136
Telephone: (703) 368-7995

Admiral William McRaven
The Special Operations Warrior Foundation (SOWF)
Specialops.org
P.O. Box 89367
Tampa, FL 33689
Telephone: (813) 805-9400

Jim Nantz
Nantz National Alzheimer Center (NNAC)
P.O. Box 4384
Houston, Texas 77210-4384
Telephone: (202) 445-9322

The Honorable Condoleezza Rice
The International Rescue Committee
P.O. Box 6068
Albert Lea, MN 56007-9847
Telephone: (855) 973-7283

Gary Sinise
The Gary Sinise Foundation
www.garysinisefoundation.org
P.O. Box 40726
Nashville, Tennessee 37204
Telephone: (615) 575-3500

Denzel Washington
Boys and Girls Clubs of America
1275 Peachtree Street NE
Atlanta, GA 30309-3506
Telephone: (404) 487-5700

Sam Waterston
Rural & Migrant Ministry
The Rev. Richard Witt
125 Duncan Avenue
Cornwall-on-Hudson, New York 12520
Telephone: (845) 485-8627

NOTES

Preface

1. Jesus's Baptism, Mark 1:9–11, Matthew 3:13–17, Luke 3:21–22, John 1:29–34; Jesus's Temptation, Mark 1:12–13, Matthew 4:1–11, Luke 4:1–13; Jesus's Proclamation that the "Time is Fulfilled," Mark 1:14–15, Matthew 4:12–17, Luke 4:14–21; Jesus Calls the First Disciples, Mark 1:16–20, Matthew 4:18–22, Luke 5:1–11.
2. Mark 12:17.
3. Dr. Todd M. Johnson, "Christianity is Fragmented—Why?" (South Hampton, Massachusetts: Gordon Conwell Theological Seminary, November 6, 2019), https://www.gordonconwell.edu/blog/christianity-is-fragmented-why/.
4. See Acts 11:25–26.
5. See, for instance, I Corinthians Chapter 12.
6. Matthew 11:28.
7. John 12:32.
8. John Stott, *Life in Christ* (London: Three's Company, 1991), p. 7–8; Cf. Stephen Neill, *Christian Faith and Other Faiths* (Oxford: Oxford University Press, 1961, p. 91); John Mbiti, *African Religions and Philosophy* (Portsmouth, New Hampshire: Heinemann, 1969), p. 277.
9. I Corinthians 2:2.
10. I Timothy 6:19.
11. Will and Ariel Durant, *The Story of Civilization—Caesar and Christ* (New York: Simon and Schuster, 1944), p. 622.
12. Will and Ariel Durant, *The Story of Civilization—The Age of Napoleon* (New York: Simon and Schuster, 1975), p. 111.
13. As quoted by John Stott in *Guard the Truth* (Downers Grove, Illinois: InterVarsity, 1996), p. 153.

14. I Timothy 6:10. (Emphasis mine.)
15. Barack Obama, *The Audacity of Hope: Thoughts on Reclaiming the American Dream* (Edinburgh, Scotland: Canongate Publishers, 2008), p. 202.
16. Luke 9:25.
17. Job 1:21 (NIV).
18. Richard Foster, *Celebration of Discipline* (San Francisco: Harper, 1988), p. 1.
19. Russell J. Levenson, Jr., *Witness to Dignity: The Life and Faith of George H. W. and Barbara Bush* (New York: CenterStreet/Hachette, 2022).
20. Acts 1:8.
21. https://statisticsanddata.org/data/most-popular-religions-in-the-world-2025/.
22. Theologian Theodore, in "Dawn Treader," *The C. S. Lewis Institution*, Issue 1.2, February 1, 2020: Cf. C. S. Lewis, *God in the Doc: Essays on Theology and Ethics*. Edited by Walter Hooper (Grand Rapids, Michigan: Eerdmans, 1970).
23. C. S. Lewis, *The Weight of Glory and Other Addresses* (New York: MacMillan, 1980), p. 92.
24. My own interpretation of what Hamlet surmised about what God puts into each creature that calls them back to God, from William Shakespeare's *The Tragedy of Hamlet*, Act IV, Scene IV, dated between 1599 and 1601.

Dr. Francis Collins

1. C. S. Lewis was a professor of Medieval Literature who taught at both Cambridge and Oxford Universities in the United Kingdom. After his conversion to Christianity, he began speaking and writing on matters of the faith and is considered to be one of the most prominent apologists of the last century. He died on November 22, 1963.
2. Constructon of Westminster Abbey began in 1245. The rose windows were designed by Sir James Thornhill and made by Joshua and William Price.
3. Francis Collins, "My Journey from Atheism to Christianity," Cal Tech, September 6, 2016.
4. C. S. Lewis, *Surprised by Joy* (New York: Harcourt Brace, 1955).
5. Dr. Collins plays both the guitar and piano. He was part of the band "The Directors," made up of former Senior Staff of the National Institutes of Health.
6. *Mere Christianity* was written by C. S. Lewis and first published by Geoffrey Bles Publishing in London, UK, on July 7, 1952, with several varying editions by different publishers in the years since.
7. A mountain range popular with hikers, which extends from southern British Columbia through Washington state and Oregon and ends in Northern California.
8. S. Vanauken, *A Severe Mercy* (New York: Harper & Row, 1977), p. 100.
9. From *Language*, p. 33; cf. P. Tillich, *The Dynamics of Faith* (New York: Harper Row, 1957), p. 20.

10. The Right Reverend N. T. Wright was born on December 1, 1948. Bishop Wright is an Anglican Bishop and noted theologian, author, and biblical expositor who has served in several posts in the Church of England, most recently as a senior research fellow at the University of Oxford, since 2019.
11. The Reverend Tim Keller was born September 23, 1950. He served as the founding pastor of Redeemer Presbyterian Church in Manhattan, NY, and was widely known for his outstanding preaching and insightful writing. He retired from Redeemer in 2017 and was later diagnosed with pancreatic cancer and then died on May 19, 2023.
12. The Gospel of Matthew, chapters 5–7.
13. The Scopes Trial, also known as *The State of Tennessee v. John Thomas Scopes* and sometimes referred to as "The Scopes Monkey Trial," ran from July 10–21, 1925, and made it illegal to teach human evolution in state-funded schools.
14. Augustine, Bishop of Hippo, was born on November 13, 354 AD and died on August 28, 430 AD and is considered one of the preeminent theologians of the early Church and Christianity. His exegesis and commentary on Genesis, entitled, *De Genesi ad litteram* (Latin), translated "On the Literal Meaning of Genesis," was written between 401 and 415 AD.
15. Dr. Francis Collins, *The Road to Wisdom* (New York: Little, Brown and Company, 2024).
16. NIV.

The Honorable Dr. Condoleezza Rice

1. Condoleezza Rice, *Condoleezza Rice: A Memoir of My Extraordinary, Ordinary Family and Me* (New York: Ember/Random House Children's Books/Random House, 2010), p. ix.
2. During the intensive years of peaceful protest to end segregation and the abusive and heavy-handed response of some elected and appointed officials in Birmingham, Alabama, 1963–1964.
3. "Nobody Knows the Trouble I've Seen" was first published in *Slave Songs of the United States*, edited by William Francis Allen (New York: A. Simpson and Company, 1867); "Glory, Glory, Hallelujah" was first published as part of the greater hymn, "The Battle Hymn of the Republic," written by Julia Ward Howe (an abolitionist) (Boston: Oliver Ditson and Company, 1862).
4. The Reverend John Ortberg has been the Pastor of Menlo Church in Menlo Park, California, since 2003.
5. Russia invaded Ukraine on February 24, 2022, and as of the time of this interview and its subsequent publication, the war between the two countries continues.
6. The parable of the prodigal son is found in Luke 15:11–32.
7. See Matthew 25:40.

8. The Terror Attacks of September 11, 2001.
9. Dr. Rice became the eighth Director of the Hoover Institution on September 1, 2020.
10. Walt Disney Pictures, released June 15, 1994.
11. Joseph Haydn, *The Seven Last Words of Our Saviour on the Cross* (German: *Die sieben letzten Worte unseres Erlösers am Kreuze*). Commissioned in 1786.
12. Dr. Persis Drell served as the Provost of Standford University from February 1, 2017, to September 30, 2023.
13. See Ephesians 2:8–9.
14. See Philippians 2:12.
15. Condoleezza Rice, *A Memoir of My Extraordinary, Ordinary Family and Me* (New York: Random House/Ember, 2010), p. 293.

Gary Sinise

1. Lt. General Lynch is a retired Brigadier General who served in many positions until his retirement, when he founded his own consulting business, R Lynch Enterprises. He travels and speaks nationally, works on behalf of Veterans and Wounded Warriors and has authored several books, including *Work Hard, Pray Hard* (Savio Republic, 2017), and *Adapt or Die* (Baker Books, 2013).
2. Gary Sinise, *Grateful American: A Journey from Self to Service* (Nashville, Tennessee: Thomas Nelson, 2019), pp. 14, 25, 26.
3. Ibid., p. 34.
4. Gary Sinise played Lieutenant Dan Taylor in the film *Forrest Gump*, produced by Paramount Pictures, 1994, and based on the book by Winston Groom of the same title. In the film, the "floating feather" represents the way in which life takes certain twists and turns to build the full story of one's life. Sinise was nominated for an Oscar for Best Supporting Actor for his portrayal of Lieutenant Dan.
5. Sinise, *Grateful American*, p. 99–100.
6. Ibid., p. 150ff.
7. You can read more about this in *Grateful American*, and specifically in pages 136–148.
8. Ibid., p. 151.
9. This would have been Friday, September 14, 2001.
10. Ella Sinise is the youngest of Moira and Gary's three children, born in 1992. His other two children are Sheila, born in 1988, and McCanna "Mac," born in 1990.
11. As noted, the subtitle of Gary's autobiography, *Grateful American*, is *A Journey from Self to Service*.
12. McCanna "Mac" Sinise died on January 5, 2024.
13. St. Augustine's Prayer Book is an Anglo-Catholic devotional book and has been published in various versions since 1947 by the International Anglican Oder of the Holy Cross.

14. Augustine's *Confessions* was written between 397 and 400 AD and has been published in numerous languages over the years. This autobiographical work consists of thirteen books and is considered to be one of the most significant collection of reflections in the history of the Christian faith.
15. The remarkable story of these two albums and several other pieces of Mac's work can be found on the website for the Gary Sinise Foundation: https://www.garysinisefoundation.org/mac-tribute.

Ambassador Nikki Haley

1. Nikki Haley, *Can't Is Not an Option: My American Story* (New York, New York: Sentinel/Penguin, 2012), p. 46.
2. Bamberg, South Carolina, where Nikki Haley was born and lived in her childhood years.
3. Punjabi is the language typically spoken in the Sikh tradition and worship. The Sikh Holy Book, Guru Granth Sahib, is written in Punjabi, and most of the hymns and prayers used in Sikh Temple worship services are in Punjabi as well.
4. Nikki Haley's siblings are Mitti, Simmi, and Gogi.
5. Nikki Haley, *Can't Is Not an Option: My American Story* (Sentinel/Penguin: New York, New York, 2012), p. 9.
6. Nikki Haley, *Can't Is Not an Option: My American Story* (Sentinel/Penguin: New York, New York, 2012), p. 47.
7. II Corinthians 5:7.
8. Nikki Haley, *Can't Is Not an Option: My American Story* (Sentinel/Penguin: New York, New York, 2012), p. 11.
9. Nikki Haley, *With All Due Respect: Defending America with Grit and Grace* (New York, New York: St. Martin's Press, 2019), p. 37.
10. Ibid., p. 44.
11. Nikki Haley served as the 116th governor of the State of South Carolina from January 12, 2011, to January 24, 2017, and as the 29th United States Ambassador to the United Nations from January 27, 2017, until December 31, 2018.
12. Reference to Luke 12:48.
13. Clark Gillespy and I grew up in Birmingham, Alabama, together and have been friends since we were in elementary school together. He served as President of South Carolina Duke Energy from 2012–2016.
14. Haley, *Can't Is Not an Option,* p. 200.
15. The "1,000 Year Storm" that hit South Carolina in October of 2015 did billions of dollars of damage and claimed nearly twenty lives; the Townville Elementary School shooting took place on September 28, 2016; Hurricane Matthew slammed into South Carolina on October 8, 2016.
16. Sarah Young, *Jesus Calling* (Nashville: Thomas Nelson, 2004).
17. Sarah Young, *Jesus Always* (Nashville: Thomas Nelson, 2016).

Notes

Denzel Washington

1. Denzel Washington, *A Hand to Guide Me: Legends and Leaders Celebrate the People Who Shaped Their Lives* (Des Moines, Iowa: Meredith Books, 2006).
2. I had sent him a copy of *Witness to Dignity* as a humble attempt to show I had some writing skill.
3. He was going to film *Gladiator II*, Paramount Pictures, 2024.
4. Cf. Proverbs 22:6 *NRSV*, as quoted in *A Hand to Guide Me*, p. 8.
5. Denzel Washington, "Commencement Address," University of Pennsylvania, May 16, 2011.
6. Michael Harris was also a major figure in the record industry. President Donald Trump pardoned him after he served approximately 30 years of a 25 years to life sentence, before leaving office in January of 2021.
7. Denzel Washington, commencement address, Dillard University, May 7, 2015.
8. Ibid.
9. *A Hand to Guide Me*, p. 22.
10. *The Hurricane*, Universal Pictures, 1999.
11. University of Pennsylvania address, May 16, 2011.
12. Teresa of Ávila, *The Interior Castle* (Dover Publications: Mineola, New York, 2007).
13. *A Hand to Guide Me*, p. 270.
14. Ibid., p. 23.
15. Luke 12:48.
16. "Take Me to the Water," Nina Simone, 1967.
17. Bishop Charles E. Blake is the presiding bishop of the Church of God in Christ, the fourth largest Protestant denomination in the world.
18. The Kelly Temple Church of God in Christ was known as the "Mother Church."
19. A reference to the traditional Black spiritual song "When the Saints Go Marching In," which originated as a hymn, but the author and date of authorship is unknown. On May 13, 1938, Black jazz artist Louis Armstrong and his band recorded the piece as "The Saints," and it remains to this day one of his most famous recordings and one of the most famous renditions of the song.

Admiral William H. McRaven

1. The Fellowship of Christian Athletes, also known as FCA, is a nonprofit, nondenominational Christian ministry that seeks to bring people into a relationship with Christ and help them grow in that relationship, through the fellowship of coaches and athletes. It was founded in 1954 by Don McClaney, head basketball coach at Eastern Oklahoma in 1954. It has grown to be the largest Christian ministry of its kind in the world.
2. Tom Landry was the head football coach for the Dallas Cowboys from 1960–1988; he died on February 12, 2000, at the age of 75. Roger Staubach was the quarterback for the Dallas Cowboys from 1969 until 1979. He currently lives in Dallas, Texas.

3. The United States Navy SEALs ("Sea, Air, and Land") can trace their roots back to World War II and were officially founded in 1962. Navy SEAL Team 3 was established in 1983.
4. A shot line is used for diving purposes and helps to anchor the boat.
5. Admiral William McRaven, "Commencement Address" (Austin, Texas: The University of Texas, May 19, 2014).
6. Admiral William H. McRaven, *Make Your Bed: Little Things That Can Change Your Life . . . and Maybe the World* (New York: Grand Canal/Hachette, 2017).
7. Ibid., p. 6.
8. Ibid., p. 9.
9. Ibid., pp. 15–21.
10. Ibid., p. 21.
11. Hebrews 11:1.
12. W. T. Purkiser, d. 1992.
13. Admiral William H. McRaven, *The Hero Code: Lessons Learned from Lives Well Lived* (New York: Grand Central/Hachette, 2021), pp. 105–110.
14. Ibid., p. 111.
15. Walter Reed Military Medical Center is in Bethesda, Maryland.
16. II Corinthians 4:16 offers this counsel, "So we do not lose heart. Even though our outer nature is wasting away, our inner nature is being renewed day by day," which seems to mirror Admiral McRaven's encouraging words.
17. Admiral William McRaven, *Sea Stories: My Life in Special Operations* (New York: Grand Central/Hachette, 2019), p. 179.
18. Located in the eastern part of Afghanistan, the Paktika Province is one of the thirty-four provinces in the country and has a population of about 800,000 residents.
19. Luke 23:34, ESV.
20. McRaven, *The Hero Code*, p. 142.
21. Matthew 27:46, NRSV. The words were foretold in David's Psalm 22:1, written sometime between 1010 and 970 BC, around 1,000 years before Jesus's Crucifixion.
22. Matthew 7:9–12.
23. Admiral William McRaven, *Sea Stories: My Life in Special Operations* (GrandCentral/Hachette: New York, 2019), p. 333.
24. Will Durant, *Heroes of History: A Brief History of Civilization from Ancient Times to the Dawn of the Modern Age* (New York: Simon and Schuster, 2001).
25. Admiral William H. McRaven, "Commencement Address" (Dallas, Texas: The University of Texas Southwestern Medical School, May 28, 2015.)

Amy Grant

1. "El Shaddai" was written by Michael Card and John Thompson and recorded by Card on his 1981 album, *Legacy*. Amy's rendition was recorded and released on her platinum album *Age to Age*, which was released under the Myrrh Label in 1982.

2. Amy Grant, *Mosaic: Pieces of My Life So Far* (Colorado Springs, Colorado: Water-Brook Press, 2007), p. 135.
3. Amy Grant, *Mosaic: Pieces of My Life So Far* (Colorado Springs, Colorado: Water-Brook Press, 2007), p. 135.
4. Kevin Moore was born in Los Angeles in 1951 but has family roots to Louisiana and Texas. He is known by the stage name of Keb' Mo' and is often described as a living link to Delta Blues music.
5. On March 11, 2011, the Tohoku Tsunami hit the coast of Japan, killing over 20,000 people.
6. Grant, *Mosaic*, pp. 1–3.
7. Ibid., p. 52.
8. Ibid., p. 105.
9. Ibid., p. 117.
10. Betty Smith, *A Tree Grows in Brooklyn* (New York: Harper Brothers, 1943).
11. This is a paraphrase of John 1:1–6.
12. Ibid., p. 191.
13. Referencing Jesus's words from the Cross, in Luke 23:34.

The Honorable James A. Baker III

1. Russell Jones Levenson, Jr., *Witness to Dignity: The Life and Faith of George H. W. and Barbara Bush* (New York, New York: CenterStreet, 2022).
2. James A. Baker III., *Work Hard, Study . . . and Keep Out of Politics* (New York, New York: G.P. Putnam's Sons, 2006), p. 5.
3. Christian Science does not promote the use of physicians or medicine for healing but, instead, promotes the belief that all sickness can be healed through prayer and those who practice spiritual healing (https://www.christianscience.com/what-is-christian-science/beliefs-and-teachings).
4. The Hill School is a private non-denominational boarding school in Pottstown, Pennsylvania. Chapel continues to be central to the life of the school, and current students are required to attend at least twice a week. The school's "Statement on the Spiritual Life of the Community" states that the school is "grounded in the Christian faith of the school's founders, the Spiritual Life program welcomes diverse religious traditions as it seeks to promote the growth of the soul in all students as individuals, as members of the community, and as citizens of the world." https://www.thehill.org.
5. George H. W. Bush was elected to the United States House of Representatives in 1966, representing Texas' 7th Congressional District. He gave up that seat in 1970 to run for the United States Senate but was ultimately defeated by Lloyd Bentsen.
6. At the time of this interview, my wife and I were living on Green Tree Road, just a block or so from the house that Mary Stuart Baker designed.

7. *Work Hard*, p. 16.
8. Ibid., p. 16.
9. Susan Garrett Baker and James Baker III married in 1973.
10. In his later years, discussions about the afterlife were a matter President Bush and I discussed many times up until his death. He never asked, "Is there a heaven?" But he often wanted to discuss what heaven was like and if he would be reunited with loved ones. My answer was always, "I do not know much about what it will be like, but you will definitely be reunited with your loved ones!" And from time to time, I had the same discussions with Secretary Baker.
11. From remarks offered at his acceptance of The George H. W. Bush Award for Excellence in Public Service, as reported by Hallie Jones, October 28, 2021 (Bryan, Texas: 15KRHD), https://www.kxxv.com/brazos/james-baker-receives-george-h-w-bush-award-for-excellence-in-public-service and also, *Work Hard*, p. XIII.
12. George H. W. Bush died on November 30, 2018, and was buried at his family plot, alongside his wife, Barbara, and daughter, Robin, on the Campus of Texas A&M in College Station, Texas, on December 7, 2018.
13. James Baker III was the sixty-first secretary of state, appointed under President George H. W. Bush, and held that office from January 25, 1989, until August 23, 1992.
14. James Baker III's father, James A. Baker, Jr., died on May 21, 1973.
15. Bowie Ken Kuhn was fifth commissioner of major league baseball from 1969–1984.
16. Eduard Shevardnadze served in several roles in the former Soviet Union. During his tenure as the minister of foreign affairs of the Soviet Union (from 1985–1991), he became a close ally of the president of the Soviet Union Mikhail Gorbachev. Shevardnadze played a key role in the diplomacy that led to the end of the Cold War on December 5, 1991. He eventually rose to the office of the president of Georgia in which he served until November 23, 2003.
17. After moving back to Houston, Secretary Baker and his wife, Susan, gave that plaque to St. Martin's Episcopal Church in Houston, and it hangs near the entrance to the Pastoral Care Center on the church campus.
18. Today, many Christians and most American military teachers use an outline of the just war theory developed by St. Augustine of Hippo (d. 430 AD) that sets out the following conditions. For a war to be considered just,
    1. It must have a just cause.
    2. It must be declared by a legal authority.
    3. It must have a just intention (to restore peace, not to wage revenge).
    4. It must be a last resort.
    5. It must have the probability of success.
    6. It must have just conduct (no killing of civilians, only military combatants).
    7. It must be enacted proportionately (the good must outweigh the evil).
19. Operation Desert Storm, also known as "The Gulf War," was launched on January 17, 1991 and ended six weeks later with the Liberation of Kuwait on February 28, 1991.

20. Pope John Paul II.
21. Peter Baker and Susan Glasser, *The Man Who Ran Washington* (New York: Doubleday, 2020), p. 221.
22. Barbara Pierce Bush died on April 17, 2018. The quote comes from Secretary's Baker's remarks in his eulogy for the president, during his memorial service at St. Martin's, December 7, 2018.
23. This closed street is used as a parking lot for employees of the Executive Office of the President, and is adjacent to the White House.
24. *Work Hard*, p. XVII.

Jim Nantz

1. I write more extensively about that day in my book, *Witness to Dignity: The Life and Faith of George H. W. and Barbara Bush* (New York: CenterStreet/Hachette, 2022).
2. Russell J. Levenson, Jr., *In God's Grip: What Golf Can Teach Us About the Gospel* (New York: Morehouse/Church Publishing/Seabury Press, 2025).
3. Jim Nantz, *Always by My Side* (New York: Penguin Putnam, 2008), p. viii.
4. Jim Nantz often refers to his friend "41," the late Honorable George H. W. Bush.
5. Dave Williams, called the "Father of College Golf" for the way he revolutionized the college golf game, died December 16, 1998; Ken Venturi was a PGA professional golfer who died on May 17, 2013.
6. Lionel Leo Hampton was an African American jazz musician who died on August 31, 2002.
7. *Always By My Side*, p. 78.
8. Ibid., p. 78.
9. John Wooden was the head coach of UCLA basketball from 1948 until 1975 and died on June 4, 2010.

Sam Waterston

1. *The Great Gatsby*, Newdon Productions, 1974; *Capricorn One*, ITC Entertainment, 1977; *The Killing Fields*, Goldcrest Films/Enigma Production, 1984.
2. Created by Dick Wolf and produced by Wolf Entertainment Universal Television, the first episode of *Law and Order* aired in 1990. Sam starred as a New York executive assistant district attorney for most of his 405 episodes, for 30 years, over nineteen seasons, from 1994 until 2024.
3. Russell J. Levenson, Jr., *Witness to Dignity: The Life and Faith of George H. W. and Barbara Bush* (Center Street/Hachette, 2022), pp. 144–148.

4. Sam and Lynn Louisa Woodruff married in 1976.
5. A reference to Jesus's teaching from Luke 11:33.
6. I hope the reader will forgive a rather lengthy reference note, but it might be helpful in setting the framework from which Sam will offer his thoughts. What follows is a brief note about each person he has included. You will be able to find out more in the suggested reading section at the end of this book.
   - William James was an American philosopher and psychologist. Often referred to as "The Father of American Psychology," he died in 1910.
   - Bertrand Russell was a British-born philosopher and mathematician. His essay "Why I Am Not a Christian" was published on March 6, 1927. He died in 1970.
   - Samuel Beckett was an Irish-born writer and lecturer at Trinity College in Dublin, Ireland. Reared an Anglican, he often included religious themes in his works.
   - Abraham Lincoln was the sixteenth president of the United States until his assassination in 1865. Sam Waterston is a student of all things Lincoln and has played him on stage and screen.
   - Karl Barth was a Swiss Reformed theologian whose most popular work was *The Epistle to the Romans*, published in 1919. He is considered to be one of the most influential Christian theologians of the last century. He died in 1968.
   - Albert Camus was a French philosopher who was considered to be one of the major voices in "absurdism." Though many claimed he was an existentialist and an atheist, he rejected both suggestions and was well known for saying, "I don't believe in God, and I am not an atheist." He died in 1960.
   - Albert Einstein was a German-born theoretical physicist and mathematician, and known as the father of the theory of relativity, and played a major role in the understanding of quantum mechanics. He believed himself to be a humanist, but not an atheist. He died in 1955.
   - Richard Dawkins is a British-born (b. 1941) evolutionary biologist, and while not antagonistic to Christianity, is best known for his public profession of atheism, and his 2006 book, *The God Delusion*. He lives in Oxford, England.
7. John 8:30.
8. Scylla and Charybdis were fictional sea-monsters associated with Greek mythology that the ancient Homer set on opposite sides of the Straight of Messina between Sicily and Charybdis. The idiom "between Scylla and Charybdis" is often a reference to the proverbial challenge of "choosing the lesser of two evils."
9. William Shakespeare, *Hamlet*. Act III, Scene 2. Published 1603 AD.
10. Ibid., Act I, Scene 5.
11. Abraham Lincoln, "The Perpetuation of Our Political Institutions," address before the Young Men's Lyceum of Springfield, Illinois, January 27, 1838.
12. Abraham Lincoln, second inaugural address, United States Capitol, March 4, 1865.
13. "Love the Lord," in Deuteronomy 6:4 and Matthew 22:37; "Do unto others," in Matthew 7:12 and Luke 6:31.
14. Psalm 46:10.

15. Albert Einstein, December 1926. This was never published, but appeared in some private correspondence between Einstein and physicist Max Born.
16. Sam played American physicist J. Robert Oppenheimer in the seven-episode television miniseries *Oppenheimer*, produced by the British Broadcasting Company Production. It ran from October 29 until December 10, 1980.
17. "The Collect for Peace," *The Book of Common Prayer* (New York: Oxford University Press, 2007), p. 99.
18. Shakespeare, *Hamlet*, Act V, Scene 2.
19. John 1:43–51.
20. "The Great Creator of the Worlds," Words: *Epistle to Diognetus*, ca. 150, tr. F. Bland Tucher (1895–1984) from *The Hymnal 1982* (New York: Church Publishing Company, 1982), Hymn # 489.
21. Sam went to Brooks School in North Andover, Massachusetts, (founded in 1926) for one year, where his mother and father taught and his brother attended as well. He went on to attend the Groton School in Groton, Massachusetts, (founded in 1884) for five years, graduating in 1958.
22. From Sam's "Class Day" address at Princeton University, Princeton, New Jersey, May 27, 2024.
23. Shakespeare, *Hamlet*, Act V, Scene 2.
24. Sam is a devotee of Father Greg Boyle. Father Boyle is a Roman Catholic Jesuit Priest who formed Homeboy Industries in Los Angeles, California in 1992. Homeboy Industries is the largest gang intervention and rehabilitation program in the world.
25. I offer a bit of filmography for my readers here. Robert Redford is an American actor and producer, born August 18, 1936. He began his acting career in 1958 and continues to act and produce. Mia Farrow is an American actor, born on February 9, 1945, and has been active from 1959 to the present. Karen Black was an American actor, born on July 1, 1939, and active from 1960 until the year of her death, 2013. Scott Wilson was an American actor, born March 29, 1942, and was active from 1967 until the year of his death, 2018. Bruce Dern is an American actor, born June 4, 1936, and active from 1960 to the present day. Francis Ford Coppola is an American producer and director, born April 7, 1939, and has been active from 1960 to the present day. Jack Clayton was a British-born director, born March 1, 1921, and was active from 1936 until 1992, before his death in 1995.
26. From "There's No Business Like Show Business," written by Irving Berlin for the musical *Annie Get Your Gun*. It was originally released in 1946.
27. Micah 6:8. (NIV)
28. Luke 15:11–32.
29. Greg Boyle, *Forgive Everyone Everything* (Chicago: Loyola Press, 2022).
30. Ned Beatty, born July 6, 1937, was an American actor whose career spanned from 1956 until 2013. He died on June 13, 2021.
31. Father Main was a British Benedictine Roman Catholic monk who taught on Christian meditation and the use of a "mantra," which is usually a sacred sound or brief prayer. Main died on December 30, 1982.

32. Born February 28, 1533, Montaigne was a French philosopher and essayist who died September 13, 1592. His most famous work, "The Complete Essays," was published in 1580.
33. Sam serves on the Board of Oceana. The Washington, DC, based nonprofit is the largest international advocacy organization focused solely on ocean conservation. Oceana's mission is to protect and restore Earth's oceans.
34. Dr. Pauly, born May 2, 1946, is a French-born marine biologist and serves on the board of Oceana.
35. William James, *The Varieties of Religious Experience*, published 1902.

Brit Hume

1. Jack Anderson was considered one of the founders of American investigative journalism. He died on December 17, 2005.
2. Andrews Airforce Base is located in Camp Springs, Maryland. The last public memorial service for the president was held at St. Martin's Episcopal Church in Houston, Texas, and he was buried later that day alongside the remains of his wife, Barbara, and daughter, Robin, in a small family plot near the George H. W. Bush Presidential Library on the campus of Texas A&M, in College Staton, Texas.
3. Sabine Baring-Gould, "Onward Christian Soldiers," 1865; Isaac Watts, "O God, Our Help in Ages Past," 1708.
4. *The Killing Ground* was a 1979 American documentary film written by Brit Hume, which portrayed the dangers of waste dump sites in various places around the United States. It was nominated for an Academy Award for Best Documentary Feature.
5. Britt Hume's work produced his book *Death and the Mines: Rebellion and Murder in the UMW* (New York: Grossman, 1971).
6. Fred Barnes Jr. (b. February 1, 1943), is a political commentator and a prolific writer on matters related to presidential and political history.
7. Malcom Muggeridge's book *Jesus Rediscovered* (New York: Doubleday, 1969).
8. Jerry Leachman played linebacker for the University of Alabama under Coach Bear Bryant, beginning in 1968. He later entered full-time ministry and, among many other roles, has served as pastor to hundreds in the Washington, DC, area and beyond.
9. I Thessalonians 5:17.

Dr. Jane Goodall

1. Rudyard Kipling, *The Jungle Book* (New York: Random House, 1989), p. xvi.
2. *The Story of Doctor Dolittle, Being the History of His Peculiar Life at Home and Astonishing Adventures in Foreign Parts*, was written by British Author Hugh Lofting and first published by Frederick A. Stokes in 1920.

3. Edgar Rice Burroughs was born in Chicago, and wrote twenty-six novels about Tarzan, beginning with *Tarzan of the Apes,* published in 1912.
4. King James Version.
5. Judy was Jane's younger sister.
6. Richmond Hill Church was originally built in 1856. The current building was constructed in 1891 and is the largest church in Bournemouth, England.
7. Luke 9:62, King James Version.
8. Jane Goodall, *Reason for Hope* (New York: Grand Central, 2000), p. 24.
9. Ibid., p. 34.
10. A reference to Paul's Sermon at the Areopagus in Rome, from Acts 17:28.
11. Jane Goodall and Douglas Abrams, *The Book of Hope* (New York: Celadon Books, 2021), p. 201.
12. Acts 17:28.
13. Goodall and Abrams, *Book of Hope*, p. 18.
14. Goodall, *Reason*, cf., pp. 79–81.
15. Dr. Goodall named many of the Chimpanzees that she studied and with whom she lived in Gombe.
16. Jane Goodall, *Reason for Hope* (New York: Warner Books, 1999), p. 87.
17. Mark 10:15.
18. *UNESCO* is the acronym for The United Nations Educational Scientific and Cultural Organization. *UNESCO* is an agency within the United Nations and is responsible for promoting peace, social justice, human rights, and international security through international cooperation on educational, science, and cultural programs.
19. First published in 1831.
20. William-Shakepeare, *Macbeth,* Act V, Scene V.
21. French-born Jesuit Priest who died in 1955.
22. A full explanation of this experience can be found in Dr. Goodall's book, *A Reason for Hope*, pp. xi., 92-94.
23. Jane Goodall, *The Chimpanzees of Gombe* (Boston: Harvard University Press, 1986).
24. See Acts 9:1–9; Acts 22:6–11; and Acts 26:9–20.
25. Read more about this conference and what Dr. Goodall learned in her book *Reason for Hope*, p. 205ff.
26. Learn more about the Goodall Institute's TACARE Program here: www.twowings.com/en/programme/tacare.
27. Learn more about "Roots & Shoots" here: rootsandshoots.org.
28. Cf. Psalm 23:4.
29. Goodall, *Reason*, p. 164.
30. Ibid., p. 260.
31. Ibid., p. 146.
32. Ibid., p. 179.

33. Goodall, *Book of Hope*, p. 58.
34. Ibid., p. 35.
35. Ibid., p. 270.

Closing Thoughts

1. John 13:34.
2. Proverbs 3:13–18.
3. Ecclesiastes 3:1, attributed to King Solomon, reigned 970–931 BC.
4. Mark 1:18.
5. Mark's Gospel, with only 16 chapters, is also the shortest.
6. John 1:35–51.
7. Augustine, *Confessions*, trans. Henry Chadwick (Oxford: Oxford University Press, 1991), p. 3.
8. Also from *Confessions*, Book 8, Chapter 7.
9. Blaise Pascal, *Pensées* (Franklin Center, Pennsylvania: The Franklin Library, 1979) 7.425, p. 116.
10. C. S. Lewis, *Mere Christianity* (New York: HarperCollins, 1980), p. 50.
11. C. S. Lewis, *Mere Christianity*, p. 106.
12. Collins, *The Language of God*, p. 31.
13. Alister McGrath, *The Unknown God* (Grand Rapids, Michigan: William B. Eerdman's Publishing, 1999), p. 12.
14. I Timothy 6:17–19.
15. Psalm 46:10.
16. Matthew 25:40
17. I John 4:7–12.
18. Annie Dillard, *Pilgrim at Tinker Creek* (Los Angeles: McGraw Hill Publishers, 2000).
19. You can read about the Jesus movement in a number of books that chronicle its birth and growth, among them Edward E. Plowman's *The Jesus Movement* (London: Hodder and Stoughton, 1972).
20. John 10: 27-28, NRSVA.
21. John 3:17.

SUGGESTED FURTHER READINGS AND VIEWINGS

Now that you have come this far, you might want to continue your reading. Below is a list of books that are favorites of the people I have interviewed for this book, and several of my own favorites.

James A. Baker III., *The Politics of Diplomacy,* published 1995.
James A. Baker III., *Work Hard, Study . . . and Keep Out of Politics,* published 2006.
Peter Baker and Susan Glasser, *The Man Who Ran Washington,* published 2020.
Karl Barth, *The Epistle to the Romans,* published 1919.
Samuel Beckett, *Waiting for Godot,* published 1953.
Dietrich Bonhoeffer, *The Cost of Discipleship,* published 1937.
Gregory Boyle, *Barking to the Choir: The Power of Radical Kinship,* published 2017.
Gregory Boyle, *Creating a Culture of Tenderness: Embracing Our Kinship with All of Life,* published 2019.
Gregory Boyle, *Forgive Everyone Everything,* published 2022.
Gregory Boyle, *Tattoos on the Heart: The Power of Boundless Compassion,* published 2010.
George H. W. Bush, *All the Best,* published 1999.
George Carey, *I Believe,* published 1991.
Francis B. Carpenter, *Six Months at the White House with Abraham Lincoln,* published 1866.

Dr. Francis Sellers Collins, *Belief: Readings on the Reasons for Faith*, published 2010.
Dr. Francis Sellers Collins, *The Language of God*, published 2006.
Dr. Francis Sellers Collins, *The Road to Wisdom,* published 2024.
Michael Curry, *Love Is the Way*, published 2020.
Albert Einstein, *The World as I See It*, published 1934.
Richard Foster, *Celebration of Discipline*, published 1978.
Richard Foster, *Life with God*, published 2010.
Richard Foster, *Money, Sex and Power: The Challenge of The Disciplined Life*, published 1987.
Dr. Jane Goodall, *The Book of Hope: A Survival Guide for Trying Times,* published 2021.
Dr. Jane Goodall, *Reason for Hope: A Spiritual Journey*, published 2000.
Dr. Jane Goodall, *The Ten Trusts: What Must We Do to Care for the Animals We Love,* published 2003.
Nikki Haley, *Can't Is Not an Option*, published 2012.
Nikki Haley, *If You Want Something Done*, published 2022.
Nikki Haley, *With All Due Respect*, published 2019.
Brit Hume, *Death and the Mines*, published 1971.
Brit Hume, *Inside Story*, published 1974.
Amy Grant, *Mosaic: Pieces of My Life So Far*, published 2008.
Nicky Gumbel, *Is There More To Life Than This?*, published 2011 and 2017.
William James, *The Meaning of Truth*, published 1909.
William James, *The Principles of Psychology,* published 1890.
William James, *The Varieties of Religious Experience*, published 1902.
Tim Keller, *Counterfeit Gods*, published 2009.
Tim Keller, *Making Sense of God*, published 2016.
Tim Keller, *The Reason For God*, published 2008.
C. S. Lewis, *Mere Christianity*, published 1952.
C. S. Lewis, *The Four Loves*, published 1960.
C. S. Lewis, *The Problem of Pain,* published 1940.
C. S. Lewis, *Surprised by Joy*, published 1955.
Abraham Lincoln, *Speeches and Writings,* published 1859–1865.
Max Lucado, *Anxious for Nothing,* published 2017.
Max Lucado, *Grace for the Moment*, published 2000.
Max Lucado, *Help Is Here*, published 2022.
Max Lucado, *Unshakable Hope*, published 2018.
William McRaven, *The Hero Code*, published 2021.

William McRaven, *Make Your Bed*, published 2017.
William McRaven, *Sea Stories*, published 2019.
William McRaven, *The Wisdom of the Bullfrog*, published 2023.
Jon Meacham, *The Hope of Glory*, published 2020.
Michel de Montaigne, *Essays*, published sequentially in 1580, 1588, and 1595.
Richard Mouw, *Uncommon Decency*, published 2010.
Jim Nantz, *Always by My Side: A Father's Grace and a Spiritual Journey Unlike Any Other*, published 2008.
Barack Obama, *The Audacity of Hope*, published 2006.
Condoleezza Rice, *A Memoir of My Extraordinary, Ordinary Family and Me*, published 2010.
Condoleezza Rice, *Extraordinary, Ordinary People*, published 2010.
Condoleezza Rice, *No Higher Honor*, published 2011.
Condoleezza Rice with Philip Zelikow, *To Build a Better World*, published 2019.
Richard Rohr, *Breathing Under Water*, published 2011.
Richard Rohr, *Everything Belongs*, published 2003.
Richard Rohr, *Falling Upward*, published 2011.
Fleming Rutledge, *The Bible and The New York Times*, published 1999.
Fleming Rutledge, *Help My Unbelief: 20th Anniversary Edition*, published 2020.
Gary Sinise, *Grateful American: A Journey From Self to Service*, published 2019.
Mother Teresa of Calcutta, *Come Be My Light*, published 2003.
Mother Teresa of Calcutta, *The Joy in Loving*, published 1997.
Mother Teresa of Calcutta, *No Greater Love*, published 1977.
John R.W. Stott, *Basic Christianity*, published 1958.
John R.W. Stott, *The Cross of Christ*, published 2006.
John R.W. Stott, *Life in Christ*, published 1991.
John R.W. Stott, *Why I Am a Christian*, published 2003.
John R.W. Stott, *Your Mind Matters*, published 1973.
Barbara Brown Taylor, *Home by Another Way*, published 1999.
Barbara Brown Taylor, *Leaving Church*, published 2006.
Barbara Brown Taylor, *Luminous Web*, published 2000.
Barbara Brown Taylor, *Speaking of Sin*, published 2001.
Denzel Washington, *A Hand to Guide Me*, published 2006.
N.T. Wright, *On Earth as in Heaven*, published 2022.
N.T. Wright, *Simply Jesus*, published 2011.
N.T. Wright, *Surprised by Hope*, published 2008.

Suggested Viewings

James Baker: The Man Who Made Washington Work, PBS, in association with Maryland Public Television/Thinkport for John Hesse Productions, 2014.

Jane Goodall: The Hope, A National Geographic Film, 2020.

William McRaven, "Commencement Address to the University of Texas Southwestern Medical School," May 28, 2015.

William McRaven, "Commencement Address to the University of Texas," May 17, 2017.

Statecraft: The Bush 41 Team, streaming on Amazon Prime.

Denzel Washington, "Commencement Address to the Graduates of the University of Pennsylvania," May 16, 2011.

Denzel Washington, "Commencement Address to Graduates of Dillard University," 2015.

Sam Waterston, "Commencement Address to the Graduates of Princeton University," May 27, 2024.